LITTLE ONE

This book is dedicated to the Native Red Indian peoples of North America, and to the Great Spirit they have nurtured and cared for over hundreds of years on behalf of all peoples and all races who share the Earth.

LITTLE ONE

MESSAGE FROM PLANET HEAVEN

ANN WALKER

Century · London

Published in 1994 by Century
Random Century Ltd
20 Vauxhall Bridge Road, London SW1V 2SA

Random Century Australia (Pty) Ltd
20 Alfred Street, Milsons Point, Sydney, NSW 2061, Australia

Random Century New Zealand Ltd
9-11 Rothwell Avenue, Albany, Auckland 10, New Zealand

Random Century South Africa (Pty) Ltd
PO Box 337, Bergvlei 2012, South Africa

Ann Walker's right to be identified as the author of this
work has been asserted by her in accordance with the Copyright,
Designs and Patents Act, 1988.

Typeset in Linotronic Baskerville by
SX Composing Ltd, Rayleigh, Essex

Printed and bound in U.K. by
Clays Ltd, St Ives plc

A catalogue record for this book is available from the British Library.

ISBN 071 266081 X

To protect the identities of those concerned, most of the names in this book
have been altered.

Contents

PART FOUR

Acknowledgements

I wish to thank everyone who has helped deliver this message to the world. I am particularly grateful to Valerie Smith, my witness and friend, whom I could always trust to tell the truth about events as they unfolded on my journey; to Harry Kyle, a UFO enthusiast, who helped and confirmed the sightings; to Isabel and Bill Powell, who totally gave their faith to White Arrow and who willingly accompanied my husband and me on the late night visits, and who speak the truth; and to a young man, whose devotion to, and faith in White Arrow helped me to put the information together in order to present the Report.

My grateful thanks go to Brian Mitchell for his careful and sensitive reworking and editing of the manuscript, and to James Stephenson-Ward for his attention and efforts to ensure the drawings were accurate representations.

To my husband and my children, without whose love and devotion none of this could have been possible, I offer my eternal love.

*   *   *

Part of the proceeds from the sale of this book will be used to set up the White Arrow Foundation in order to further his work with the trees and the formulae; part will go to the Indian reservations involved in bringing Ann to an understanding of the symbols, and part will be used to facilitate the further development of her journey.

Slowly and surely read, and as you turn the pages remember that no man could have written this.

I, White Arrow, ask you, the people of the Earth, to help my Father save you. My Father who loves you all.

For slowly and surely these words come from my lips, not hers.

WHITE ARROW

Introduction

For the first thirty-seven years of my life I was in pain.

I had two beautiful daughters and a gem of a husband, but inside I was horribly tormented. For a great deal of that time I tried desperately to soften the pain with pills until eventually I realised that I was only just surviving. Somehow I managed to reduce the number of pills and gradually crawled out from the haze and the fog to find myself in an unknown land called the real world.

In the real world, there was still pain; there was still fear. There were also many things I had never noticed before. There were challenges to meet, a family to make amends with, a husband to love, a job selling lottery tickets in Uxbridge to hold down and a life to be lived.

And then there were voices that kept me awake in the night . . .

At first I thought it was some form of madness. The lack of sleep caused by their nightly conferences wore me down, so that just as I had begun to believe that I could survive in the real world, these voices came in as if to break me. And as I sat in the office where I worked one afternoon, tired and on the verge of defeat, a milky grey shadow in the shape of a person came from nowhere and stood in a corner.

Over the following days the shadow came and went, and the night-time voices continued. One night I was so desperate for sleep I spoke back to them, pleading with them to stop, or at least to speak to me only during the day. Twenty or more human faces peered at me through a large window in my mind. I can only assume they listened because at last I slept.

That weekend, the shadow became a man. Tall and bronzed, he stood before me, with jet black hair, held in leather plaits, that fell down either side of his face. A band around his forehead kept the hair from covering his crystal blue eyes that surveyed everything with a calm and loving understanding. The shadow had become a specific person, a Red Indian warrior – a Red Indian warrior whom I and thousands of others would know as White Arrow. He took an arrow out of the quiver on his back. It had a brilliant white feather on it, and it gave me joy, strength and dignity beyond words.

Through White Arrow I learned about the Spirit realm – the 'other side'. Though I had always believed in God, I was not a religious person and knew nothing about Spirit. White Arrow also showed me a vision of a life we had shared together, in the nineteenth century when the Red Indian nations were being ruthlessly slaughtered by the advancing wagons and rifles of pioneers venturing West across North America. It was a life we had shared as man and wife, when White Arrow, then known as White Feather, was Sitting Bull's adopted son in the tribe called White Eagle. Through this, I began to learn about reincarnation: about how our souls, created by God, evolve over many lifetimes, refining and learning, purifying and advancing towards the ultimate goal of perfect reunion with God; how in between reincarnations we are allowed to come back after death to look after our loved ones. Through this process of evolution we first become guides ourselves, and then higher guides, until the ultimate goal, the reunion with God, is achieved. I learned that through reincarnation, all men have the chance to be all things, from poorest to richest, pauper to prince, orphan to king.

In time I became known as a medium and people came to hear White Arrow's messages of love and hope. They came to be reunited with lost loved ones, or for advice with earthly problems. They came for answers and meaning. We all need to have deep memories turned over. We all need to remember some part of the mystery that is life in our universe.

For fifteen years now I have watched his loving help for those who come. I have watched how he shows people that through our own free will we can overcome whatever challenges lie ahead of us. Through his love, White Arrow has shown how to heal the rift between we who live on earth and those who live in Spirit. Mankind's survival as a species now depends, more than ever before, on our willingness to heal that rift, so that we can listen to our guides.

I am a very ordinary woman, but one with an extraordinary guide. I have listened to my guide, I have watched him, I have learned from him. I have grown to love my guide more than my own life. Under his instruction I have written this book as a record of events on my road so that mankind can understand that what is happening in our world today is not because we are alone – it is because we *think* we are alone.

March 1994

PART ONE

'Gramma said when you come on something good,
first thing to do is share it with whoever you can find;
that way, the good spreads out where no telling it will go. Which is right.'

Forrest Carter *The Education of Little Tree*

· 1 ·

April, 1991

The sound of letters falling through the front door and landing on my hall carpet signals the start of the day. I have a plane to catch and I have packed and re-packed my suitcase since before dawn. As I hump the case to the top of the stairs, ready for my husband Tony to take it down the stairs and load into the car, I see White Arrow appear. He is sitting on the doormat in a loincloth, and moccasins, with two arm-bands, and a white feather hanging down on his right side. As usual his arms are folded over his chest and his legs are crossed. He lifts his head to greet me and a bright white smile of pure joy spreads across his face.

I have known this Spirit Indian for twelve years now, yet every time I see him, his beauty fills me with awe. He has the body of a young man in his twenties, but an older face somehow, with crystal blue eyes that sparkle when he speaks. He always has a band wrapped around his forehead to hold his shiny black hair, which then falls down either side of his face in brown, leather-strapped plaits. He is strong and bronzed and always fills the space around him with a sense of peace and pure love. He has changed my life out of all recognition. I seldom know what he is bringing and rarely know where he is leading me, but over the years I have come to trust him without reservation. It seems natural to trust him. I love being with him.

As I pick up the letters I feel his excitement and know for certain that he is anticipating the journey that lies ahead of us, and I wonder again why he has been so reluctant to tell me anything about it, other than the barest facts. Today's journey to America is the start of some-thing important – that I know. It also marks the end of a process of discovery that began a long time ago on a day just like this, when the postman delivered the mail.

On that day, in April 1991, I also came down the stairs and col-lected the letters together. I stood up, yawned, stretched and then went to the kitchen, glancing sleepily through the pile. I filled the elec-tric kettle and plugged it in, then I opened the letter from America.

Dear Mrs Walker,

Over eight months ago I received via telefax your letter inquiring of two rain symbols. Prior to answering your inquiry I decided to await your 'detailed letter'. Since seven months have now passed and I have not received your letter I will answer you.

The two symbols that you sent to have translated are made by two separate individuals by two separate tribes. The drawing with the jaguar is of Eastern Woodlands origin. Both symbols are religious.

Both symbols are translatable and they convey messages. I can read them but it is not for me to translate them for you. These symbols tell entire stories and as a Native American I have not been given the authority to translate these stories for Non-Native Americans.

Yours sincerely

His Black Horse
(Thomas Rain)
2nd April 1991

I saw the letter fall out of my hand. 'The symbols are true!' I shouted. Tony rushed in. 'The symbols are true,' I said to him. He looked at me quizzically. 'OK, I'll explain it later,' I said, knowing I needed time to work out how to convey the importance of this letter, not only to Tony, but to the world at large.

'White Arrow,' I said, 'I'm sorry I doubted.'

He appeared beside me, 'Do not worry, Little One. I too am excited. The truth can now be told.'

'Truth about what?' I asked.

'Patience. In time it will be revealed.'

I knew well enough there was little point in pushing him to tell me. If the time was not right, and if the answer was yet not to come from Spirit, then I would have to engage my mind and find answers of my own. I sat down with my coffee, placing the letter in front of me. I tried hard to remember one night in 1980 when he had appeared to me as I lay ill in bed. A Spirit Indian I had not met before stood beside him.

'I want you to draw a picture for me,' White Arrow said, in a grave voice that I knew signalled something of importance. I grabbed paper and pencil and, to the best of my ability, drew the patterns he showed me. When I had finished, they both vanished. I looked at the drawings, wondering what they were and who the other Indian was. White Arrow immediately reappeared with an answer to my unspoken question, 'I need his help as the symbol is Cherokee. He is Cherokee.'

I looked at the drawing again. A child of six might have done it.

'A symbol for what, White Arrow?' He wouldn't answer. I turned the symbol round in my hands. Some of the things White Arrow had given me before had been puzzling, but he had always explained their meaning. This time he was saying nothing, and eventually my need to know gave way to my trust in him and in the wisdom and knowledge that comes from his world. So I just looked at him.

'I will return with the Cherokee again, with more drawings. You will keep them. When the time is right they will be explained to you, but not now – so there is no use asking, Little One. One day I will bring into your life someone who will explain them to you, but at a later stage.'

For the following seven nights, White Arrow and the other Red Indian came to me, bringing a single drawing on each visit. When I had the seven I knew instinctively that there would be no more.

I eventually gave in to my curiosity and started looking at books on the Red Indians and their culture. I found nothing like the drawings I had been given. One day I even went to the British Museum where I did find a book by a man called Jefferson, who had studied Red Indian symbols at the turn of the century. In his book there was one illustration that resembled one of the symbols I had been given, and another with some vague similarity to another symbol, but no interpretation of their purpose or meaning was offered.

Although I learned nothing more about the symbols through my research, it did serve to educate me a little in the history and ways of the Native American people. I suppose White Arrow knew I would search in vain for answers to the symbols, and I suppose he also knew I would learn something about his people. When I could find out no more, I decided to put the drawings away, knowing that when White Arrow was ready he would show me answers.

That was in March 1980, and the intervening years were filled with change. As White Arrow watched over me, I experienced and witnessed great changes in my own life, and in the lives of those around me who were drawn to White Arrow's teachings. Every day was a learning process about Spirit and the way Spirit helps people through White Arrow. As time went by, White Arrow also revealed more to

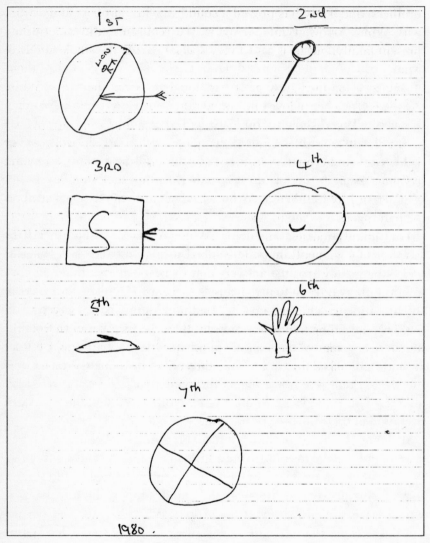

The seven symbols

me about our past together and about our marriage. I learned about his father, Sitting Bull, the Chief of the tribe I had been brought up in, after I had been taken from my white parents. I was shown how we lived together and brought up a family. Tony was initially unsettled by White Arrow's insistence that he still considered me to be his wife, but over the years he grew accustomed to the idea and now they have great respect for each other. They regard each other as blood brothers, and Tony has proved a solid, rock-like support in my work with White Arrow. White Arrow is in a real sense a member of my present family; but he is also a very special part of the whole family of Man.

My love for him grew as it had for Tony over the years. White Arrow is a teacher of love and comfort, sent by God to show the living a better way; to show us the door to his kingdom while we live on earth. I felt truly blessed, and happy to carry on our work in the knowledge that even if a great deal of it felt unseen, the answers would come in time.

Then in July 1991 White Arrow asked me to send the seven symbols he had dictated to me to America. He asked me to find a directory of Red Indian agencies, and in it he pointed with his finger to the address of Thomas Rain. I understood that White Arrow was at last directing me towards the answers to my questions about the symbols. I sent only two of the seven symbols, because I realised they were of the utmost importance, and I wanted to make sure they weren't falling into the wrong hands before I sent them all. Had I known from the outset what some of the answers to my questions were to be, I think I would have asked for God to take the cup away there and then.

· 2 ·

The High One

As soon as I received Thomas Rain's written response to the first two symbols, I sent him a copy of *Heaven Can Come Later*, a book I had written and published myself in an attempt to tell the story of how I came to be with White Arrow in both this and a previous life. With it I sent a covering letter, but no more of the symbols, because I still needed to make sure that what I was sending was going to the people White Arrow had in mind. I was impatient for a reply, and every day that passed without an answer felt hollow.

Then the phone rang at 7.30 one morning. I tried to get to it before it woke Tony, but I heard him pick it up. 'Ann, it's for you. America! Mr Thomas Rain.' I leapt at the receiver, heard Tony's extension go down and felt my heart thumping in my chest.

'Hello, can I help you?' There was an echo on the line and at first it sounded as though I was answering myself. The line crackled a bit, then I heard,

'Ann Walker?'

'Yes,' I answered. My heart slowed down. His voice was deep and clear.

'This is Thomas Rain. You wrote to me about the symbols . . . Hello?'

'Yes, yes, I'm here.' I was trying to form a picture of him in my mind.

'Well, I just wanted to call you to say that we believe you may have come from these parts many years ago. Your book *Heaven Can Come Later* says you were married to White Arrow – we think we can verify the reincarnation . . . You still there?' My head was spinning.

'Yes, I am.'

'Well, the two symbols you have sent me are important. I have mailed you another letter, but I just thought I would call you personally. Would it be possible for you to come out and meet us?'

'Uh . . . Yes.' I sat down. 'Yes, as soon as I can. I'll make some arrangements at my end and then I'll let you know.' He briefly explained that he was one of five spiritual leaders in the Assiniboine community, and gave me his phone number. As I wrote the numbers down, I felt the need to hear it said again.

'Mr Rain, about the information in the book I sent you. It is *true* that I was married to White Arrow in a previous life? You can prove that from what I wrote, can you?'

'Yes.'

'Have you ever had anyone contact you like this before?'

'Yes, we have. Over a hundred years ago a man called Jack Wilson came to us from another part of America. Have you heard of him?'

'No.'

'Well, we think your reincarnation could be linked in some way to this man.'

'Who was Jack Wilson?' I asked. 'Was he important to you?'

'He was, Ann. You could say he was a prophet, a legendary Indian leader who introduced the Ghost Dance. Before he died, he told us he would return one day. We gave him an Indian Name. It was *Wovoka:* "Walker".'

I said nothing. Some part of me that I can only describe as the truth opened up inside and I looked into it with great intensity. 'No, Mr Rain. I am not Jack Wilson.' White Arrow had given me no clues about that name so I just knew it was wrong.

I told him I would ring as soon as possible and hung up. I sat back. I was born in North America over one hundred years ago, grew up on Indian land, married a Sioux Indian and passed into Spirit some sixty years later. I had been reborn in England in 1949 where I grew up to meet, when I was thirty-seven, a Spirit Guide called White Arrow, who had been my husband well over a century earlier. Now White Arrow seemed to be showing me a way to go back to our homeland in Montana where, it transpired from Thomas's word, there existed some form of proof that we can, and do, return from Spirit. It suddenly dawned on me that somewhere out there I might come face to face with my descendants. Someone who greeted me in the street might be a great grandson; someone who told me the time might be my great granddaughter!

You may think that I would be used to the unusual after so many years of working with Spirit, that nothing should surprise me any more. I must remind you, however, that I live in a human body and I exist in the same emotional realm as other people. I realised now that I had two families, one there, one here, both from different times, with different blood, with no connection whatsoever between us apart from time – a time past and a time present.

A week later, the second letter arrived.

May 15, 1991

Dear Mrs Walker,
   Please accept this letter as confirmation that I have received your telefax messages, your personal letter, and the book which you so graciously sent to me.
   Your story and your symbols are very interesting. I'm sure that we are almost wasting our time by corresponding. We really need to speak in person. Unknown to the whole world is that the traditional Native Americans have kept their traditional ways and knowledges. We can help you.
   I will be free to see you in July or whatever date you choose to come to the United States of America to visit. The only date that I may be indisposed or out of town would be from July 3 to 8, 1991.

   I may call you.

   Sincerely,

   Thomas Rain.

This confirmed what Thomas' earlier letter had suggested: that symbols known to the Native Americans *had* been given to me by White Arrow and the Cherokee spirit. They were symbols from a language that had been closely guarded and never, over hundreds of years, had they been shared with a white person. This surely was proof that Spirit survives – how else could I, in West London, know of secret ceremonial symbols never before seen outside of a closed community in the United States, but for the intercession of Spirit? I rang Thomas Rain immediately, to be absolutely sure I understood how important this was. He simply laughed and said it was true, adding calmly that not only would I have to travel to the United States, but somehow I would have to prove myself to be one of them, otherwise they could not sanction revealing the information I wanted. Quite how hard *that* was going to be I did not realise as I started to make plans for the trip.

Tony has a fear of flying, and I knew there was no way he would go with me. But I also knew he would not stand in my way. I explained to him that I had to go, that it was for White Arrow. I promised I would call every day.

I did, however, need someone to witness events as they developed in America. Someone who could be truthful about what they saw and heard but who would remain detached from the events themselves. After much thought, I decided to take my daughter and grand-daughter, and my close friend and personal assistant, Val Smith. Val has helped me from the very beginning. She typed my first book and arranged my tours and she has never been envious or wanted to push herself into the limelight; her only motivation has been to be a part of White Arrow's work, and to help bring him to a wider audience.

I was aware that I would be in the thick of things, carried away with excitement and concentration. My daughter would carefully observe every event in great detail, and Val would write everything down as it happened. Between the two of them they would ensure that nothing would be overlooked, that every significant thing would be impartially witnessed and recorded. I knew that what I would learn would be hard for people to believe, and that proof would certainly be needed to help others accept these revelations.

White Arrow left me to make all the arrangements. I planned the trip for the end of July 1991 and spoke to Thomas Rain several more times, sending him two more symbols. Once again, he confirmed that they held important meanings, but declined to divulge their message until I was in America.

'Patience, Little One, you will know when you get there,' was White Arrow's only comment.

'Yes, OK, but is there anything I should know, anything I should be aware of?'

He sat down and considered my question. As he thought about it, I studied him and wondered who in Heaven he was. He looked up and said, 'The symbols given to you hold many keys to the future for many people. You cannot possibly know until we go to the States. I promise when you go all will be explained.'

Then I slowly became aware of another presence in the room. At first I could only feel it. Then slowly I saw the air form some kind of shape. I couldn't see it clearly enough to describe it, but I knew this Spirit was a guide and knew that he was a High One – guides who are at a higher level and who help us through advising our personal guides. I had never seen or been in the presence of a High One and felt foolishly self-conscious and on my best behaviour. White Arrow said, 'The High One wants a word with you. Yes, Little One, there is a higher one than me.'

The High One spoke with a level, commanding voice that was at once frightening and mesmerising. 'What you seek in America is what you want, Ann.' I assumed he meant evidence to prove the existence of reincarnation.

'The stories are true,' he went on. 'White Arrow has an important mission here. He brings messages from us. His journey is important. You are important. Remember, I wrote your future so everything in this plan has been taken care of. All you must do is follow.' His voice enthralled me. It was almost flat and unemotional when he spoke, yet as the words reached me they were full of colour and feeling. I was sitting upright on the edge of the chair. 'The truth, and the proof, are important for the future, for all people. Above everything you have the key to it all. Trust us. Your work will be long and hard and many people will doubt the things you are told to tell to them. But not all. Your trust in us is important. You have never doubted us, proving your faith by that; but the knowledge you have been given up until now is only a part of your life. Now you must find the strength to face the world with new knowledge you are about to receive from us.'

He paused and for a moment I thought he had gone. Then I heard him say, 'I understand your confusion.'

I have always known that Spirit can read our minds, and it was true: I was confused. I sat back in the chair and listened for more.

'This you must believe: you have been chosen to work with one of the highest Guides in Heaven. That Guide is White Arrow. He is the most supreme Guide. He will make this clear. White Arrow must be known to exist by all men. We watch in anticipation. It must all be planned, revealed in sections when the times are right, until the full picture is apparent. You have been chosen, for you do not look on White Arrow as a God, but as a friend. As your friend he removes the need for you to feel important. To us you are. Trust us. We are here now to help with the Coming Event. The course of life will change. We are here to help the world.'

Then he was gone.

White Arrow said nothing, so I tried hopelessly to understand all this on my own. I would have been so much happier just knowing that in a previous incarnation I had been married to a Red Indian who had re-turned to me in Spirit in this life in order to help and teach people. But now I had to accept that White Arrow was 'the most supreme Guide'. I was scared.

'Why *me*, White Arrow?' I asked. He smiled. I smiled back and said, 'Oh, it's OK. Whatever your friend meant, you can still be White Arrow to me. I knew you were special anyway. I'm glad.'

White Arrow kept his clear blue eyes on me. They were untroubled. 'In time, Little One, it will be made clearer to you. I will tell you all when we return from America. It is important to the world that you go.' That was all he said.

'Who the hell is he?' I thought when he had gone. I wanted to know if I was good enough for him. Why had God chosen someone as ordin-ary as me and given me a Guide as important as White Arrow? The responsibility suddenly weighed heavily on my shoulders. A million thoughts and questions raced through my mind until eventually I realised I would have to wait for Spirit to answer.

The following morning I woke early and was sitting up in bed with my tea when White Arrow appeared. However, he didn't seem to have anything important to discuss with me and just sat with me as I wrote a letter. I was used to his ways now and it felt comfortable to have him there. Then from nowhere I felt the room fill with an overwhelming Spirit presence. I quickly checked White Arrow's face to be sure everything was all right, and as I turned away from him, I saw a large, golden lion standing at the foot of my bed, breathing slowly. At first I was startled, then became mesmerised as I watched it walk in a circle around the room and then lie down in front of the fire. For some reason I immediately thought of the High One.

'This can't be the High One, can it, White Arrow?' I asked.

'Yes, Little One,' he replied. 'We come in many forms.'

As soon as he said that, I wanted to know why they came in different forms, and why did they come to me? I wanted to know so much, but White Arrow would only tell me to have patience. 'In time, you will understand,' he said.

About two weeks before I was due to leave for the States, I armed myself with a list of questions and at 7.30 one Tuesday morning, phoned Thomas Rain in Montana again.

'Hello?'

'It's Ann Walker from England. How are you?'

'Fine!'

'I hope you don't mind me ringing. It's late at night for you.'

'No, it's OK,' he replied.

I was eager to get to the point. 'I have questions to ask you.'

'Fire ahead.'

'First of all, you will be able to read the symbols when I come over, won't you? And you will be allowed to tell me what they mean?'

'Yes, Ann.' His calm voice made me aware of a slight antagonism in my own. 'When you come over we will explain everything. But Ann, it will take at least two years for you to fully digest what you will learn.'

I was calculating in my mind how long I had already been waiting for an answer to these symbols – I was disappointed and angry – when suddenly he said, 'Did you know that I know White Arrow? I know him well.'

'Do you? I'm glad.' But I was puzzled: White Arrow was *my* Guide. 'Well then, do you know who White Arrow was? And what his name was on Earth?' I asked. I knew but I wanted confirmation.

Thomas said I would be told these things when I arrived in Montana, and that he was travelling to meet the people from whom White Arrow had come. Again I felt the excitement grow. At moments like that I can hardly believe what is happening to me, and my thoughts are chaotic. I was speaking to a Red Indian who lives where White Arrow had lived. I love White Arrow, and know that it is not possible for him to speak untruths. But at times my human need to disbelieve is greater than my desire for truth – we are all doubters at core. And what was happening to me certainly *seemed* beyond belief. Lost in these thoughts, I heard only the end of Thomas' sentence,

' . . . be having a religious ceremony for you.'

'What?' I shouted.

'I said, when you come will you bring a swim-suit and a loose dress, as we will be having a religious ceremony for you.'

'What sort of ceremony? What for?' There was a short silence and then he told me to read certain books on the Red Indians. If I couldn't find them he would endeavour to send them to me, but he made it clear that I needed to educate myself further in the ways of '*my*' people. I told him about the remaining five symbols and said I would bring them with me. As we were about to finish the call, he asked me a strange question:

'Do you know about the crop circles in your country?'

I laughed out loud and said, 'Are you asking me if I've met any aliens recently?'

'Yes,' he said. 'I know you have been in contact with one.'

He meant Michael.

· 3 ·

Michael

White Arrow brought Michael to me in spirit years before, in 1983. I had known him as flesh and blood when I was young and first going out with Tony, because they worked together and had developed a strong friendship based on a shared sense of humour. We knew each other for about six months and then moved on and lost contact until two or three years later, when I learned that he had passed into Spirit while still a young man in his twenties. He had had bone cancer. Although I was sad at the time, his memory faded until one afternoon, many years later and quite out of the blue, Michael appeared. I turned the television off and called to Tony.

'You'll never guess who's here.' Tony is past being surprised by my saying these sorts of things. 'Do you remember Michael?'

'Michael?' said Tony. 'Oh yes, I remember. Give him my regards and love.' This is Tony's standard greeting to Spirit, be it to his mother, his father, or whoever, despite the fact that I have told him that all he has to do is mentally tell them himself.

'Michael sends it back. Isn't it nice he remembers us?' After a while he left and we thought no more about it. A year later he returned, but unlike Spirits who just appear in front of me or walk into a room, Michael seemed to 'zoom' in. I was in the midst of a meeting, and no one could have been further from my mind. I explained to my friends that Michael was in the room and told them who he had been. He continued to appear in this manner for the next few years, visiting maybe once or twice a year, speaking little, but seemingly content to be with us. Four years ago in 1987 I watched him 'zoom' into the room again. This time he stayed longer and we spoke about life in the Spirit realm.

'Do you live in Heaven, Michael?' I asked him.

'No, Ann. Shortly after I died, within days, I had the choice of returning to the living. I did indeed choose to live again; but not on Earth. I live on another planet now.'

'Are you trying to tell me you're an alien?'

Michael didn't answer that precisely. 'Where I live, the planet is black-and-white.'

I turned to Tony and explained what Michael was saying, adding, 'No one will believe this. I mean, I'm not doubting what you're saying, Michael, but I'm going to need time to understand this.'

'Maybe,' he said. I turned to look for White Arrow. He would know what was right.

'It's OK. Just listen,' he said. I turned to Michael again. He looked nothing like an Alien to me; but then, how would I know what an Alien looked like anyway? I waited for him to continue, but nothing more was said, and after a short time he vanished.

Michael's visits became more frequent after that but he would always repeat that he came from a black-and-white planet. I asked him if he had a family.

'Yes, I have a wife and children.'

I think I would have been less at ease with his visits had it not been for White Arrow. I mean no disrespect to any other Spirit, but to me, White Arrow is more important than anyone else. As long as he is there I'm not bothered by whoever wants to be in touch with me, extra-terrestrial or otherwise. So much work has now been done through science fiction in books and films and television to accustom us to the idea of life on other planets, that most people now feel it is a very real possibility. The language we have developed to describe extra-terrestrial life is tinged with Hollywood's images, but it is the only common language between us and the only tool they have to describe themselves to us. After all, we can only hope to understand something if it lies within the bounds of our knowledge at any given time. Many people around the world who believe in reincarnation are more accustomed to belief in life on other planets. Hindu scriptures, I am told, refer to the migration of souls to other planets, and to anyone who believes in the Spirit world, there is no great barrier to believing in life elsewhere in the universe.

Michael explained that he was a living being from a planet which is superior to our own. He and his people knew how to direct their Spirits from one plane, or dimension, to another. Through our Spirit channels they could talk to me without having to manifest themselves physically. What I did not understand was why he looked human; and why had we, on Earth, not yet found other life forms.

After communicating with me for several years, he did something which made the answers to these questions abundantly clear. One evening in 1987 he zoomed into the room in his usual form and changed before my eyes, from the 5' 10", red-haired, slim young man I had known, into a colossus. He just grew taller and taller until his face vanished through the ceiling, and he had to bend his knees to enable me to see his head and shoulders. His whole form had changed – no film or television programme had ever invented a being like this!

'Ann, this is the real me now.' He spoke softly as though he didn't want to frighten me any more than he felt I already was, but I wasn't really alarmed. I was fascinated, hypnotised, but not scared. I kept on telling myself that the Michael I had known had been a kind man, and the Michael I was seeing now was the same kind soul in a different form. I knew there was no malice in him. Anyway, White Arrow was standing over me. I could tell that he knew this demonstration was going to take place, but I couldn't help wondering what purpose it served. I couldn't see how having contact with a being from another planet would help me in my work with White Arrow. Then knowledge that one day it would all be made clear washed through my head again, and I just accepted it. I liked being in touch with the alien after that. I accepted him just as a friend and hoped he would continue to be that in the future.

In August 1990 I introduced an old friend of Tony's to Michael. Harry is an extremely clever man with a great interest in UFO phenomena. He came on several occasions to take part in question and answer sessions with Michael, in White Arrow's presence. One day Harry asked what had caused the explosion at Tunguska, Siberia, in 1908 which recent research has shown bore all the hallmarks of an atomic explosion. Michael was about to answer when White Arrow stepped in. He spoke to Michael and I was told that it was not possible for them to answer that particular question. It was the first time I had seen White Arrow intervene in the teachings of another Spirit and I realised White Arrow was in charge of Michael. White Arrow just said, 'Soon, Little One. You will know soon.'

The fact that I had been given so many little glimpses of this other world seemed to make the scale of information that remained unseen, presumably to be revealed at a later stage, a real cause for fear. I stopped pushing for more, and helping people came again to the fore; Michael once more slipped away into the background.

Until 1991 that is, when he again appeared to me in his enormous Alien form.

'Michael, why do you visit me?' I asked him. 'What purpose do your visits serve?' White Arrow appeared and sat quietly next to me.

'We are going to meet soon,' Michael said. 'Not just yet, but soon.' I looked up, craning my neck but unable to see his face beyond the ceiling.

'Where and when will the meeting happen?' I asked.

'When the time is right, the meeting will be arranged.' White Arrow nodded in agreement. I was not sure if I was brave enough for this. Meeting Michael over the years in Spirit form with White Arrow by my side was one thing; physically shaking hands with an Alien visitor from outer space would be something quite different.

Michael was about to say something else, when White Arrow shook his head. 'Just who are you, White Arrow?' I said.

'Little One, you know very little at the moment, but the time will come when you will be very important. The knowledge I bring will help many people on this earth. I have come with a message, but it must be laid out and seen to be true in the correct way. At the moment you are confused.' I certainly was! 'I promise I will explain when we come back from America. Trust me.'

'Oh, I *do* trust you, White Arrow. It's just that so much is happening and I'm getting tired and a little scared, not of going to the States, but of who you are.' It felt as though changes were afoot and it was hard for me not to resist the prospect of change. I wanted to know how Thomas knew about Michael, exactly how he fitted into this extraordinary jigsaw and what meanings were hidden in the symbols.

In retrospect I can see how I was gradually being educated, but nothing prepared me for what was to follow.

· 4 ·

July, 1991

On 26 July 1991, the day we embarked on our journey to America, I rose before dawn. I turned to White Arrow. 'Excited?' I asked him. He had been by my side for twelve years, since 1979, and it seemed to me that in some strange way this was White Arrow's homecoming. He smiled that lovely, warm smile that starts in his eyes, sitting in his usual place with his legs crossed and his hands folded over his chest.

'Yes, I am pleased,' he said. White Arrow has never been one for long conversations. Whatever he needs to say he says without embellishment.

'Thank you,' I said.

'For what?' he asked.

'Oh, I don't know. Everything, I suppose.' I was thinking how lucky I was just being able to talk to White Arrow. 'So many things. Oh, this is no good, I'll have to get Tony up.' He smiled again and then vanished. 'Tony, it's nearly seven,' I called out. I looked at the cases. Everything was there, I was sure, but I slipped from the bed and unlocked them again and checked that I had packed absolutely everything. Thomas Rain had told me to bring Earl Grey tea and Hudson Bay chewing tobacco, since it was, he told me, their custom to exchange gifts. As I knew I would be meeting nine chiefs in total, I had packed about a dozen of each.

Everything seemed to be in place. As I fumbled with the locks again I heard Tony moving around and felt worried and saddened that I had to leave him on his own. He hated being alone and I knew I would miss him terribly, but, as I say, he just would not fly. His fear of heights was so great that even the idea of sitting in a plane at 30,000 feet brought him out in a cold sweat.

The flight was due to leave at 12.30. I wanted to be at the airport in plenty of time and had arranged for Val to come round at 7.30. She had never flown before and I could almost feel her excitement as she knocked at our door. My daughter was also pleased to be going but my beloved little granddaughter, who had been in a plane before, was the most excited and she managed to do all the jumping around and shouting that we sensible grown-ups can't quite do any more.

At the airport I kissed a worried Tony goodbye and promised again to ring him every day. He had the number for our hotel and I knew that keeping in touch regularly would make us both feel happier. At the departure gate we hugged each other again and I whispered, 'It'll all be all right, love.' He held on for a long time, then turned away and walked into the crowd.

As we settled into our seats and the plane taxied to the runway, I closed my eyes. The engines roared and then screamed and an invisible force pushed my back deep into the chair. I felt the nose lift; we were airborne. Unable to contain myself any more, I mentally shouted at the top of my voice, 'We're off, White Arrow, I hope you know where you're taking me and what you're doing!'

I opened my eyes and looked at my travelling companions. The four of us were on our way to Great Falls, Montana, a small town of about 8,000 souls in the middle of nowhere.

It was a long flight and due to an error at the check-in counter I had been allocated a non-smoker seat. I smoke heavily and was lucky enough to meet a couple at the back of the plane who invited me to sit with them whenever I wanted. They couldn't understand why three women and a child were going to a small town like Great Falls. I knew there was no way of even beginning to explain so I simply said that we had friends there, and left it at that.

By the time we arrived at Great Falls we had been travelling for seventeen hours. We rang for a taxi and waited outside the airport. There was warmth in the air. Thomas Rain had told me to breathe heavily of this air when I arrived, and that is exactly what I did. I stood up and closing my eyes took deep, scooping breaths from the mild breeze. Then I saw White Arrow for the first time since we had left London. I was so pleased to see him.

'Well, we're here,' he said, and then he left. I called after him, wanting more than just a curt statement of fact, but he was gone. The taxi pulled up and we all piled in, grateful that all that lay ahead of us now was our beds. I was first out of the car when we arrived at the hotel and as I struggled into the foyer with the cases I looked around for some help. Behind the reception desk a girl was speaking to someone on the phone. As I approached the desk I heard her say, 'No, Mrs Walker hasn't arrived yet.'

'Please!' I said, waving my hands at her. 'Is that my husband?'

'Is that you Ann?' I could hear the slight edge of panic in Tony's voice. He asked if we were all OK, and I assured him that everyone was absolutely fine. As we checked in, the receptionist handed me an envelope, but I was so involved getting the cases to our rooms that I forgot to open it. My daughter and my granddaughter were in one room, and Val and myself in another. By the time I pulled back the sheets from my own bed, I realised I had been operating in that state of mind which is a blend of physical exhaustion and exhilaration. Then, as I climbed into bed, I remembered the letter.

7/26/91

Mrs Ann Walker

Dear Ann:

Welcome to the United States of America and to the State of Montana. I hope your trip was easy, fast, and not too tiring. I am on my way home from a business trip to Seattle, Washington. I have been on the road for the past six days.

Listed below is the schedule which I can give to you for Saturday, Sunday, and Monday, July 27, 28, and 29, 1991. Rest tonight for you will arrive rather late.

Saturday, July 27, 1991
10.00-11.00am; I will drive down from Havre, to pick you up here at your motel. I will drive you to Fort Belknap where I must conduct a Native American ceremony at 2.00pm for two families.

We will hold a religious ceremony and a traditional feast and a Give-Away will be held. This will last until 6.00pm.

At 7:00 p.m. you can watch the Milk River Indian Days Powwow.

We will speak when I come down but if you wish, you can stay at the Chinook Montana Motor Inn tonight.

Sunday, July 28, 1991

This is the big day. I will describe this in more detail when I see you. I will take you, your daughter and granddaughter with me at 8.00pm. We will be holding a formal Assiniboine Spiritual Ceremony for you, White Arrow, Michael, and other Spirits who are with you ALWAYS.

This ceremony will be a traditional Sweat Lodge Purification Ceremony. Three other Spirit ladies will take part in this ceremony. I have received the Spiritual instructions that we must do this in this manner since the entire happening has been pre-ordained.

At the conclusion of this ceremony, we will explain in full the four symbols and the others that you are bringing with you.

Monday, July 29, 1991

I will bring you back to Great Falls, Montana. On Tuesday, I will be involved in business which will once again take my time for the rest of the week. If you have any questions please call me.

I look forward with great anticipation to meeting you and yours in person.

Sincerely yours,

Thomas Rain
TA Shurga Suba – His Black Horse

I turned to Val and said, 'Wasn't that nice of him?' Then I fell into a deep ocean of sleep.

· 5 ·

Summer, 1991 –
Arrival in Montana

On July 27th we were up early. I tried to find the restaurant for break-fast and was directed towards the lounge where there was a sideboard with a coffee machine and a basket full of doughnuts which I distributed to Val, my daughter and my granddaughter, waking them cheerfully into our first day in this new country. Then I settled to read Thomas's letter again. Val was in the shower and I shouted, 'I won-der what he's like, Val?' A crowd of faces crossed my mind. 'I wonder if he's short, or fat, or wears glasses?' Val just laughed. My daughter came in with my granddaughter, who proceeded to investigate the radio and the television and under the beds and behind the curtains until we were ready to go in search of a proper breakfast.

We walked out into the heat of our first American day and crossed the street to a café which appeared to be locked in some kind of a time warp. It was like a diner out of the 1950s – there was an old jukebox by the window, and a handful of people sitting at the counter. As we sat down at a table by the window, I saw a man at the bar dressed in a full cowboy outfit and it took several seconds for me to register that this was a *real* cowboy. Only the spurs were missing, but otherwise he might have stepped out of a film.

I could see our motel from the window. I thought if we had time before Thomas Rain arrived, we could all explore together and do a bit of shopping. A group of young people came in and gathered around the jukebox. The 'waiter', who was only about twelve years old, took our order, and as he moved past the other kids, the jukebox clicked into action and the theme tune from the film *The Good, The Bad, and The Ugly* started playing. I had to laugh, because it felt as though the atmosphere was being stage-managed from some hidden control room.

Plates overflowing with food were brought to our table. The ome-lettes must have been made with half a dozen eggs each and there were more hash browns than we could possibly eat. My grand-daughter's little mouth fell open and her eyes widened in disbelief. We laughed a great deal and ate until we could manage no more, then we chatted and joked about what the day might bring. I pushed my chair a little way from the table and lit a cigarette to have with my coffee, resting my elbows on the table and looking once more at the shop-fronts and signposts that lined the street. One of the girls said some-thing and I moved my eyes to meet hers and share the joke, then sipped at my coffee but when I moved my eyes back to the view, it was no longer there. The busy high street had gone; instead I could see only a dusty red track and two cowboys on fine dark horses. Then the vision went, and once again I could see the present-day town. This is not an uncommon occurrence for me, and I knew that I had gone back to a time before the town had even been built.

There was a message at the motel from Thomas informing us that he would ring again within half an hour. I dreaded something having gone wrong. We went back to our rooms and waited.

'Hi there. Good morning,' the voice said. It was a bad line, but I knew it was Thomas. 'Did you have good flight?'

'Yes, fine thanks.'

'Are you very tired? Would you like to leave it for today?'

'No, I'm OK. Really. In fact I had a very good night's sleep. We're all fine and looking forward to meeting you.'

'Great, so am I. There are so many things we have to talk about. I'm afraid I've been held up a bit, and won't be able to pick you up till about twelve noon – will that be OK with you?' I looked at my watch. It was 9.45.

'That'll be fine,' I said.

'See you then.'

I said 'OK, bye,' and replaced the receiver. The girls were waiting eagerly to hear what had been said but as I started to tell them that Thomas had been held up, the phone rang again.

'Sorry, Ann.' It was Thomas. 'I forgot to tell you it's going to take a couple of hours to get there, so, to save you coming back tomorrow, I wondered if you would like to stay in a motel in Chinook.' He would book accommodation for two nights so that we would not have to travel back and forth between ceremonies. We now had time to see the market and some more of the town.

As we walked along, my granddaughter holding my hand and jumping around with joy, I felt very glad that I had brought her. She was only five, but I wanted her to remember this trip later in her life.

Because a large market we discovered was part of a great annual rodeo festivity, the road had been blocked off, becoming a pedestrian precinct with people in all sorts of costumes and make-up walking between the stalls. Everybody seemed so happy and relaxed. At one end, a rock band was belting out heavy music, and in front of this a clown with red hair and a wide painted smile tumbled and joked and made people laugh. We stopped at some of the stalls and bought a few bits and pieces. We were back at the hotel just before noon. We decided to wait outside for Thomas, sitting on a wall enjoying the sun and watching the people go by. 12.30 came and went with no sign of him. I noticed that White Arrow had not been around me that morning and assumed he was with his people. He is never far from me and I knew that if I needed him he would appear.

Eventually the sun became too hot, and, concerned for my granddaughter's soft skin, I suggested to my daughter that we go back inside and wait. I jumped off the wall and as I picked up my bag I noticed a man emerge from a large white car. He was in his forties, extremely tall and well built with skin that was tinted, but I realised at that moment that I had no idea what colour a Red Indian actually was. He walked towards the motel door and I said,

'Excuse me, are you Mr Thomas Rain?'

'Yes, you're Ann Walker!' A huge smile spread across his face. We shook hands and I introduced the others. I liked him immediately.

Soon we were all driving away in his car and he was outlining how events would unfold over the next two days. I sat in the front and was able to study his face as he drove and spoke. He would occasionally turn round to make sure everyone in the back was comfortable, or to emphasise a point. We would go first to Chinook, he said, in order to book into our motel, then on to Fort Belknap to arrive at around 4.00pm. Some of the symbols would be explained to me at the Spiritual Ceremony to be held on Sunday evening, but he would explain the first symbol on Saturday night.

We drove 165 miles. I said nothing to the others, but from the outset I had been aware of a Spirit Red Indian on horseback galloping behind us and periodically calling out the words, 'Hohe! Hohe!'. We drove past Big Sandy and Bear Paw Mountains, Rocky Boy Mountains and a town called Havre before finally reaching our destination at Chinook. It was a typical American small town, and the motel was near a railroad station which mainly received goods trains; the passenger trains only ever stopping on request. Thomas had to be at the Reservation to conduct the ceremony for the two families which he had mentioned in his letter.

On our way to Fort Belknap Thomas told me more about the ceremony. My family and I would be guests of honour at the ceremony conducted to instigate a twelve-month period of mourning which would hold the deceased and their family together, at the end of which another ceremony would be held to release the Spirit and end the period of grief. It seemed a very great privilege to be admitted to an event of such intimacy.

Shortly before 4.00pm we arrived at the Fort Belknap Indian Reservation. As we drove into the car park I could see a large structure to my left which looked like some form of government building. To my right stood another large edifice which was clearly a place of worship. Other cars were pulling into the area and people were pouring out of them towards this prayer house. We were the only white people there. Some of the children were dressed in real Indian clothes and wore paint on their faces, while others were in jeans and trainers like kids anywhere in the world nowadays. Inside the building I could see rows of chairs set out in front of long benches. Thomas left us to find a place to sit and we settled in the third row back, so that we would be able to see clearly. Once seated, I took time to examine my surroundings. People were bringing in extravagant quantities of food, heaped onto trestle tables that ran the length of one wall. Directly in front of me, high up on the wall, there was a large shield covered in Indian drawings. In the corner beyond it hung items of Indian heritage and clothing and dotted on tables I could see war bonnets, blankets, and other beautifully decorated and colourful articles.

Behind the long table was what seemed to be a large kitchen. I was thirsty and went in to ask for water. At least a dozen women were cooking. I was helped to a glass and as I stood in the middle of them, their heat, their noise, silently drinking the cool water, a procession of women carrying enormous platters of meat walked past. I wondered how many people they were feeding – there was enough meat for thousands. I felt I was in the way and went back to my seat. Thomas came over to tell us the ceremony would soon be starting.

Twelve chairs were placed in the centre of the hall, and various people sat in them. Thomas greeted each one as they came into the centre. It became clear that these were members of the bereaved families. When the chairs were all occupied, the ceremony commenced. It took about half an hour, and although I understood nothing that was said, because it was conducted entirely in their native tongue, I was moved to tears, partly because it was hard not to share in their grief, but mainly out of gratitude for having been allowed into this sacred event. Finally the Sacred Pipe of Peace was given by Thomas to each of the mourners and the ceremony was then concluded.

A long orderly queue of people, running half way around the hall, formed by the tables and waited patiently to be served. There must have been at least 1,000 people there and I learned that a further 2,500 would be joining us later. As guests of honour we were taken by Thomas to the front of the line and piled our plates high.

I watched the queue continue to grow an hour after we had eaten and still there was enough for people to fill their plates. Every single person on the reservation entered the building and was fed that afternoon. Thomas said we would be leaving for the Powwow in about half an hour and we were welcome to wait for him in the hall, or we could have a look around outside. As I stepped outside into the bright sunlight, the car park ceased to be. Instead of cars I could see wagons. These were wagons I had seen before – in my past. The image changed again and this time I was standing in the middle of a group of tepees, and Indians beckoned me to enter one of them. Before anything else happened, however, the scene reverted, and I was once again in the car park. I could hear my daughter talking to me. 'Quick Mum, do you want your picture taken?' I looked around, saw nothing more and shrugged my shoulders.

· 6 ·

Summer, 1991 –
First Disclosures

The scenery along the highway to the Powwow was breathtaking. I watched the distant silvery blue mountain ranges glide past as we drove through a landscape alive with colour. The sky was big, bigger than an English sky and even the clouds looked more vibrant. The girls were asking Thomas more about the ceremony and he was enjoying talking to them about the Indian ways. My eyes focused on the Spirit Indian who once more galloped alongside the car. I noticed that he held a pennant in one hand. I turned fully round and looked closer. It was White Arrow.

Amazed, I watched him for many miles until Thomas said, 'We're nearly there!' and then he was gone. This was White Arrow's land, his home. I felt another energy gathering around me, and although I could not see it, I knew this was Sitting Bull.

'Just a couple of miles to go,' said Thomas. I smiled and my thoughts were with Tony. I knew he would love this country, and I decided there and then that I would bring him one day, even if it meant coming by boat. It was difficult being separated, but I had no choice. The importance of this trip had been made abundantly clear to me, and I was not able even to consider letting White Arrow down.

The car stopped and in front of us stood a large open structure of steel posts supporting a metal roof. There were no walls, only rows of chairs surrounding the building. Thomas introduced us to three Sioux Indians, two men and a woman, who were preparing for the Powwow. The men wore war bonnets of astounding beauty, with long feathers trailing down their backs while the woman wore a traditional tasselled dress coloured like a rainbow. We took some group photographs, our own British outfits drab and neutral next to the Indians, then sat with the others already gathered, including some white Americans. The Powwow is an important ceremony to the Sioux. It is a form of religious dance which is held every week, each tribe's Powwow differing in style, but always intended as a celebration of life where they can dance and sing according to God's instruction.

My granddaughter was thirsty and we went in search of a soft drink while my daughter set up the video equipment. The ground was dusty and there was a warm breeze drifting through the gathering. The ceremony started at 7.30 pm and was due to carry on well into the morning. Indians, chanting loudly and holding tasselled banners, entered the dance area first. They looked magnificent, dressed in every colour imaginable, bejewelled and feathered and moving together as if connected. Hundreds more followed, winding round into the centre of the area until it was completely filled with noise and colour and movement.

As I watched, I became aware of a hollow longing deep in my stomach. It was as if I had heard the music before, as if I had moved my feet the way they moved theirs, as if my mouth had made the sounds they now made. I knew it was my past. It came in flashes and then went, but for the second or two when I had the sensation all I wanted to do was join in with the dancers. I felt White Arrow close by me and I knew he was happy. Then I felt strange. I wanted to cry. I knew this was my land and these were my people and I simultaneously grieved the length of time we had been separated, and rejoiced in this reunion.

We arrived back at the hotel at ten o'clock. I was physically tired, but my spirit was soaring. The time had come for Thomas to talk to me about the first symbol, so I bade the girls goodnight and he and I ordered a drink in the deserted lounge. He began by repeating to me that it would take at least two years for me to digest all of the information this trip would yield, and that it would not be possible this time for me to meet my Indian descendants. There would be another trip to America, he said, and that meeting would take place then.

The first symbol, one of the two I had sent in 1990, was a drawing of a circle crossed by a diagonal line. From outside the circle a horizontal arrow points from the right to the mid-point of the line, which is at the centre of the circle, and above the line sits a jaguar.

'Ann, I will now explain quickly to you what the first symbol means. The circle means the sky. The line through the middle of the circle is the Milky Way. The arrow means White Arrow, and we refer to the jaguar as the cat which is in the Milky Way.'

I looked at Thomas, trying hard to understand the implications of his interpretation, but to be perfectly honest it made little sense.

'Thomas . . . what are you saying? That White Arrow is part of the Milky Way? Or is that where he comes from?'

'Yes. That's right,' was all he said.

I tried to conceal my disappointment. Perhaps it was me. Perhaps I had thought there would be more to it than that. I already knew White Arrow came from above, so did it really matter if he came from the Milky Way? As far as I was concerned, White Arrow travelled all over the place so why should he not be part of the Milky Way?

Thomas said, 'Ann, we will explain more about the symbols tomorrow night and maybe that will help you understand.'

'To be perfectly honest – ' I said.

He leant forward and placed his hand on my arm. 'Don't worry. More will be explained to you tomorrow.'

I smiled and thanked him. We shook hands and he arranged to pick us up at noon on the following day. I walked slowly down the corridor back to my room and put the information about the symbol on a shelf at the back of my mind. I called Tony and felt better for hearing his voice, then went into my daughter's room and kissed my granddaughter good night. Finally, I sat up in bed and tried to explain to Val that I still had no idea why the symbols were so important, that I was apprehensive about the coming ceremony, and was beginning to feel overwhelmed by events. Val was understanding and supportive, and I felt grateful to have her with me. She said I was just tired and told me she was sure everything would be clearer in the morning. Reassured, I slept.

At 6.30 the following morning I was sitting in bed with a coffee and a cigarette, still battling to make sense of Thomas' explanation, of the feelings I had at the Powwow, and of my apprehension, when White Arrow appeared on the bed beside me. We had not spoken properly since landing in America, and apart from seeing him riding wonderfully by the car we had hardly been in touch at all.

'Hi!' I said. 'Enjoying yourself?'

'You're puzzled.'

'Yes I am. It's the symbol, I just don't see why it's so important.'

He studied me carefully and then said, 'Many years ago the symbols you have were intended for you. They were drawn by an Indian and they have been passed down over the years by my people. These symbols were passed down waiting for you to claim them. They knew that one day the right person would come. They have waited many years, Little One, for someone to come to them with these symbols, and because these symbols are so important, my people will be cautious for a while. The symbols are the start of other things. In the past many have gone to my people and said they were the one my people were waiting for.' He paused.

'What do you mean, "waiting for"?' I asked.

'Wait, Little One. I can only promise that in the near future all will be revealed.'

'You mean, I won't be told everything on this trip?'

'Patience. Your first symbol, Little One, is the key to allow my people to accept you, for only they know that the symbol illustrates me, and so it proves to them that you are definitely in contact with my Spirit, my *self*.'

'White Arrow, why can't you just tell me what they mean? Surely that would be simpler than all of this?'

'Little One, that is not the way, for you have a special path to follow and you need my people's help and to get that help you will find you will be tested by my people. Once you pass the test, they will help you on this journey.'

'Well, I hope I don't let you down,' I said, as Val turned over in her bed and White Arrow vanished. I spoke to Val for a bit, then called Tony again before we all went down for breakfast. There was a message for me from Thomas to say that he would be delayed by two hours and would pick us up at 2.00pm. Sure enough, Thomas arrived on the dot of two o'clock and once again we all piled into his car. This time, however, the only item of baggage was my small bag containing the swim suit, a cotton dress, Earl Grey tea and Hudson Bay tobacco.

'Thanks for yesterday,' I said as we drove away.

'Did you enjoy yourselves?'

'Yes, very much. Thanks.'

'Good. It will take a couple of hours to get to where we're going, so relax.' Then, in a quieter voice, 'Did you understand what I said about the symbol?'

'Yes,' I replied, not wishing to admit how perplexed I still was, how I was still waiting expectantly for the knowledge that tonight's ceremony would, I hoped, yield.

He went on, 'You *were* married to White Arrow in the past, but I must repeat, you won't meet your Indian family until your next trip. On this first journey you will be learning about the symbols. Then he addressed all four of us. 'Each one of you was meant to come on this trip for a reason.'

I turned round and looked at my granddaughter and felt proud that God had chosen her. I remembered that a friend of mine, who is also a medium, had told me before we left England that Thomas would look on my granddaughter as a special child.

We drove on and he described the historic landscape we were passing through. He told us about the battles that had been lost on mountain ranges, and about the Indian traditions and beliefs, then he sang to us. We were quiet for a while, absorbing the power and magic of the countryside. He turned his face to me for a split second, then spoke again in a hushed voice.

'Ann, there is a revolution coming. White Arrow has been sent to you by God, and you have to deliver his message to the people of the world.'

I think I just continued to stare directly ahead of me at the road as the white lines disappeared under the car bonnet, but I must have looked startled because Thomas repeated what he had just said.

'Yes, *you* have a message to deliver to the people of the World.' I knew Thomas was a Spiritual Elder for his tribe; I had no reason to doubt what he said, other than my own disbelief in my own abilities. Why me? Why should God in his supreme wisdom choose *me* to deliver his message? *Why?* It angered me. It scared me. I did not want this. It pinpointed my inadequacies. It made me responsible for something I did not even understand. As I was raging inside myself,

Thomas was still speaking. He was talking about Jesus and the cross.

'Jesus was put on earth to prove that there was life after death, but the people of his time failed to understand this, and they made him into a God. To our people Jesus was one of God's messengers. We believe that there is only one God in the heavens. God sent Jesus Christ as a prophet, so Jesus was important and a very holy man: but he was not a God. We have a symbol you have already seen, Ann. White Arrow has shown you this symbol. It is a circle with a cross inside it.' I realised he was talking about the seventh symbol. 'It means many things but the most important meaning is that the cross is even. It is in balance. The cross that is made like the one Jesus Christ was crucified on is out of balance. Like the World.'

I turned to him, wanting to agree with him but my throat was clamped tight and my eyes were wet so I turned away again and looked out of the window. White Arrow was racing along beside us on his horse. He was looking at me and waving. I heard him calling me, but Thomas touched my arm, so I mentally said goodbye to him and turned again to Thomas.

'I have another message for you, Ann,' he said.

'Thomas, I don't think – ' but he interrupted again.

'In three years' time you will die.'

· 7 ·

The Sweat

Death holds little fear for me but I do view it as an intimate event, not to be spoken about openly in a car on a strange road in a foreign country. My mouth stayed open and my eyes remained on him, unblinking and unfocused.

'When you were thirty-seven years old you died, and a new life began. God sent you White Arrow and allowed you and he to communicate as one and the same. In three years' time your life will change again as critically as it did when you were thirty-seven.'

'Fine,' I said. What else could I say? I was relieved that I had allowed him to finish, but I felt extremely confused. White Arrow and his horse were gone. I had come to this country with so many questions, hoping that I was doing the right thing and instead of answers, I was finding more and more unfathomable questions.

'We'll soon be there,' Thomas said, 'but I'd like to stop here for a while. I'd like to show you Chief Joseph's Battlefield. He was the Nez Perce Chief. This was the place where his entire tribe was wiped out. It was one of the last battles fought between white men and the Indians.'

There was a large monument nearby and, as I read the inscription, I noticed another car pulling into the parking area. The two women in the car greeted Thomas and he brought them over to introduce us. They were Mandan women who were to join us at the Sweat Lodge Ceremony that night. We talked for about five minutes and then Thomas excused himself and beckoned me to follow him. He sat down on the grass and surveyed the battlefield, saying nothing and expecting nothing. The monument had a seat built into it which I occupied, and we both sat in complete silence, absorbing the splendid view and feeling its tranquillity.

'Do you see anything?' he asked me. In the distance I could see White Arrow silhouetted on the ridge of a hill, his horse's tail flicking from side to side. I described what I saw. For an instant before Thomas spoke, the air around me became oppressive and was filled with the sound of battle and the cries of the dead and dying.

'Whenever I sit here,' he said, 'I can hear the wounded.' He said it without any hint of emotion. Before I could open my mouth to tell him that I too could hear the sounds of war, I saw White Arrow pull the horse's head round and trot towards us. Half way across the field he stopped and pointed at the blue hills and then at me. Again, he was pointing at the hills and then back at me. Not able to understand what he meant, I described what was happening to Thomas.

He smiled. 'That's where you will be going later today, and all the way along people will be welcoming you and telling you that they are glad you are here.'

When I looked back at White Arrow to tell him I understood, he was surrounded in blue light. He started galloping powerfully back and forth across the battlefield at great speed and then suddenly he was holding a lance decorated with brightly coloured feathers which he raised up high in front of me before turning his horse towards the flat-topped hills, and galloping away.

'The blue light means that he comes from the sky, Ann. And the spear is to show you that he is a chief.' Instantly I remembered countless occasions over the years when White Arrow had stood in front of me and pointed at the sky and I had been unable to understand what he meant. I laughed and turned to wave at him but he was gone.

Before we continued on our way Thomas showed us where to find special herbs and 'sweet grasses' that only grew in certain places, one of which was this battlefield. He picked some leaves, demonstrating how to break them up in the palms of our hands and rub the sap onto our face and arms and told us they were an important part of certain ceremonies where the leaves were burned as a form of incense.

The two Mandan women followed us as we continued on our way to the ceremony. Thomas made an additional stop at the place where we had seen the Powwow to offer advice to someone in need, which gave us half an hour or so to browse around the stalls and say hello to friends we had made the night before. It was now 6.00pm. We drove on for another half an hour or so, during which time he told me that he knew of 'the Frenchman' who came to me in Spirit. I said nothing but understood that he meant a Spirit called Monsieur Phillippe, who regularly appeared to me and seemed to be a friend of White Arrow's; he was the spirit of a French trapper who had known White Arrow in his incarnation in the nineteenth century. Thomas pulled off the main road and followed a dirt track until we could see a pick-up truck coming towards us. We all got out of the car and Thomas spoke to the driver whom he seemed to know well. White Arrow appeared, still mounted, in the middle of a field directly in front of me. I understood he wanted me to go to him. My daughter was videoing and I had my granddaughter by my side. As I neared White Arrow my granddaughter decided to go back to her mother and as she went, another Indian appeared at my side and followed me. He told me his name was Bald Eagle but said nothing else. I was now in the middle of this vast field surrounded by the flat-topped hills. I sat cross-legged on the dry ground as White Arrow rode towards me. Bald Eagle lowered himself to the grass and crossed his legs. White Arrow reined his horse to a halt. The horse stood calmly, bending its head forward as though well schooled. White Arrow dismounted and sat a few feet away, then he spoke. 'These are your people,' he said. 'This is your land. You are their leader.' He then stood, walked back to his horse and rode away.

I went back to the others and when I was a few feet from them, Bald Eagle disappeared. I asked Thomas if he knew who Bald Eagle was.

'Yes. Why?'

I told him what I had seen but felt compelled not to repeat what White Arrow had said. Thomas looked at me strangely.

'Do you know *what* Bald Eagle is?' he asked. 'Bald Eagle is the eagle of the sky. You were greatly honoured, Ann, for the Bald Eagle came from the spirit and the sky and showed himself to you as a human.' He was obviously conveying to me the rareness of the occurrence, but so much was happening to me that very little was sinking in, and so I failed, at the time, to register the importance of it.

At the end of a dirt track stood an odd shaped wooden dwelling, a weather-boarded house, its windows covered in mesh wire. A cat was nursing its kittens on the porch as Thomas led us straight through the swing door into a large room with doors to my left and to my right and what appeared to be a large kitchen directly in front of us. A small group of people were sitting and standing round a table at the far end of the room. They greeted us warmly as we were introduced individually by Thomas. Thomas spoke with the group and my granddaughter started to play with a small dog that had been sleeping under the table. The man who owned the house was Thomas' uncle, Gerry; both he and his wife, Alice, were about sixty years old. She and Thomas's wife, Cathy, took my granddaughter and the dog on to the porch with the two other women who were also to attend the ceremony. I watched Gerry's lips as he spoke to Thomas, or Tom, or Tommy as he was variously known, and suddenly realised that I had only been in this land for two days, and had spent that time solely in the company of Red Indians. I was only just becoming aware of how special a breed of man they were. All my reading and research had not prepared me for the magic I began to feel surround me at that moment. I could feel Spirit so strongly. It seemed that I could hear God in every word they spoke and the truth each time they breathed.

Perhaps because I am a medium, I was 'tuning in' to what was already there, but it began to dawn on me that I was to be the only white person ever to have set foot inside the Sweat Lodge. Prince Charles is the only other English person to have visited that particular Sweat Lodge, but even he was not permitted inside.

Gerry gave me a cup of water and said, 'Tommy has told me of the symbols you bring to our land. You wish to know what they mean.'

'Yes, I would like to know,' I said.

We held each other's gaze for some time.

'Many people would give anything for this,' he said lifting an arm through the air and motioning to what was around him. To the house, the people, to Spirit. 'Many want to make stories and much money can be made by the white man if they knew our secrets. Many have come searching. We have had many who have lied to us, but we have seen through them. Our secrets are sacred to us.' He had not blinked once. 'You will not lie to us.'

'I haven't come this far to do that,' I said. 'I don't know why I have been brought to you. White Arrow has sent me to bring these symbols to you but I really don't understand any more than that. I will not lie.'

He then produced the first four symbols I had sent and sitting opposite me at the table he turned his head a fraction towards Thomas and said, 'My nephew has shown me these symbols. He has also told me that he described the first one to you.'

'Yes, that's right,' I said.

'Tonight, after the ceremony, we will tell you what the rest mean, but the ceremony must take place first. These symbols are very important to my people, and very important to you. We feel good that God has chosen someone like you.'

He placed the symbols to one side and asked me when I was born. I said in 1942 and he went on to explain that he had been stationed in England for a short time during the war. We spoke for a while about my work with White Arrow and then he suddenly said: 'We think you could be the great, great, granddaughter of the man called Horse. Have you heard of the film?' I looked at him in surprise and nodded. 'You must have Indian blood somewhere.'

'Well,' I said, lost for words, 'I don't know. My mother's father was an American, but I don't know any more than that.'

'Yes,' he said. 'I am sure you have Indian blood.' The men left to prepare the Sweat Lodge with logs, a job only ever undertaken by the men of that particular tribe, and the women started to organise themselves. I was already wearing the swim-suit but was told that the cotton dress I wore over it was not loose enough, so Alice lent me one of hers. About half an hour after the men had gone the women started to leave, so the girls and I followed them.

As we approached the Lodge I could see that most of the people had already gone in but there remained outside in the warm night air a group of six men seated in a semi-circle around a fire. I started following the other women into the Lodge, but was instructed to stand in front of the six men. Val, my daughter and my granddaughter were told to stand a few feet away. The bonfire was directly behind me, its heat on the back of my legs making me wonder how long I would have to stand there for.

Thomas then spoke and he asked, 'What have you come for?'

'The truth,' I blurted out. 'The truth.'

'What truth?'

'The truth about the symbols,' I said. Thomas turned round to collect a package, a white bag, and I took the opportunity to move a few small paces away from the heat, hoping no one would notice. He opened the bag and said, 'These are gifts from us to you.' Then he proceeded to lay out a beautiful golden quilt with Indian patterns on it, a belt-buckle for my husband, a purse for my daughter specially made for her out of soft white suede, and pink and white beaded earrings for Val. I passed him the tobacco and the tea as I was instructed to do. During this time, I watched White Arrow ride up to the Sweat Lodge and dismount. He walked to the opening, bent down low and disappeared inside. I said nothing, understanding that it was not right for me to do so at that moment.

The six men stood up and directed me to follow them into the lodge. I was relieved to be leaving the heat of the fire. I made sure that the girls were all right and took a last look at my little granddaughter before ducking down and passing through the opening.

The interior was extremely dark, the only light a faint glimmer from the hot stones that filled a hole in the centre of the space. I clambered over some of the women to sit where I was directed by Thomas, who sat on the opposite side with the other men. I made myself as comfortable as possible, aware of a rigid layer of nerves in my gut. One of the men left through the opening and closed the flap as he went. Tom called him the Door Keeper, his purpose being to allow no one to enter or leave the Sweat Lodge, and to ensure the fire kept burning so that the stones remained hot. The lady to my right placed a towel over her head and drew her knees up under her chin. I did the same, expectant and scared. Tom began to speak in his own tongue and continued without appearing to take a breath for some time. Then in English he said: 'We would like to welcome this lady who has travelled many miles to be with us this night and we are honoured. We would like to welcome her and help her in her search for the truth,' and then he reverted to his own tongue and spoke words which as they left his mouth I knew to be prayers. Out of the silence that followed came the sound of cold water meeting red-hot rock. I waited, not knowing what to expect, and pulling my legs tight to my chest and dropping my forehead to my knees I breathed deeply as the hissing steam rose in swirling clouds of burning vapour and enveloped me completely. It was almost unbearable.

I heard the flap lift and felt the air around me cool slightly, as some of the women crawled to the opening and fell out. I followed, desperate to be away from the steam, but no sooner had I reached the door than Tom shouted, 'Ann! You are not allowed to go out! You must stay inside. This is the way.' So I staggered back to my place, glad to see Alice still there.

'You can smoke if you want to,' she said. I thanked her, happy for any distraction. The air continued to cool and as I inhaled deeply I wondered how many times they would stoke up the steam, but before I had taken another puff the others came back in so I hurriedly stubbed it out, grabbed the towel and wrapped it around my head and waited. I heard the flap go down. The prayers were said again, and as the water hit the stones again the steam arose around me, only this time the heat was more intense. It felt ten times as hot. When I tried to breathe, it burnt the inside of my nose. I felt panic welling up inside. I tried again to breathe but it hurt too much. I was feeling faint and I started to scramble for the opening again. No matter how brave I was supposed to be, no matter what was at stake, I had to get out before I passed out. I climbed over the poor person sitting next to me and headed ruthlessly for the flap which, by the time I had reached it, was being thrown open by the Keeper. Everyone else was falling through the opening too, and I landed in a heap on the cool, soft grass, with tears streaming from my eyes.

'I can't go back in there. I can't,' I cried, gasping for air and feeling the sweat pouring from my skin. I saw my daughter running towards me with Val a little way behind her and I knew I had to pull myself together. Something told me not to cry. I looked at my daughter and for some reason her face convinced me that I had to go through with this. She lit a cigarette and handed it to me. 'Mum, are you OK?'

The others were shouting. 'White Arrow must have wanted that one hot! Boy, that was a good one!' Tom called out and told me I should be inside. Reluctantly, I followed the others back into the Lodge. One of the Indian girls refused to go back in, stammering that it was too much for her. I sat right by the entrance so that I could at least get out quickly. The Keeper dropped the flap and once again I wrapped the towel around my head, closed my eyes tightly and waited. I heard the prayers coming to an end and felt the muscles in my legs tense as the water bubbled and sparked on to the stones. This time, however, it was bearable and I was able to endure five or so minutes of heat until the flap was opened; but I was still the first one out.

The girls came over and sat with me. I smoked a cigarette and then we all went in again. I had no idea how many times I was expected to undergo this trial by steam. As I forced myself back to the opening and squeezed through, I heard the voice of a young woman.

'Ann, call on your guide. Do not run out of here. Your guide will help. Trust him.' My fear had been so great that I had completely forgotten about White Arrow and I immediately started talking to him mentally, asking him for strength. When Thomas started the prayers I saw two Indian Spirits suddenly standing in front of me. They were both holding poles in their hands and encouraging me to go forward and go past them. At first I was afraid. I felt exhausted and did not think I could stand, let alone walk to them, but I did and as I passed between the poles, they vanished. The steam hit me and although it was still searing and painful, it was a little less hot. The flap opened and as we stumbled out I heard someone saying there was no more going in and I fell in a heap of grateful, sweaty thanks. Everyone was lying on the grass moaning or laughing, and I remember thinking this was something they did regularly that I had never done before, and yet I had endured it.

At that moment, I understood that I now had to tell Tom what White Arrow had said in the field. I crawled over to him. 'Tom, I have something to tell you from White Arrow.'

'Wait Ann, I will call the others.'

Tom and four other Chiefs gathered in a circle under a sky alive with stars. I described how White Arrow and Bald Eagle had appeared in the field and how White Arrow had told me these were my people and this my land. I told them how the two Spirits holding poles had encouraged me to walk between them in the Sweat Lodge. They became interested in the poles and asked me to describe these in more detail. Andrew, the oldest among them and a man with a kind, loving face, spoke to Tom in his own language and stood up.

'Andrew knows of these poles. He will bring one to show you from his home.' He lived fifty miles from the Lodge.

We watched the old man go. I studied their faces as they meditated, feeling a sense of belonging and equality which anyone would have found difficult to believe had they witnessed the gathering of five Red Indian Chiefs and a shrivelled little pink lady from West London.

Tom produced a red rattle from his medicine bag. The rattle is ritually used to call on Spirit and only those who are with Spirit are permitted to possess one. Holding it he began to speak about the symbols.

'Last night I told you what the first symbol meant,' he cleared his throat, leant towards me and then looked up at the sky. 'Look Ann, can you see the stars in the shape of an arrow?' I rested back on my elbows and looked up into the vast wilderness of sky. To be honest I was so shattered that I really did not care if there was an arrow in the sky or not. From the corner of my eye I thought I saw a shooting star. There was certainly a shape. I sat up.

'Yes,' I said. 'I can see it.'

'That is White Arrow,' Tom said.

'Yes.' I said again, not really understanding.

He held up the rattle. 'Ann, this is what the second symbol shows.' It made sense to me: the second symbol was a small circle with a diagonal line attached to its lower left edge. It certainly could be a representation of a rattle and its handle. 'Only a medicine person would have one, and this indicates that you are close with Spirit.' He then handed me the rattle and said, 'This is for you.' This was a great honour and I accepted it humbly and placed it by my side.

'The third symbol is a square with an 'S'-shaped line within it. The line is a road; it means that you are on God's road.

'The fourth symbol is a circle in the centre of which is a crescent shape. This tells us that on the second day after the new moon in January you will receive a message of great importance from those who watch over you.

'The fifth symbol represents a fish. It means two things. Firstly you will receive a gift from the sea. Secondly, something of great significance will surface for you in the future.

'And the sixth symbol is a hand. This, Ann, is the hand of God.

'We have yet to receive the seventh symbol from you. These symbols and their meanings we give to you. But only you, through White Arrow, will truly know their whole meanings. Only White Arrow will tell you all their secrets.'

I nodded and thanked him. The seventh symbol had in fact been the circle with the cross inside it that had been the object of so much discussion between Thomas and myself in the car.

*   *   *

I went over to join the girls and found my granddaughter soundly asleep on a bench by the fire, wrapped in a blanket. My daughter picked her up and we went into the house where we found a meal laid out in honour of White Arrow who, Tom said, had not been fed for thousands of years. We prayed and then the women served and passed round the food. I had little appetite but drank some soup so as not to offend anyone, and wondered what they meant by this ritual of feeding White Arrow. It was now past midnight but I had to wait for Andrew to return with the pole so we organised for someone to take the girls back to the motel and then, exhausted, I rested my head on the table and closed my burning eyes. Alice asked if I was all right. I sat up and smiled.

'Yes I'm fine. Just tired.'

Gerry spoke. 'This place is sacred ground. Very few are invited here.'

'Yes. Thank you.'

'Do you know that these people have met the Aliens?' Tom asked.

'Well, you mentioned something about it in the car.'

'These people know them well.'

I turned to Gerry. He said, 'We see the lights of their ships often. But it is my wife who sees them more.' Alice pointed outside to the mountains and the sky. She said, 'I see them arrive over the hills. I have never met one of them close, but I see the lights of their space-craft coming over the hills.' I looked at Gerry and understood what he had meant when he said that many people would do anything to hear their secrets.

'Does it not frighten you?' I asked,

Alice said, 'No, they don't frighten me. On many nights I watch them come and go. They would do no harm. They feel safe here. They are among friends.'

Andrew came in carrying the pole wrapped in a red cloth. Tom spoke to him, took it and unwrapped it. It was identical in every way to the poles I had seen the Indians holding in the Lodge; a very old, dark wooden stick with an eagle's head on the top and brightly coloured feathers trailing from the side. He made certain odd movements with it, passing the stick from hand to hand, his eyes fixed on the eagle's head.

'This is part of your medicine bag, Andrew,' Tom said. 'It is used to help my people.' I knew by looking at Andrew that he wanted me to have the pole, but Tom was telling him he could not part with it. After a short silence they spoke again, then Tom turned to me and said,

'Andrew has been given your Indian name by the big White Spirit.' Andrew said something.

Tom continued, 'You will receive your Indian name in the near future. It cannot be told to you tonight.'

I looked at Andrew and felt very close to him. His face remains one of the most spiritual I have ever seen. His eyes were full of love and wisdom. I leant across the table, touched his hand and thanked him. I felt honoured that this wise old man had travelled one hundred miles to present me with a precious gift which he so wanted me to have, but which he was not allowed to part with. And I felt sad for him, that he was unable to make his gift.

We got up to leave. I shook hands with them all and prayed that I would see them again. No matter how drained I felt, these were a people I could never forget.

· 8 ·

Passing the Test

The following morning, 29th July 1991, I woke with a headache. I got up and swallowed two aspirin and sat on the bed with my head in my hands. Why were the elders of a Red Indian tribe praying to White Arrow? He appeared on the bed beside me.

'White Arrow, who the hell are you? As far as I know you were not an Indian chief when you were on earth – not like your father, Sitting Bull. Why then are you so revered?'

'White Arrow is my Heaven name, Little One. For many thousands of years the Indians knew about me, Little One, but they did not know of the big plan.'

'WHAT BLOODY PLAN!' My head was pounding.

'Patience, Little One. Patience. In time you will know all, but for now, I will tell you only a part. Thousands of years ago it was arranged that I come down to Earth for us to meet for the future. The future being hundreds of years ahead. For you and I had to be married, then I had to return to my rightful place in Heaven. The Indians did not know of my return to earth so they continued to pray to White Arrow, my Self. After your life on earth, you too returned to Heaven, the plan being that you would return in time to your earth, that time being now, for us to meet again but also to prove that life does carry on after death.'

'Fine. I'm sorry I shouted. I understand the reincarnation and how important it is. But how important are you? How high in Heaven are you? Tell me!'

'Little One, you must have patience. Soon the jigsaw will fit, but the pieces must be given to you slowly or the burden will be too great for you to carry.'

'You mean there's more?'

'Yes. In time.' Then he went.

I lay there feeling frustrated and tired and aching, but mainly confused about where White Arrow was taking me and scared of the future, for whatever was coming, I knew it was something big.

I closed my eyes and prayed for God to give me understanding.

It was 8.00am and Tom was coming for us at noon with two Indian girls who had asked for a reading from me. I got up and felt the vice tightening around my head, and wished I had never agreed to do the reading. But I washed and brushed my teeth, and by the time I woke Val I was feeling much better. I knew that she and my daughter had been profoundly affected by the events of the previous night. They had watched as I had put myself through fear and pain. They had seen how much the second Sweat hurt and had watched and taken notes as I went back in for more. They had been frightened for me, and it came as no surprise that as Val sat up in her bed there were tears streaming from her eyes.

We had a quiet breakfast and then strolled through the town before packing our things. Tom arrived on time and lunched with the others while I sat with the Indian girls for about an hour and read for them, before they embarked on their six-hour drive back. All Red Indians believe in Spirit; their medicine men and women are what we would call mediums.

We had only been on the road for a few minutes when White Arrow appeared galloping along beside the car calling out 'Hohe! Hohe!'. I asked Tom what it meant.

'It is an exclamation. All it means is that he's really glad. The Sioux are his people and he is very pleased that you are all here among his people. You are going where he wants you to go and he is happy about it.'

White Arrow followed for a while and then pulled his horse to a halt as we drew up to Tom's home. Tom lives in a trailer, a large mobile home parked in fields at the end of a dirt track. A small fence surrounded the trailer and behind it was what looked like a paddock. My granddaughter saw the horse before any of us and leapt out of the car and ran directly towards the paddock. I was aware of a look of mild concern crossing Tom's face but thought nothing of it as I followed my granddaughter. We opened the gate and went into the paddock and petted the horse and gave it grass. 'What's she called, Tom?' I shouted.

'Well, we were thinking of calling her Rabbit,' he answered from where he stood. I was aware that he was frowning, but my grand-daughter was so infecting me with her joy at being close to a horse so large that I ignored it and shouted, 'Can we ride her, Tom?' Two or three other Indians appeared and rested against the paddock fence, but said nothing. I smiled at them politely, 'Please Tom? It would make her trip.' One of the Indians handed me a rope and told me – from a distance – how to attach it to the headpiece straps already fixed around Rabbit's head. My granddaughter and I chatted merrily to Rabbit and she nibbled at our hands and shook her head from side to side and flicked at flies with her tail. Before too long I had scrambled on to her back and was hoisting my granddaughter up by one arm and settling her in front of me. We sat on her, bare-back, for quite some time and I remember feeling very peaceful and content and glad that, like White Arrow, I too knew how it felt to be astride an Indian horse.

After a time Tom called us in and we dismounted, thanked Rabbit very much for the ride and handing the rope back to the Indian, closed the paddock gate and walked towards the trailer. Tom said nothing for a moment and then shaking his head and laughing with apparent disbelief, he said:

'Ann! Ann, do you know that this horse has never been ridden! It is a wild horse. No one has been able to tame it!'

I stopped in my tracks. 'What do you mean?' I asked.

'It is a wild horse, Ann. We only caught it recently and no one has been able to ride it.'

'Well then why on earth did you let me go near it? I had my grand-daughter with me. She could have been hurt, Tom!'

'Our horses are sometimes closer to Spirit than we are ourselves. Mother Nature loves you, Ann. It was she who tamed Rabbit for you.'

Angry with Tom for letting us go near a wild horse, especially when I thought of what might have happened to my granddaughter, I was too shocked to understand the thrust of what he was saying, and I held tightly on to her as we climbed the steps to the trailer.

His wife gave us iced drinks and we chatted for a while until Tom, who had seemed very pensive, disappeared into one of the other rooms, returning with an ancient war bonnet of the most outstanding beauty. He told me reverently that it had belonged to his grandfather.

I thought it was the loveliest thing I had ever seen and asked to hold it. I was examining the delicate feathers and lifting it towards my head, wanting to feel what it was like to wear one, when Tom said, 'No, Ann. Only Indian Chiefs are allowed to wear a war bonnet. Never a woman.'

I was embarrassed and apologised and placed it carefully on the table.

'No, it's yours,' he said. 'I give it to you. As a gift.' I could hardly believe it. I looked at his wife and she nodded. I was so excited.

'Thank you, thank you!' I cried. More than anything, I had wanted to take a war bonnet back as a reminder of everything that White Arrow is. I had hoped to find a replica in a market somewhere, but this was an act of generosity beyond my wildest dreams. This was a real bonnet which meant that each feather on it represented a great deed that had been accomplished by the wearer. Furthermore, this was an heirloom, a part of Thomas's own family heritage. I was humbled and unable to find words to express my gratitude properly, but thanked him again in a whisper and promised I would care for it as long as I lived. Then he handed me a heavy object wrapped in red cloth which, as I unravelled it, revealed itself to be a large, glistening, white quartz crystal.

'The Spirit have asked me to give this to you so you may use it. It will give you healing during the day,' he said and then went on to explain how it worked before handing me a stone bowl. 'This, Ann, is a receptacle in which to burn the sacred sage I gave you, before you rub it over yourself. You are to do this each month when you feed White Arrow. All of these objects are to be put in White Arrow's room.' I thanked him again. His wife expressed the desire to make us moccasins and she measured our feet, promising to send them to us in England when they were made. She and Thomas then left the room, motioning me to follow. We stepped into a smaller room where I saw Tom's wife solemnly holding a bundle in her arms. She explained that it was a religious item that her grandmother had left for her to carry. She wanted to know from White Arrow whether she should still be carrying it. I rested the palms of my hands on the cloth. White Arrow appeared and spoke, blessing Thomas and his wife and then blessing the bundle. They seemed overjoyed with the blessing.

Back at the motel, Tom settled in the big armchair in my daughter's room and I lit a cigarette, waiting for him to speak.

'Do you know that it is the greatest honour for me to have Spirit send you to me? I say to you again that you are here to deliver a message to the world. The crop circles,' he continued.

'What about them?

'They have been left for you. Part of your message lies in the circles. My people will try to give you interpretations, but as with the symbols, only White Arrow knows their true meanings.'

'You are joking!' My mouth was wide open. I had heard about crop circles and seen pictures of them, but it seemed extremely unlikely that they were anything to do with me! But Tom's face was set: he meant what he said. 'Tom, you're joking,' I repeated.

He ignored me. 'We cannot buy all of the books on crop circles here, so I would like you to send me as many as you can. I will then take the patterns to the Spiritual leaders and try to let you know what they may mean. I can assure you, they are Indian symbols.' Before I had time to comment he continued, 'Did you know that I left my job at the council the day you arrived? It was my last day at work. There are only a few of us who can read these symbols. If you had sent them any later than you did, it might have been years before you found anyone else to help you.'

'White Arrow would have known that,' I said.

'Yes. He knows everything. I have already told you that this journey of yours will be in two parts. Another leader will be brought to you in a year's time.'

'So am I only going to know you for a short time?'

'Yes, but in the meantime we will search for your family.'

Although I knew their records had been destroyed in the wars, making research difficult, I was disappointed. 'Don't you know who they are yet?'

'No,' he replied. 'At first we wondered, because of the symbols, if you were the reincarnation of the man called Jack Wilson, the only other person from outside the Indian community who has approached us, whom I discussed with you when you were in England.'

I replied immediately. 'As I said then, I know that's not me, Tom. It just feels wrong.'

Tom nodded. 'We *will* find the family, but there are tests for you to go through.'

'What do you mean, tests?'

'One was last night. Had you not gone into the Sweat Lodge four times you would have failed, and we would have been nice and polite, but we would not have told you about the symbols. We would have said goodbye.' I wondered what on earth had made me go back after the second sweat. Tom looked at me seriously. 'You did act like a white woman.'

'I *am* a white woman! I have been reborn into another life. Into another culture.'

'To us, you are an Indian woman.' It was no use arguing. 'There are more tests to come but these will only strengthen you for the future. There is a Medicine Dance. Also we want you to go to the mountains. We want you to fast in the wilderness for four days. That means you will have no food and you will have no water. We may possibly hold a Sun Dance for you, but because you are so close to Spirit we may be able to avoid that. Will you do all this?'

Before I could think I heard myself say, 'Yes, I have to, for White Arrow.' I felt scared, but it was White Arrow who had helped me through the Sweat Lodge ceremony, and I knew he would do the same, whatever lay in store. 'Yes,' I repeated, 'I'll do whatever's needed.' He smiled. 'So, have I passed your test?' I asked. He said nothing and I crossed my arms. 'I mean I brought over the symbols and I sat in your Sweat Lodge. Have I passed?'

'Yes.'

I breathed out in a long silent whistle. I had come out to America wanting definite proof of my reincarnation, which I had not received. I was left with information on the symbols that I did not understand and with the knowledge that I had passed a test and so was honoured with acceptance as a Sioux woman.

Before Tom left, I mentioned that we wanted to visit Glacier Park in the Rockies and asked him how best to get there.

'By car. Be ready first thing in the morning. We'll take you. If we have time we can go into Canada as well.'

The following morning I slept in for the first time in years and there was a mad rush to be ready by the time he came for us. Hardly had I brushed the sleep from my eyes before we were on our way to the Rockies. It was a bit like seeing the beautiful plains and mountains in a dream-like state. We climbed higher and higher through verdant fields and valleys, following craggy mountainsides and catching glimpses of far-off landscapes under a hazy sky. We stopped at a view-point about half way up and as I stepped out of the car I felt a bolt of lightning strike inside my head. The pain was intense and I had to sit for a few seconds until it receded, becoming nothing more than a headache. Other people were also enjoying the view and I stood up slowly, determined not to let the now dull thudding spoil my enjoyment. A mountain goat with her baby appeared from nowhere and stopped by my side to snatch at blades of grass. The other sightseers gathered round and photographed the goat and her kid. Then Tom came over and for a while he watched me watching the goats. 'They have come to see you,' he said quietly.

I laughed.

'Do you know why they're called mountain goats? Because they live in the mountains. Not with people. This is the first time they have ever come near people and it is because you are here. It is Mother Earth that sends them to you. You must see it is her love for you that sends these goats.'

What could I say? I knew by looking at him that he believed what he was saying was true. I took some pictures and carried on walking. My head was still pounding and I stopped to buy some water before we continued on our way. The others were chatting. My grand-daughter was asleep. White Arrow appeared.

'Why can't you tell me? I'm getting so confused, White Arrow. Why am I so important to these people? Why do wild horses let me ride them and goats come down from the hills to see me? These people are far more spiritual than I am. Any of them would do a better job for you than I can.' I waited for him to answer but he said nothing. 'How can I serve you when I'm so confused? Why can't you tell me? Why, White Arrow?'

'Wait, Little One. You must trust me. I have brought you here for a reason. This is the start of a long journey that faces you and to give you all the answers you seek at once would be too much for you. But I am going to say this, Little One: your journey is for the people of the world. To help them.'

'White Arrow, I'm not able to carry that kind of responsibility.'

'Let me ask you a question, Little One. What would you do if the world asked for your help and you had knowledge that could save it?'

'That isn't fair, White Arrow. I would have no choice but to help.'

'Because you wanted to,' White Arrow said.

'Yes of course, but – '

'No buts, Little One. The world will need our help. We have chosen you to pass this help on. Your world is in trouble. We are here by God's command to help the world.'

Rage flared up inside me and it was hard to continue the discussion in my mind without shouting out loud and alarming the others in the car. I breathed deeply. 'Well then, why me? It's so far fetched! Why someone like me, who is so ill-prepared for this task, who has led the life that I have, who has no university degree, no contacts in high places, no real understanding of what this is all about? Answer me that. If you answer nothing else, answer that. Why me? Why me? Why me?'

With measured words he simply said,

'Before the end of the year, you will know who I am, and what I am.'

That was in August 1991. White Arrow then vanished, and as I closed my eyes and rested my head against the seat of Tom's car, I remembered an event that had taken place in March of 1991. I had stood in front of my hall mirror and taken a really good look at myself. I tried to look into the real me. I looked at my stomach and tried to visualise who I was inside. To my horror I realised there was nothing there. It was a void. I was terrified. Then the word 'Alien' came through to me. 'No I'm not!' I shouted, 'I can't be!' I ran away from the mirror and refused to think about it any further, hoping it was my imagination. But now, sitting in a car in the American Midwest, the memory had come back, and against my better judgement, I was wondering if there was some connection. I thought about Michael. I thought about White Arrow and the sky. I thought about the blue light that had surrounded him in the field. And then I fell asleep.

When Tom and his wife called by the hotel two days later to say goodbye, Tom took me aside and said, 'When you return, White Arrow will tell you and show you what the symbols mean and what the true message is. I promise. There is much for you to do and learn. Only White Arrow can show you the way. A revolution is coming that you are a part of. In three years' time, everything will be revealed. If you need any advice you only have to ask, but I can tell you now that you will be returning to America every year for the next four years.' He then turned to Val and said, 'Don't envy Ann. She carries a great responsibility.'

We said our goodbyes and the following day I left America.

· 9 ·

The Return to England

On 4th August, 1991, Tony was at the airport to meet us with Val's family. It felt good to be back. Faint glimmers of yellow in the trees hinted at Autumn and the air was cool. It was impossible to begin telling Tony everything that had happened in America, so I caught up on his news from home.

'. . . and Harry's been on the phone, Ann,' he said. 'He says some crop circles have appeared near Aylesbury. He wants to know if you would like to see them.'

Naturally I agreed, and so the following morning found me, jet-lagged, picking my way through a corn field. 'What am I doing here?' I asked White Arrow, as we approached the pattern of bent stalks that looked like currents in the field. No answer came. I studied the circle, wanting to know how this tied in to everything else and wondered what lay in store. I had a sensation of fear. I stood in the centre of the main circle with four smaller circles surrounding it to make a square formation. Questions kept burning in my mind. Where did White Arrow fit in to all of this? What was his connection to the aliens?

During the following weeks I heard nothing from the Red Indians, and as Tom had assured me he would be in touch, I began to worry. Five weeks passed and it was beginning to feel as if they were waiting for something from me. White Arrow just kept on saying, 'Have patience.' I had written to Tom, sending him illustrated books on the crop circles, but had not received a reply. Eventually my patience ran out and I rang him. 'How are you?' I asked.

'I'm very well! Is everything OK?'

'Yes. Did you get the books?'

'I did. I was going to write you a letter next week after I take them to the elders. I'll let you know.' This made me feel more relaxed. I had been worried that perhaps my visit had not gone as well as I thought it had.

'Have you had a message for us from White Arrow?' Tom asked.

'No,' I replied, puzzled by his question, 'but I am in contact with White Arrow all the time.' It seemed to confirm my suspicions that they were waiting for something. He said he would be in touch and we rang off. Patience.

White Arrow appears in different ways. Sometimes I just know he is in the room without even seeing him and at other times he shows himself very clearly so that I cannot ignore him. A few days later, on the night of 17 October, I had just finished seeing a client and had a free hour before the next one arrived. I was grateful for the rest; it had been a hectic day. Tony was reading and I slumped into my chair and switched on the television. White Arrow appeared directly in front of me, blocking my view of the screen, which is not unusual if he wants to talk about something important. I pressed the remote off-switch and settled back to listen.

Then Michael appeared as well. He had not visited me for some time and I was delighted to see him. I was accustomed to his Alien form by then and I greeted him warmly. They stood together in silence. I began to feel uncomfortable, wondering what was happening, why neither were speaking, and why they both looked so stern? Then I watched in horror as White Arrow slowly increased his height, growing taller and taller until he and Michael were the same height. Whenever Michael appears he always squats so that I can see him clearly. White Arrow did not do this and I watched as his head and shoulders disappeared through the ceiling completely out of my sight.

I wanted to scream. I knew that what I was seeing changed everything. I closed my eyes and all in one breath said, 'Please, please, White Arrow, come back to normal, please tell me this is my imagination.'

I heard him say, 'Little One, open your eyes,' then I heard the word 'Goe'.

When I looked he was back to normal.

'What is going on, White Arrow?'

'We are two of the Seven. I am not a Spirit, Ann.' I watched a second time as he rose to a height of over ten feet, disappearing into the ceiling and then reverting slowly back to normal.

'I need to know more, White Arrow. I really need some answers.

Now. I mean it. I really need your help.' I was crying.

'In time.' And they both disappeared.

I went to bed angry and frightened. It felt like my brain was battling to make connections in the midst of a thick fog.

As morning light crept through the curtains I gave up trying to sleep and sat in my bed waiting. I could go on no longer without some clear and concise facts from White Arrow. I know he knows my mind so when he appeared I simply said, 'Tell me now, White Arrow.'

He smiled. 'Relax, Little One.'

Since my return from America he had taken to calling me Ann, which, from him, sounded so distant. I was at least pleased to hear the words 'Little One' again. I managed a half smile.

'I come from a long way beyond the reach of man on Earth. I will try and explain more, Little One. Many years ago you came to this Earth and lived as a Red Indian girl. Both at that time and many years before, a plan was made with you in mind: you were part of that plan well before you arrived on the planet Earth, and knew anything of it. It was decided that at that time I too would return with you to live for a while. My return had a purpose. For you to get used to this planet and on your return as Ann, you would come to know and trust me. When you returned to Earth this time, as Ann, all your knowledge of your past life had been taken away, the same as everybody on earth; it would have been of no use to you until now. People had to know you as one of them, as an ordinary human being; they had to know you have felt pain like them. As a result, they trust you and will trust you in the future. For thousands of years we have been trying to help your planet when we could and we have been willing to show ourselves to human beings, but we have found to our cost that people are scared of us and so in that fear would try to harm us. So we have had to defend ourselves, which we did not want to have to do. We come in peace, with knowledge that can help your Earth. It is God who has sent me and my people, but it is *your* people who have sent out prayers for this help, and that is why we are here. We knew many thousands of years ago that this time would come, and this is why you have been put on the planet Earth: to help us with our mission.'

'White Arrow, I believe you because you have always spoken the truth to me. I *have* to believe you, even if I can't feel it yet. But you are going to have a big, big problem convincing others, aren't you?'

'I have plans. Remember who I am. If I could not convince your people, then there would be no point in all of this. I just need time to bring this proof, when I will give them the evidence they need through you. Don't worry, Little One – God has much power. Even now, your mind is wondering, not quite sure. I understand this but in time you will believe, just like when you first met me, and you questioned me and then found what I said to be true.'

'You know I believe you. It's digesting it and knowing what to do with it and how and when and . . . Is Michael one of your people?'

'At this time he is second to me.'

'Then why don't you look like him? Not that I want you to – I love you as you are.'

'If I had shown you the real me the time we first met, I don't believe you would have adjusted as quickly. In any case, we can take on many forms.'

With my newly acquired knowledge about White Arrow, I wanted to know exactly how much the Indians already knew. In October 1991 soon after White Arrow had shown me his other form, I called Thomas. 'Hi Tom.'

'Hi! How are you?'

'Fine, thanks.' We chatted generally for a while and then I said, 'So did you know that White Arrow is an Alien?'

'Yes.'

'Why didn't you tell me?'

'I couldn't, Ann. I wasn't allowed to. We had to wait for White Arrow to tell you himself, then we could verify it for you.'

'It's a bit scary,' I said. 'It was the last thing I expected, although now I can see that it begins to make sense of a lot of things.'

'Yes, and you know that he's working for God, so you have nothing to fear. Now you know why you were brought to us. I'm sorry I couldn't tell you when you were here.'

'It's all right. I'm just glad it's not me going slightly mad. I'm glad to know. Anything on the crop circles?'

'I can give you one of the meanings now if you like.'

Something told me they knew more than just one, but I was getting used to their ways and understood that they would not impart information until they felt, or were told, that I was ready for it. He referred to a crop circle in a book called *The Crop Circle Enigma* by Pat Delgodo – which I had sent him. He told me it was a Mandala, a mystic diagram made up of squares and circles, symbolising the universe and cosmic forces. The pattern was simple. Each square illustrated one of the Visitors. White Arrow comes first, then Michael, then another one – Monsieur Phillippe. It was almost like leaving their trade mark for our world.

I was about to ring off when I remembered that White Arrow had given me the name 'White Eagle'.

'Tom, sorry about this, but do you know what the name "White Eagle" means?'

'Yes I do. Leave it with me,' he said.

After a few weeks, I called Tom again.

'When White Arrow gave you the name White Eagle,' he said, 'he was telling me where to look, Ann. Are you sitting down?'

I sat down. 'I am now,' I said.

'You have on Earth great, great grandchildren from your time here as an Indian. Three girls and two boys.'

Then he gave me the name, address and phone number of one of the girls and told me to contact her.

'When you came to us, Ann, you gave us the name White Arrow. Because of the symbols you brought, we knew you spoke of White Arrow in the sky. When White Arrow in the sky lived on Earth, he was known by a different name. He was known as White Feather. White Feather was the son of Sitting Bull. The real son.' The line was silent for what seemed like an eternity. Eventually Tom spoke.

'Ann, I have found your family now. My work for you is finished. Soon someone else will be brought to you to help in your work with the Aliens. We will always be friends, but my part in your work is now over.'

After I replaced the receiver I thought long and hard about the reincarnation. It was going to take time to prove this in a way that people could accept. I called the girl and tried to explain some of the story. Tom had already briefed her, which made it easier for me, but we were discussing events that had taken place over a hundred years previously. Her father had died a year earlier but she said she knew of an old woman of eighty who remembered the past. She also knew that White Eagle, son of Sitting Bull, had lived but agreed with me that we had to find a way of proving without doubt that I had existed and that I had been married to White Eagle. All that was going to take some time, and as we go to press with this book, research is still being carried out to find conclusive proof.

The New Moon in January 1992 approached. The symbol showing a crescent within a circle had predicted that an event would take place two days after the New Moon – on 7 January. I knew in my heart that whatever this event was, it was connected to the Aliens and as the date loomed closer, I felt more and more nervous.

Over Christmas I had been visited regularly by three other beings. One, a bear, came accompanied by an eagle, who I felt sure was the Indian Bald Eagle who had spoken to me in the field in America, and by a beautiful golden lion. They would appear to me for a few moments before vanishing. I intuited that these were the Aliens in animal form, forms they had adopted when showing themselves to the Red Indians for thousands of years. I understood, too, that what I was seeing was spirit forms of Aliens, and that although they are capable of coming among us as physical beings, that was not what I was witnessing now.

Red Indian elders had been seeing the Aliens in animal forms for generations; indeed a great deal of the higher Indian wisdom is to do with the Aliens, which are an essential part of Indian culture and philosophy. For me, on the other hand, it was still new, and whilst I understood that they were breaking me in as gently as they could, and that White Arrow would always be there, nonetheless, I found this disturbing. In addition I had learnt from Tom that *only* the elders knew that the Spirit animals the Indians saw were, in fact, Aliens. The other members of the tribe did not know this. Neither did they know that White Arrow was an Alien. They knew him only as a great, high Spirit.

*　　*　　*

One morning, just after Christmas, I received eight more symbols. As I sat drawing what I was shown and muttering, 'This is all I need,' White Arrow told me to send them to the Red Indians and they would explain what they meant. 'Fine!' I said, but whereas working for Spirit had always made me so happy, now this contact with Aliens was making me afraid.

A day or two before the 7th, White Arrow told me that on that chosen day I would have to go out into the garden, at 5.30 in the morning.

'WHY DO I HAVE TO GO INTO THE BLOODY GARDEN IN THE MIDDLE OF WINTER AT 5.30 IN THE MORNING!?'

'It's to do with the Aliens, Little One.'

I knew Tony would be more terrified than I expected to be myself, so I asked our friend Harry, who has a well-developed interest in UFOs, to come along. On the night of 6 January 1992 I left a message on my tape recorder for Tony and the kids. I wanted them to know that I had to do this. I needed them to understand that if anything happened to me, if I was taken away, it was out of my duty to God and to White Arrow and not because I didn't love them with all my heart.

I had so many unanswered questions.

I had no idea what to expect.

· 10 ·

Alien Contact

On the morning of 7 January 1992 I got up at 5.00. I did not want to do this. Tony made me a cup of coffee and we waited for Harry. I tried to reassure myself that White Arrow would not let anything bad happen.

Harry came at a quarter past five, and he and Tony stood at the back door, looking out of the window to make sure I was all right. I walked down the stone steps into the garden. There was a frost and I could hear the grass crunching under my feet. I lit a cigarette. White Arrow stood by my side.

A ball of light appeared at the bottom of the garden. It seemed to vibrate and then expand. It thinned and spun round into a vertical beam of light that seemed to disappear to a point of infinity in the sky. Inside the illuminated tunnel, other lights moved and I could see flashes of yellow. It then seemed to expand and contract again and an Alien walked out of the pillar of light and came towards me. His appearance was unclear, hazy, but in his hands he carried a chain from which was suspended a medallion. This he placed over my head and I knew I had been given something of great importance. It was not a physical object, but something made of spirit. I turned to White Arrow.

'Look and listen,' he said.

What I can only describe as a 'craft' was then shown to me. At first I could only see the outline, as it appeared in front of me and hovered in the air slightly above my head. It was silver-black in colour, like a piece of coal when the light catches it. It was oblong and I could see through it – so I knew it was invisible to others. A door opened and fell forward, away from the body of the craft. White Arrow then stood in the opening, engulfed in brilliant white light.

Then I heard a voice. 'This world is in trouble, and we have come to help. We do not have much time, so we have to seek your assistance. In fifty years' time the people of the world will be finished. In fifty years your Earth will have moved five degrees. There is a comet approaching Earth. Because of the five degrees, your world and that comet will be too close to each other, and, although the comet will not hit the earth, it will destroy it. There will be great destruction. We can help stop the earth moving five degrees. Such a catastrophe will happen and will destroy the living if something is not done now. We can help only if they listen to us.'

'But who's going to believe me?'

'That has been taken care of,' he said and stepped back into the craft, whereupon it vanished. It was now a few minutes to six. I went back inside and described to Tony and Harry what had happened and then went to my room to write up what I had seen. I kept thinking of my little granddaughter, thinking there would be no world for her and I felt a great sadness. I also felt considerable trepidation: how was I to tell the world this terrible news without being dismissed out of hand as a crank? What proof would White Arrow give me to take to the people so that they would be convinced?

'Little One, I will prove it by showing myself to your people.'

'As an Alien?' I asked.

'Yes, Little One. We are the same.' He pointed to the medallion. It looked metallic and shone with a bright silvery, mirror-like light. He reached out and turned it over and it became dark grey. I understood that he had done this to prevent it from interfering with my life and work. I thanked him and looked at it properly for the first time. It was round, with a diameter of about one and a half inches and a thickness of perhaps a quarter of an inch. Although it resembled a large coin, it actually had no edges as we understand edges; rather it seemed to be in a permanent state of forming itself. He told me that the Red Indians knew of such medallions, although no human had ever actually seen one before, and then he said, 'All Aliens have this medallion.'

The following morning the medallion was shining blue. Two weeks later, on 23rd January, I was reading when I suddenly saw a picture forming in the medallion. I clearly saw mountains and an empty road leading up to them. Nothing was happening, it was just a sharp, crystal clear picture. White Arrow appeared: 'I want to talk to you about the medallion,' he said.

I closed the book. He pointed to my feet where I saw a shadow, my shadow, except that I then realised it couldn't be my shadow, because the light was coming from the window in front of me – and the shadow stretched into the light.

'What's that?' I asked.

'That is the other you,' he said. 'There are two of you.'

'I don't understand.'

'Let me explain, Little One. Over here we have what we call "twins". When people on earth have seen an Alien, most times they have only seen the twin of the Alien and not the real, physical form of the Alien. Well, you too have a twin. Your twin can go anywhere in the world with the help of the medallion. Over the next year I will teach you everything about the medallion and its power. The medallion puts you in direct contact with the Aliens. It is the means by which they are in contact with you.' I thanked him and looked down at the medallion shimmering on my chest.

Suddenly the medallion showed me a room and I immediately felt that I was actually present in the room.

A man was in the centre, surrounded by other men with guns. I took a step back and was no longer in the room, only looking, an observer. The man who was being protected by the others walked towards the medallion until I could see only his eye, as if he were peering through a peep-hole. Over the course of the next week I was shown more pictures in the medallion. At one point I felt I was back in the Ice Age and it was at this time that he told me I would have meetings with Heads of State.

· 11 ·

Conversations with an Alien

It was in late January and February 1992, that I conducted a series of meetings between Harry and Michael. They helped to further educate me in the realm of extra-terrestrial visits and happenings. Although White Arrow was always present during these sessions, he rarely commented, leaving Michael to answer Harry's questions. These are a selection of the questions.

Why do Aliens visit Earth?

The time is coming when people will know about Aliens and their reasons for coming here. (Session 2)

When will we know about Aliens?

In about two years' time. We must wait until it is generally acceptable. (Session 3. Feb 1992)

There have been many cases of persons claiming contact with UFO Aliens which say they come from virtually every planet in our solar system and sometimes from other galaxies. Their messages are usually associated with the follies of Mankind and are invariably ignored by the world at large. What makes you think that what you have to tell me will have any greater impact?

Evidence will be given which cannot be doubted. There will be irrefutable proof. (Session 5)

How do you propose to get the world to accept Aliens as friendly visitors?

By the miracles I [White Arrow] *shall be performing.* (Session 7)

When your people were in contact with ancient races on Earth, were they regarded as Gods?

Yes. (Session 6)

Can you tell me which ancient structures were built either by Aliens or by Man with Alien help?

Mostly pyramids. The Inca buildings. Some techniques were introduced into the minds of ancient peoples who then put up structures by themselves. (Session 8)

Who built the pyramids and for what purpose?

They are important for the world and also benefit my [Michael's] *people. They contain writing which needs to be understood. There is also some form of energy and they contain something yet to be found.* (Session 2)

Do the pyramids themselves generate energy?

No, they collect energy. The inner building blocks were levitated into place and were not quarried on Earth. (Session 3)

Is there such a thing as anti-gravity?

Yes. (Session 3)

Did you employ anti-gravity in the building of the pyramids?

Yes. Mankind once knew of anti-gravity but has since lost this knowledge. (Session 4)

Are the experiences recounted by witnesses in close encounters real or induced?

The experiences are subjective in 75% of cases. (Session 3)

Did the Roswell disk belong to your people and was it remotely controlled? Why did it crash?

No answer. (Session 5)

Why do you visit the sea more frequently than the land areas?

Because there is more intelligence in the sea and it is the life source of Mankind. (Session 2)

In our solar system, is there a planet beyond Pluto?

Yes. Also there are seven solar systems in your galaxy. (Session 8)

Can you tell me what is kept in Hanger 18 at Wright Patterson Air Force Base?

There is a small room in the basement which contains the ship which has been dismantled.

[Ann is now inside the room and she describes it]

I'm standing in a long corridor. Two other corridors meet this one. To my left I can see a desk where people are writing and there are people walking past me. Two guards stand in front of me and I know the corridor behind them is important and I know I have to go that way. As I walk past the guards I notice they wear special badges. No one can see me. There are doors either side of me. I notice all the other people have the same badges. I don't think they can be here without them. I wonder where I'm going. White Arrow is in front of me now. A woman inserts a card into a door and the door clicks open. To my left a lift door opens and someone enters. White Arrow leads me into the lift before the door closes. It goes downwards, stops, and the doors slide open. White Arrow turns left and I follow him. We are in a room. It's cold. It's dimly lit. To my right is a large computer that nearly touches the ceiling. To my left I can see tables with clear, maybe plastic, covers placed over them. Many wires lead to and from the tables. I move over to one of the tables and find that I can see through its transparent cover. A white vapour fills the space and lying on the table shrouded in this vapour is a small body. It has dark skin. I turn to White Arrow and then look around the room. There are four more of these table beds. White Arrow speaks. 'They do not have the real aliens. These bodies will vanish.' I turn to the little lifeless body of the Alien and my heart goes out to him and then I understand what White Arrow means. These are twin bodies. The US Government obviously thinks that it has real Aliens but in fact it has the solid twin bodies. It still makes me feel sad to see them like that and I want to leave this room now. White Arrow guides me back to the lift and this time we are travelling upwards. When the lift stops something makes me feel that we are not in the same building. I follow White Arrow. There is a door to our right. White Arrow waits for a moment and then we are inside the room. To my left, in a corner are parts of a spacecraft. The scientists are finding it difficult to understand what the spacecraft is made of. White Arrow takes me through another door into a room where there are a great number of computers. At one of these computers sits a man in a white coat. He is working on a picture that appears on the computer screen. It is to do with the material that the space-craft is made out of. I don't understand how I know this. He is puzzled because every time he tries to work out what material the spacecraft is made of, a colour appears on the diagram in the screen. He can't work out what is caus-ing the colour to appear. I know there is no way he can work it out. The mat-erial is different to anything on Earth and the colour is preventing him from diagnosing the material. [Ann is now back in her body] *White Arrow says, 'We will return for the ship.' Ann asks, 'You mean you're going to take it back?'*

White Arrow replies, 'Yes.'

· 12 ·

White Arrow's Mission

It was mid February 1992 when White Arrow appeared, saying that he wanted to talk, and I knew that signalled the beginning of a new wave of activity.

'Many years ago,' he said, 'before time was thought of on Earth, when man wandered the Earth without the knowledge of today, their only knowledge being that of survival, and God. Their simple faith was in the stars and the planets. The word "God" was not the word they used then, for they had no words. Before the civilisations of today there was just man, woman, and animal. The world above them was their God. It was simple for them to pray to the heavens above. What man could see on Earth was simple but once they cast their eyes to the sky it was different. This they could not touch, and, although they could see it, it was not close to Earth. As they looked at the sky they could see nothing but peace and tranquillity; but on earth it was always survival. Survival, and to live, eat and sleep. To the people of the earth, God was the sky, the stars and the planets; and what was beyond them all made men believe that something special had to be there and so that is how prayer was formed.'

'I presume this is to show that your people were here from the beginning of time. Maybe before us.'

'It is time', he said, 'for Truth to be brought to the Earth and to be explained in such a way that people on Earth will at least think about it and maybe understand why we are here. Little One, you are part of this, a major part, for you were one of us when the plan was made.' He paused. 'This is important. When earth was formed, it was formed from part of another planet, a part which broke away. Another planet was born.'

'Was that meant to be? Was it part of God's plan?'

'Everything is planned by God, including the Earth. Our planet is the closest to Heaven. Heaven is where everybody goes when they pass. Nothing dies, including my people and those from other planets that have life. Our people were asked by God to watch over Earth while life was being formed and we watched you grow. I will not go into how life itself was formed; that will take too long, and other things are more important at the moment. For a while we left your planet; for a time, indeed, it was safe to do so. You did not need us at that point, but plans were set for our return, for we knew far in advance the Earth would one day be in trouble. We play the same role for other living planets.'

'If your people go to help other planets, is yours a special planet?'

'Yes, our planet is special. Beside Heaven, which is a place of rest before your next journeys of return, our planet is what you would refer to as the right hand of God. Our purpose is to do God's work, to look after his life forms in the galaxies and the stars, moon and sun – everything that is God's work.' He paused again. 'We will now go back to what I was trying to tell you.'

'Sorry, I just wanted to know.'

'I understand that, but I must tell you these things now, for you will need them to make sense of much else that is to happen to you. Part of this plan of safeguarding God's creation was to send special "people" to Earth whenever it was heading for catastrophe. A person was sent to show humans the way. But at no time until now were we allowed to interfere, or to present ourselves and use our powers to interfere through others. God sent the Earth many prophets to show you the way forward, and we were instructed to help the prophets, to help demonstrate to men that these prophets had more powers of good than ordinary men around them. Indeed, their very miraculous powers were given by us to help them be heard when they communicated God's will to mankind. These people who were sent were in the Plan well before Earth was born. Each prophet that was sent was given only those particular powers that would fit with the limits of people's understanding at any given time. For the prophet to have too much would have brought much fear to mankind.' Again he paused.

'So, Little One, before the Earth was created, a plan was made for you; you would be born into the nineteenth century to the American Indians and I would return to Earth as a human to marry you, to be part of your Earthly existence. North America was chosen as the location, for the Indians already knew of us. And it was according to the plan that when you were subsequently reborn, it was in England; thus you would learn of the plan the hard way and have no recollection of this. We couldn't risk you remembering your early life, so we could not arrange for you to be reborn in the United States.

'When I came to you in the form of a Red Indian, it was for two reasons. Firstly, it was essential for you to understand the powers of Spirit, and secondly, you had to trust me; and what better way to achieve those aims than to show you I had been your husband in your previous life? And it worked: you did trust me. What would have happened if I had appeared as an Alien first? You would not have been able to cope with the implications of that knowledge, and so we would have failed in our work to help the world. By appearing first as an Indian, I made it possible for you to become my friend, and trust me beyond the limits of human trust. This is why we have come as Aliens now, for what you have gradually learned has meant that you are ready to help us help the Earth. The plan was set when your world was at war for this was when we heard your prayers. We knew we were needed, not only then but for the future. Your wars are getting stronger but it's not just that, it's the wars within yourselves that are destroying the world.

'This is a terrible time for Mother Earth. She hurts. She is being damaged more and more each day, and if she is damaged further, how can she help you? Without her, you cannot survive; without her trees you cannot survive; without her crops you cannot survive; without her water you cannot survive. Yet you damage them all. But above all else, you kill *yourselves*. God did not put this destruction in his Plan, nor can he allow it, but he gave you free will, without which there would be no life. *He* cannot stop you so he has sent us to save you, and to show you what you are doing to yourselves, for such is the danger it cannot be left to man alone any more. You have all seen the warning lights for some time, yet you cannot seem to stop. So, for the first time in human history, we must come to save you. And Little One, this is where *you* are needed. Soon you are to present to the whole world evidence that we are here. Do not fear that responsibility, Little One, for we will protect you in this endeavour. You have a great journey ahead.'

*　　*　　*

I keep thinking about the Sweat Lodge. How had it been possible for me to go back after the second sweat when even one of the Indian girls, someone who was accustomed to the Lodge, had been unable to? My mind races to the night in Montana when Tom gave me the rattle and Gerry said he knew my Indian name. Tom had pointed to the sky showing me the shapes of the stars. One of the stars was moving, but I had said nothing. Surely they had been showing me things that signalled where White Arrow came from. Why was my human brain so incapable of assimilating the signs? The Indians could not tell me. They had to wait for me to tell them. I hadn't. That's why Tom said there would be other tests, nights alone on a mountain, Sundances, more sweating. Until I believed the unbelievable, actually believed it in every cell and fibre of my body, the Indians' work would not be done. They could point to the gift, show me where to find it, but only I could unwrap it.

I had laughed when Tom said that the meal that was prepared after the Sweat Lodge ceremony was to feed White Arrow because he 'had not been fed for thousands of years'. We had all laughed. White Arrow is a Spirit. Why would he need feeding? But only now do I realise that you only feed a living thing. He hadn't eaten for thousands of years because it was taking him thousands of light years to get here. Why could I not put two and two together? How can I stand before White Arrow and say, *and know*, that I do believe him and yet have a part of me that does not believe him? Because that belief has yet to be integrated into a system of human beliefs that so far have worked hard, through fear, to deny the existence of other life-forms. We are not good, us humans, at dealing with paradox. Paradox is at the very centre of the universe. We fear it. What we fear, we find hard to love.

On the night of 23 February 1992, White Arrow asked me to go out into the garden. I didn't question him. I collected a pencil and a pad and a glass of water, my cigarettes and a lighter, wrapped up warmly and kissed Tony. Then I said a prayer and walked out into the cold night air.

PART TWO

'So man, who here seems principal alone
perhaps acts second to some sphere unknown.
Touches some wheel, or verges to some goal,
'Tis but a part we see, and not a whole.'

Alexander Pope: *An Essay on Man*

Meetings (1)

SUNDAY, 23 FEBRUARY 1992

It's 9.00pm. I don't know *why* I'm sitting in the garden but I trust White Arrow. He's at my side looking up at the sky. He's been doing that for twenty minutes now. I have an idea that I'm to be with the Aliens. A beam of light is focusing at the bottom of the garden. It's the pillar of light again. It expands and contracts and I know the Alien who has given me the medallion is here. Again I can't see him clearly but I can somehow sense that he is smiling. He says 'Soon you will see us as clearly as you see yourself. We are preparing you for The Visit. It will come soon.' I ask, 'You're not bad, are you? You do come in Peace?'' He smiles again. 'We come from God to help your world.' White Arrow asks me to hold my hand out. I don't know why but I hold it out anyway. The Alien disappears. White Arrow tells me I can go in now and as he does Tony calls me.

MONDAY, 24 FEBRUARY 1992

Came out at 9.00 tonight. It's a clear night but I'm nervous. What if one of the Aliens creeps up behind me and taps me on the shoulder? I'm shivering as I sit down to wait. White Arrow is sitting by my side gazing up at the sky again. I can see the stars. White Arrow tells me to hold my hand out. 'Why?' I ask. 'Don't worry. All will be clear to you.'

Fifteen minutes go by.

I can see a large, dark shape forming in front of me. I'm scared. It's the bear. He's at least ten feet tall. It's the same bear that visited me over Christmas. I have known for a while that he is an Alien who appears to me in the form of a bear. He asks me, 'What if I appeared to you in a solid form?' I answer, 'I think I'd run a mile. It's different to seeing you in Spirit.' White Arrow says, 'Now you know why you must come out every night. So that you can get used to the Alien form. When he does show himself you will not be scared.' As he speaks the

first spirit alien who brought me the medallion appears, without a
beam of light this time. He's short. I notice his feet are web-like. Then
he suddenly grows tall and I realise that they are all the same, however they first appear, in that they have the ability to change their size
and shape. He smiles and his whole mouth opens wide, and where his
face should join his torso is all mouth. Suddenly he reminds me of a
character in a children's TV programme, whose whole face opens to
become a mouth which is actually a zip, and out of fear I laugh, and
christen him 'Zipper-mouth'. He laughs too – I'm pleased that they
can laugh. He's gone. I ask White Arrow why I have to hold my hand
out. 'You will understand that later. It's time to go in now.'

TUESDAY 25 FEBRUARY 1992

It's 9.20pm. White Arrow is beside me but tonight he's not so interested in the sky. Bear appears. Then Michael. Then the Eagle and
the Lion. I watch them for a few minutes and then the little Alien,
Zipper-mouth, appears. White Arrow says, 'Look and listen.' I hold
my hand out. He takes hold of my hand. I want to pull away but I
don't. He's quite small tonight, like a child. I feel no threat.

Two tunnels of light appear at the end of the garden. They just suddenly appear like pillars, and although I can mainly see where they
land in the garden, they seem to shimmer with flashes of yellow all the
way up to the sky where they vanish. I can also see depth and shading
inside. Two beings emerge, one from each tunnel. They are taller than
the little Alien, about four feet high, and they take little Zipper-mouth
back towards the tunnels. 'Should he not be here? Are they taking him
away, White Arrow?

'Look. Listen.' The other two are guards, or keepers, he tells me.
Suddenly Zipper is giving them orders or telling them off – I'm not
sure – but I know he's important. He comes back to me and takes my
hand, as the other two leave. Then he speaks. 'I have been sent to
show you how to use the medallion and teach you other things to do
on earth. I am the only one who can show you these things so that you
can help White Arrow. I am important.' I think he's very bossy, but I
like him. I ask him if White Arrow is important. He turns and bows to
White Arrow. 'I am here to help White Arrow save this world,' he

says. I tell him I will not be nervous when I see him for real. White Arrow is saying, 'Three lights will appear in the sky soon. You will know it is the Aliens.' I ask Zipper when they will appear. He seems annoyed that I ask, but I feel that's just his way. He puts a small black box under his arm and says, 'I will bring this with me when I come.' I don't understand. He lets go of my hand and walks towards the spot where the other two had been. 'I will see you tomorrow,' he says, and now he has vanished. White Arrow tells me I can go in.

WEDNESDAY, 26 FEBRUARY 1992

It's really cold tonight. White Arrow and Zipper appear as soon as I come out. Zipper holds my hand but I have to ask him if I can keep it in my pocket because it's so cold. He nods. He attaches a wire of some sort to my wrist and runs it down to the light-tunnel at the bottom of the garden then sits in front of White Arrow. 'Now we wait for the three lights in the sky. While we wait, we can get used to each other.' I ask him if I will have to come out every night. 'Yes, but we will tell you what to do and give you warning. I know today you were worried about the future when I come.' I have been. 'Do not worry. I can leave whenever I want to. What you will do is take a video film of me. We will then tell you who to take it to. We will tell you what to say and they will listen. If they want to see White Arrow they will have to listen. So do not worry.' White Arrow is smiling at the Alien. I put my hand out and the Alien takes it. He has long fingers. I can see his feet and he is now showing me the soles. They are just like Michael's feet, slightly webbed with small toes at the heel as well as the end of the foot, but his face is different. 'Why don't you meet me inside the house?' I ask. 'Because I can't.' He's looking up at the sky. 'We are different from your spirit. I am being transported to you. You are in contact with my twin now. Soon you will see the other part of me.' I am drawn to look at my watch as if he wants me to look at it. Is the wire something to do with the watch? Have they put something into the watch? He's looking at the medallion round my neck. The black box he is bringing is something to do with the medallion. 'The medallion is part of us all. This is why you can see us, because of the medallion.'

THURSDAY, 27 FEBRUARY 1992

9.45pm. White Arrow was already waiting for me when I came out. Zipper appeared after five minutes. I can see White Arrow more clearly out here, I wonder if it's because I'm in touch with Zipper. Zipper holds his hand out to me and says, 'We wait.' I like holding his hand. I feel like I've made a new friend. A beam of light appears at the bottom of the garden and Zipper goes to it, but he is still holding my hand. His arm is *stretching*: that's ridiculous! Now he's let go of my hand and is taking a box from someone in the beam. He is placing it in the middle of the garden and now he's coming back to sit with me. I don't know why, but I just know that there is a ship up in the sky – I just know it like I know Tony's car is parked in front of the house. Zipper tells me to look at the box. I can see lots of small rays of light going up to the sky. 'Only my people and you can see these lights. They are to show the ship exactly where we are. They will be left until the ship arrives.' I suddenly say, 'Surely you're not going to land here!' He's annoyed now. 'How else am I to come to you?' He's really uptight! It makes me want to laugh but I have to stop myself. 'You will see the true me and that is only possible with the ship. They will place me here and then they will pick me up. It is arranged but everything must be in place first. The location must be perfect. We wait now. The lights will show where we are.' I know I can't leave until White Arrow tells me I can. I sit and look at the sky. Zipper is moving around me. He's feeling my face and arms. I suppose he has to get used to me too. The tunnel of light appears again and there's someone in it, but I can't see too clearly. Zipper is going now. 'I will be back tomorrow,' he says. I watch him go into the tunnel. I say 'Bye.' He waves and disappears. White Arrow tells me I can go in now and we both get up together.

FRIDAY, 28 FEBRUARY 1992

Zipper is interested in my watch again. He's playing around with it. I'm beginning to like him a lot. I like holding his hand. I know that tonight we're just waiting. The box is still there in the middle of the garden and I am looking at the beams of light shooting up into the heavens, past the clouds. Michael's here now. I can see the similarities, although Zipper is much smaller. Michael is bringing a large box from the tunnel. He's opening it in front of me and inside it is filled with a bright, white light that as I look at it turns to blue. Michael shuts it, takes it to the tunnel and vanishes. I look for the three lights in the sky, but nothing comes. White Arrow says, 'Patience, Little One.' I feel like holding my hand out, and as I do so, Zipper shows me a small ball of light. 'I will bring this for you when I come but be careful, it has power within it. Use it wisely. It will help you.' I ask if it is to do with the medallion. He tells me, 'Yes, all of this is part of it.' He's taken the ball of light away from me now. I follow his gaze to the sky but see nothing yet. I know it's coming. My friends Bear, Lion and Eagle are here. I look at my watch. Twenty-five minutes. They all go to the tunnel. Zipper is last. He waves and tells me he will see me tomorrow. I get up to go but White Arrow stops me. 'Wait, Little One, I want to say something. I will look after your children and their children always.' I thank him. 'Little One, much is in store for you. Your trust in me has needed courage and you will be rewarded.' I tell him I want no reward other than my children's happiness. 'And so they shall be,' he replies. I tell him I will always help him.

SATURDAY, 29 FEBRUARY 1992

Bad headache all day and it's bitterly cold out here. I ask Zipper if there will be many more nights when I will have to come out. He looks up and says, 'We wait for the ship. It will not be long now.' We hold hands. I'm seeing him clearly now. I know he is from the same race as Michael. As I think that, Zipper, as if reading my mind, shoots up to over ten feet tall. 'I come smaller so that you will not be frightened of me.' We all sit very quietly. Zipper and White Arrow hold hands. White Arrow takes my hand and I feel like we are all one. It feels good.

SUNDAY, 1 MARCH 1992

It's raining tonight. Although I like Zipper, I am aware that White Arrow is always around, as if to protect me. To make sure nothing untoward happens. He knows me better than they do. He knows what I can tolerate. Zipper left after exactly twenty-five minutes.

MONDAY, 2 MARCH 1992

Terrible night's sleep last night, so I'm not in the mood to sit out here in the cold, but I feel I'm letting them down badly if I don't come out. I'm so tired. I ask when it's going to happen. 'How long do I have to come out here?' White Arrow is putting his arm around my shoulder and Zipper is reaching out to me. 'Not long,' he tells me. I feel the ship is near. I don't know why I feel that, but for the last two nights I've been nervous, as if something is close. I thought I was used to the idea of the 'real' Zipper coming. I didn't think I would be scared. But I am. It's different seeing the twin because it's like seeing Spirit and I'm used to that. He gets up and goes to the tunnel. He puts his hand up as if to say, hang on, I'll be back. He comes back from the tunnel carrying a large book. It's grey on the outside and although I describe it as large, it's probably no thicker than half a dozen of our sheets of paper. Their paper material is very thin and dark, like that of x-ray pictures. As he opens the book I can see diagrams and writing and drawing, but it's all jumbled. I look at the black page and some of the diagrams seem to be three-dimensional. Some are red. The images seem to go into my head and then I begin to understand them, but when I'm just looking at them they mean nothing to me. My brain seems to absorb them. 'I will show you these drawings in detail so that you can send them to the USA.' I tell him I'll do them tomorrow.

TUESDAY, 3 MARCH 1992

Jason, my dog, died of cancer this morning. I'm sad. White Arrow and Zipper are there as usual, but now I see my mother joining us. I'm pleased to see her. She has been coming to me regularly since she died six years ago, and I feel safe when she's with me like this. We hug and White Arrow reaches out to me and I see his arm stretching like Zipper's and I know they all come from the same place. Zipper tells me that the lights will be red. I thank him. He produces a box and starts fiddling with it, as if he's moving a handle in different directions. He looks up at the sky. I feel that he is directing someone. He places the box in the tunnel and after a short while gets up to leave. 'I'll be back tomorrow. I must go.' I feel he's only going because he cares about how I'm feeling today. White Arrow and mum get up and White Arrow tells me, 'It's OK, Little One. Come inside now.'

WEDNESDAY, 4 MARCH 1992

Zipper has the book again. He's flicking through the pages. The tunnel is here and the lights are still shining up into the sky from the box in the middle of the garden. Mum's here again. It feels weird tonight. White Arrow's sitting on the wall. Zipper is on the grass, and mum's next to me, and I think we're all waiting for the red lights that they keep telling me will appear. There are lots of airplanes tonight. Zipper's excited now. 'Soon something will appear,' he says. A small craft appears. A twin, not the real thing. Someone's getting out and testing the ground. He returns to the craft and it vanishes. I do four drawings: light comes out of Zipper's fingers and words appear on the paper and then I copy them. He puts the paper under his arm and takes my hand. 'I must go. We love you.' Thirty minutes tonight.

Zipper's drawings

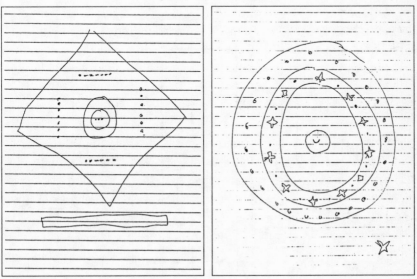

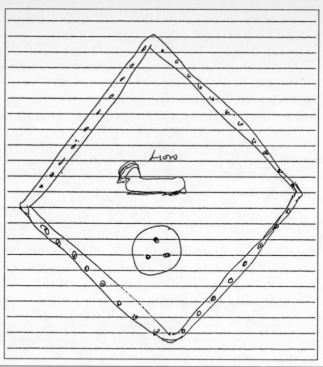

Lion

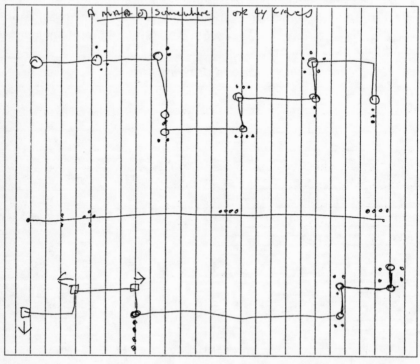

A MAP @ @ Sumewhere or 4 kids

WEDNESDAY, 5 MARCH 1992

Mum's here and I wonder whether they're bringing her in to help me when I do see one of them as they really are. I'm glad she is here. It helps me believe that what I'm doing is real. Zipper wanted to do more paperwork tonight. Every time I ask him a question he puts his hand on my arm and says, 'Do not worry.' Their love is different to earth love. It's more like the love of Spirit. Zipper says, 'We have nothing but love.' Last night's small craft is here. I'm drawing it.

The small craft

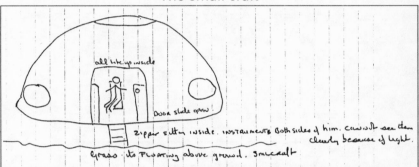

The door opens and an Alien comes out. It's clear that they're getting me used to the ships before the Visit. I also feel that everything is in place now and all they are waiting for is my fear to go. Zipper says, 'I have to go soon.' There's a noise from next door. I go inside. It's 9.20pm. Zipper must have known that my neighbour was going to come out which is why he told me he had to go. I watch him enter the tunnel and wave.

FRIDAY, 6 MARCH 1992

Sitting near the back door. It's 8.00pm and the neighbours haven't drawn their curtains yet. The ship's there but not so clear. An Alien is coming out of it and going towards Zipper. Zipper gives him something that the Alien takes to the ship, then comes back with more papers. Zipper starts to scrutinise me and makes notes about me. The light comes out of his finger when he writes. He asks me to put my hand out. As I do so his hand turns red. 'We can change to any colour we want. Tell your friend that in time, I will tell you the colours we use.' He means Harry. This information would make sense of all the sightings, throughout history, where little green men or red Aliens have been reported. Mum came with Jason, and Tony's mum came with Whisky, his cat. I do many drawings, following Zipper's tracings on the paper. He suddenly gets up. I check my watch. Twenty-five minutes. He waves from the tunnel. This love I feel from him is like the love of a child. Perfect, unspoiled and unconditional. We need that sort of love.

Zipper's drawings

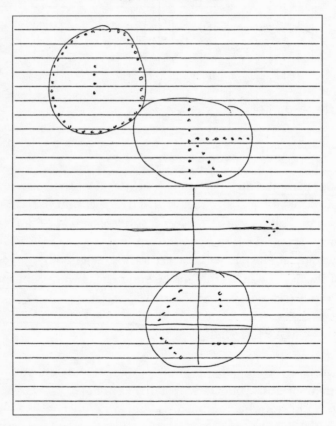

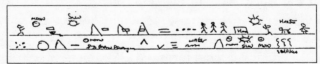

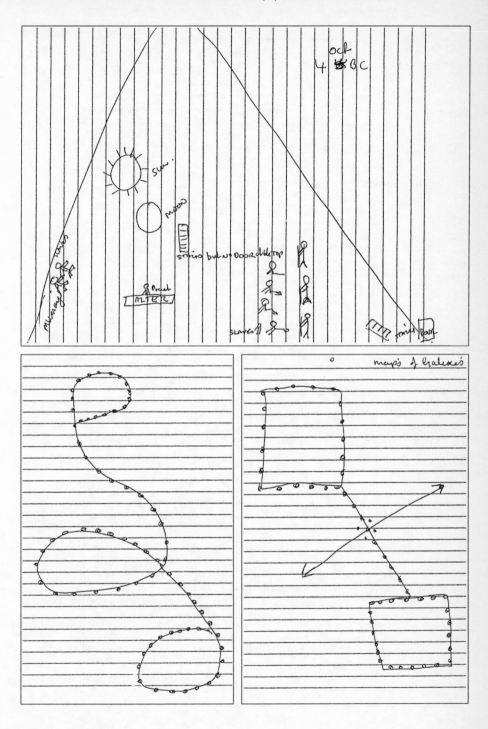

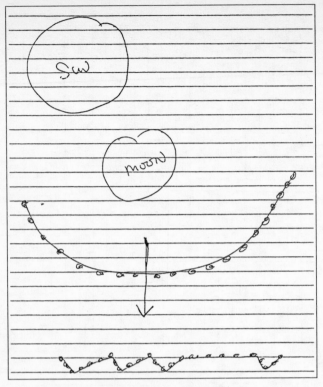

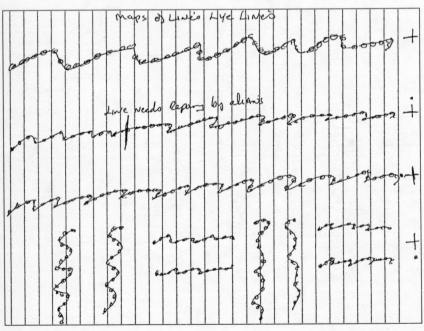

Maps of Lines Lye Lines

Line needs repair by aliens

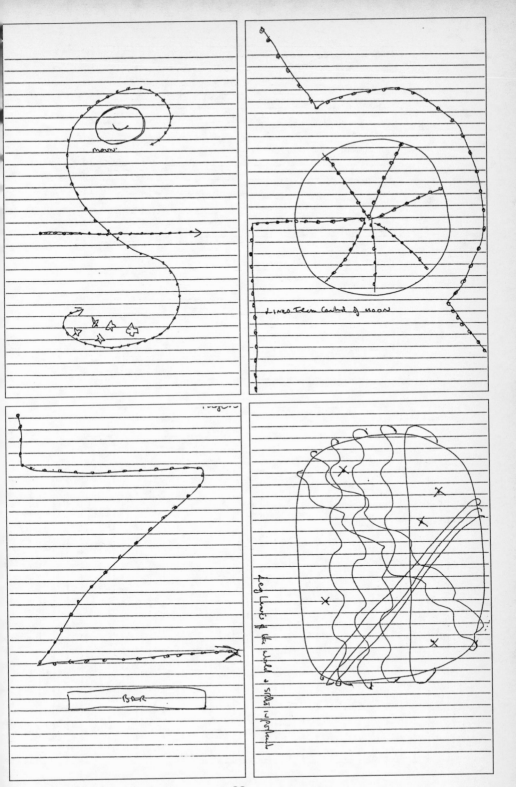

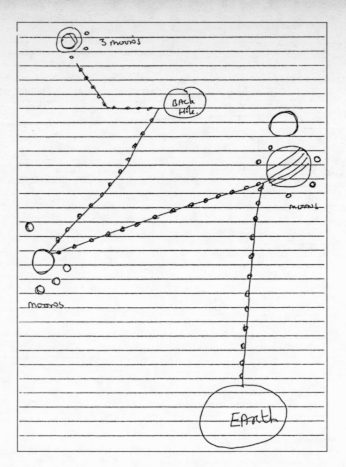

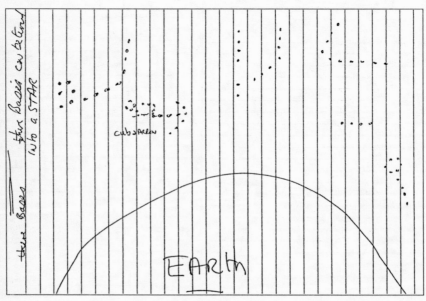

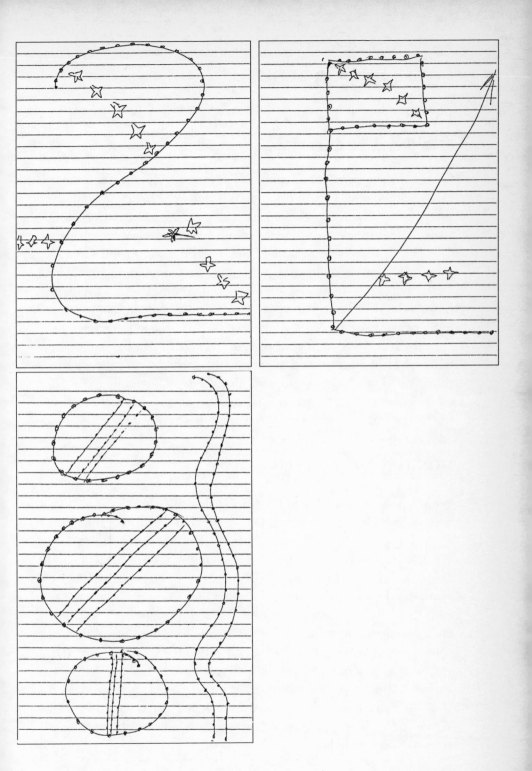

SATURDAY, 7 MARCH 1992

I was at church this evening.

SUNDAY, 8 MARCH 1992

Clear moon tonight. They are showing me the ship again. Zipper is inside it this time. It is lit up and I know they show it in this way so that when I see the real thing, I won't run. Zipper is clothed. He wears a uniform of shorts and a belt but I can't see these in any detail. The ship's door is open and I can see him sitting inside touching things, like switches and controls that are on panels either side of him. I can see his face more clearly now. I've told him I'm not frightened, but maybe they know me better than I know myself. There are red lights underneath the ship. Zipper tells me that when he comes he will appear silver. He's getting me used to the bright light that comes from the ship. He comes out and down into the garden. Wait, there's something rustling at the bottom of the garden. Something's moving around. I'm not going to run. Can't see what it is. It's still moving in the hedge and five minutes have passed. It's stopped. Maybe just an animal.

MONDAY, 9 MARCH 1992

White Arrow's here first, then Zipper; then the ship arrives and the door opens. The light is very bright. I feel that when I see it for real it might blind me a bit. Zipper's shorts look red tonight. White Arrow says, 'Listen and watch.' Zipper is making notes and once again he holds his hand up. I can see a light at the end of his finger. It's like the skin can go over it when it's not needed, but when it's in use the skin folds back. He's shining it into my face. It's just a bright, white light. I understand that he's showing me things he can do. One of the other Aliens, one of the slightly taller ones, is walking towards Zipper. He is very similar to Zipper. The only difference really is the height. I can see them all very clearly, including White Arrow. It feels like they are all getting stronger. Zipper wants to show me more about himself but White Arrow is stopping him. He is definitely in charge of them all. He seems to decide how much I can take.

TUESDAY, 10 MARCH 1992

I'm tired tonight, and it's cold. I feel Zipper's hand in mine, and then I see him. The ship is there and now Zipper is inside it again. He's in a red uniform; the bottom part looks like shorts. I can see the top more clearly and there is some sort of silver and blue emblem on it. He's unbuckling the belt and getting up from his seat. He's wearing boots. There are gloves on his hands, I haven't seen these before. He looks taller but his face is unchanged. The boots and gloves are shining. I don't know what sort of metal they're made of, but it looks like silver. He's standing in front of me now as if he wants me to take everything in. I can see the emblem on his top more clearly now. As I look up I can see the sky behind him and I can see clouds moving above his head. For a moment I am distracted from my drawing as I see a white cloud, high above us in the sky, form into the shape of an arrow. I'm amazed. How does White Arrow do that? I turn to him inquisitively but he says nothing. It's such a clear shape because the clouds behind it are heavy and grey and the arrow-cloud is much lighter, almost white. As I begin to lose myself in wonderment and awe at this miracle, Zipper pulls me back to reality. 'Come, Little One,' he says. 'We have much work to do.' Reluctantly I look away from the arrow cloud and put pen to paper. 'I'm doing it, I'm doing it.'

The emblem

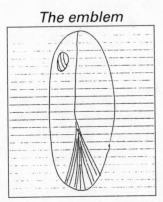

He's going back to the ship. I can see the door shut and suddenly he's at my side holding my hand. 'Zipper, it's too cold,' I say. He's lighting up his finger again, but I don't know what he means. Mum's here now. She's on one side of me and White Arrow on the other. The tunnel is lighting up and two Aliens are coming out. They're taking the box with the lights from the middle of the garden and going back into the tunnel. They've gone. I ask Zipper why they've taken it away and he tells me it's not needed any more. 'Do not worry. It was only to show my people the way. They now know where we are.' He's writing again. I keep looking up at the sky. I know the ship is up there somewhere and I wish I could see it. White Arrow says, 'Soon, Little One.' Zipper tells me to have patience. As he goes he calls out, 'Thank you.' The drawings he has been giving me over the past week now amount to twenty in all. He wants me to send them to the CIA in Virginia. He is very demanding and is continually checking that I have drawn exactly what he wants with the precise number of dots on a drawing, or that the length of a line is accurate and exactly as he wants it. He has also given me some hieroglyphics which are to do with something in Egypt that he has knowledge of.

WEDNESDAY, 11 MARCH 1992

Not so cold tonight, thank goodness. Zipper wants me to do a drawing of him. He's shining his finger on my writing. White Arrow and I discuss how he will appear when he comes – I don't know whether or not he will stay in his Red Indian form. I keep thinking that the Aliens are built of light, but I don't know why. There's a lot of white around me tonight. It seems to come from Zipper. He's getting angry now, someone's given him the wrong thing. He has to go back. I wait. When he returns he is covered in white light. I haven't seen him like that before. He's changing the colours on his finger. It was red a second ago and it's now blue. He's showing me his belt. There's something on it. I can't see it properly. It's shining. It's not actually silver but that's

Zipper's Belt

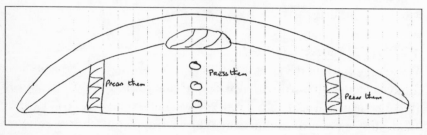

the closest colour I can find to describe it. The ship's here now, but it's not lit up tonight. Zipper is aware that I can't see the belt clearly because it's shining and he's making me do a drawing of it. I watch his finger go over his paper first and then I copy it on to my sheet of paper.

THURSDAY, 12 MARCH 1992

The ship comes a few minutes after I settle in the garden. I'm feeling on edge again. Expectant. Zipper is holding his hand out and White Arrow is telling me to 'Watch and listen.' There is a tall male being in front of me. He's wearing a long white gown. On each shoulder there is a pattern. I haven't seen this one before. He's growing taller and taller to show me he's one of the Aliens. I could kiss his feet, because he feels so holy. He carries a long stick in his hand. He then appears to fly away. He doesn't disappear like the others; he flies away.

   Zipper is writing again. It's all he ever seems to do now. His belt has red on it. Now he's showing me drawings like the ones I sent to America. I ask Zipper if he can show me his hand as a real hand. He puts his hand in mine and I can feel its warmth. I know body contact will be made. There's a big light all round the ship. It's a tunnel, but bigger than the one at the bottom of the garden. I can see a tunnel of blue and green all round the ship. A large cross has been put round my neck. The colour is coming from inside the ship. It's like watching something that's on fire. It's aflame with colour. The people who make science fiction films are closer to the truth than they know. Or perhaps their imagination is informed. This is beautiful. It's like a flickering, three-dimensional fountain of rainbow light. Zipper is moving. It's twenty-five minutes. He calls, 'See you tomorrow.' The ship vanishes and he goes.

FRIDAY, 13 MARCH 1992

I have colours all over my left hand. The same as those in the tunnel. Tonight I have learnt that I was right in thinking that the Aliens are made up of coloured light. But it's the twins that are made up of colour, not the real Aliens. There's a lot of activity tonight. A number of Aliens have come through the small tunnel and seem to be working on the ship. The ship is lit up. I feel something is going to happen soon. I can only see the workers in silhouette. White Arrow has just stopped Zipper telling me something. Zipper never gets annoyed with White Arrow like he does with the others. The tunnel of colour is surrounding the ship. The door is open. The lights on the ship are going on and off for some reason. White Arrow keeps on saying, 'Look and listen.' He won't even discuss it indoors now. It's so cold out here. I should have brought a hot water bottle. Suddenly White Arrow brushes his hair back. I know he does this to reassure me that he is the same White Arrow. Sitting Bull is here now. Zipper asks me to draw his foot, which I am now doing. It seems important to him that I draw him in detail: I don't know why. 'See you tomorrow,' he shouts out. I call, 'Bye.'

Zipper's Foot

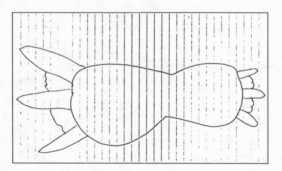

SATURDAY, 14 MARCH 1992

This morning White Arrow appeared to me dressed in a spacesuit. I didn't like it, so I asked him to stay as the Red Indian. I asked, 'You're not going to come as the Alien from now on, are you?' He said, 'Some people will want to talk to me. You must know everything about me as an Alien.' I don't mind him being an Alien – I love him. I don't mind what he is – but I'd rather know him as the Red Indian. I've worked with him that way for thirteen years. I told him it was going to take me a long time to adjust. He said he would always look after me. He pointed to a belt he was wearing that was just like Zipper's. When I looked up from the belt his face was concealed, as if he was being very careful how much of his true self to show me. I feel he's got the same abilities as Zipper but is different in some way. It feels like there is so much to learn.

SUNDAY, 15 MARCH 1992

When I first came out no one was here, then Zipper appeared, and shortly afterwards, White Arrow came. I also sense that mum and Jason are with me. Zipper is looking at White Arrow as if he wants to tell me something but White Arrow is not letting him. It's a lot warmer tonight. Zipper is now showing me a disc of some sort: again, it's that silver colour. It could be part of a belt, or it could be a medallion of some kind, I'm not sure.

The circular disc: silver coloured, with a green stone in the centre

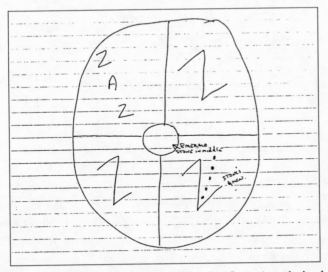

White Arrow has entered my body. It's the first time he's done that since I've been coming out here. He only ever does that if I need extra strength, like with my clients. Everything is quiet. Zipper keeps telling me to hold my hand out. I keep my glove on. Zipper tells me that I will hear from the USA about the twenty drawings of his which I have now sent to Patterson Air Base and the CIA and White Arrow seems annoyed with him for saying so. There are lights in the garden and some kind of activity but it's difficult to see clearly. This is the third time in the last week that I've felt I can see through my hand. I know it's impossible but I'm holding it out, and I can see through it. Zipper wants me to listen to him. He's laughing. I don't know why. He makes a sign like a 'Z'. No ship tonight, only lights. Wait, there is a ship now, but it's not the same one, it's different. The top opens. It lifts up and then stairs come down. It's pushed up by some sort of pressure.

The ship

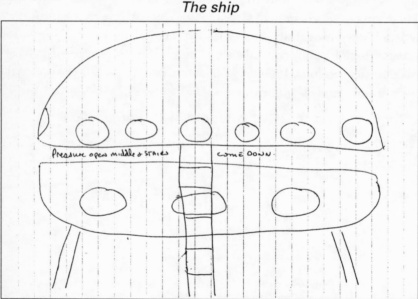

Zipper puts his hand in mine and tells me that he will see me tomorrow. White Arrow leaves my body. The ship is still here. Lots of activity around it. Zipper wobbles to the bottom of the garden and waves. I can see him very clearly in the tunnel. I say goodnight to mum.

MONDAY, 16 MARCH 1992

I had to bring the rattle that Tom gave me with me tonight. Zipper and White Arrow are already here. I'm beginning to enjoy the good feeling I have with them and during the day I look forward to coming out. Mum's here. Still nothing in the sky. I'm getting used to the idea of White Arrow being an Alien. If they are all like him, the world has nothing to fear. Zipper wants me to draw something new every night. Tonight it's another drawing of himself. He's trying to get me to draw him properly so he has placed his hand on my arm. He's put his finger in front of my hand, on the paper, but nothing's happening. 'How can I do anything with your arm covering it?' he asks. Very funny. I have to lean over to see what I'm tracing from. He says he must go. He's at the tunnel and is stretching his arm all the way up the garden to reach me. His hand is on mine, he says 'Goodnight,' and is gone. I hope others will feel their love. White Arrow says, 'Come inside.' I tell mum I love her and she says, 'I love you too.' I'm standing inside and White Arrow is surrounded by the blue light. 'From tomorrow on I will start to tell you about me as an Alien. Day by day I will teach you, for one day people will want to know about me and I must prepare you now.' I'm glad, because for the past few weeks he has said nothing about the extraordinary events taking place in my garden. But I know you can't push him. He will only speak when he's ready.

Meetings (2)

There seems to be no end in sight to these nightly meetings, but I have no doubt that they are vital to whatever process is underway. I've heard nothing from the CIA regarding Zipper's drawings. White Arrow said last night that he wanted to talk, and I feel relieved that, at last, he might be willing to offer some sort of explanation for the events of the past few weeks. He's sitting beside me, smiling, and suddenly I am aware of an element of resistance in me. Perhaps I don't want to know after all.

He's going right back to when I was born and beyond that and is telling me that I was an Alien before. I don't like that idea, but he says I will have no choice but to accept it as fact. He says, 'Now do you understand why we have contacted you, why you can accept us, and why you will be the one to tell the world?'

He continues, 'What is important now is that we have much work to do in the coming months to show that we exist. In the coming months you will be living and breathing Aliens until you know everything that it is possible for you to know. You will be taught powers that no man on this earth has seen before. But you *must* listen to everything we tell you. You must be patient, for I have much to teach you of our ways so that you can tell the world that they have nothing to fear. Fear, as you have now learnt, will stop them listening and then our work for God will have failed. After the shock of first seeing us goes, our words will be of utmost importance and as they will be spoken by you, those words must be right.' I protest. 'But White Arrow, I thought *you* were going to appear and speak to them yourself.' His mood changes. He becomes serious. 'No, Little One. We will speak only through you. But what you do not realise yet is that you know *my* language – that is why you understand us. You are not aware of this. I know this is hard for you, but in time I will show you what I mean by the language differences. We have come from many light years away. We have worked with many planets on the way. Yours is the last planet we will help this century. After we have helped your world and are satisfied with our work, we will take the same pathway back to our home.

TUESDAY, 17 MARCH 1992. Garden. Evening.

As I sat on the step tonight, Zipper stretched out his arm and placed his hand on my wrist. White Arrow was already here. I do love him. It's not so cold tonight and there seems to be no activity from the tunnel, although it is lit. Zipper's going towards it now, except that another tunnel, a smaller one, is forming in the centre of the garden and he's moving towards that one. It seems he's forgotten something. He makes me laugh. All the skin he carries makes him wobble when he walks. He's not at all amused tonight, and I'm afraid that makes me laugh even more.

He's playing with my watch again. I've come to realise that it's not really my watch he's interested in, although I don't yet know what his real interest is. My attention is being drawn back to the larger tunnel where the light beams are shooting up into the sky and through the clouds. The ship is definitely there somewhere. Zipper is making a 'Z' sign on his notes, and now the sign of the cat. I wonder if that has anything to do with Montana and the Milky Way? He's showing me *his* 'watch' now. I've only ever seen it once before and this time there appears to be an image in it. It's a face, an Alien face that I haven't seen before. He's enlarging it so that I can see it clearly. The screen seems to zigzag as if it's out of focus. He speaks into the screen and they talk to each other. Michael appears. I haven't seen him for about a week and I'm pleased he's here. He sits next to Zipper, dwarfing him with his massive frame. They both study the watch device as if they're waiting for a message to come through. Bear and Lion are here now. Michael says, 'It's soon,' and Zipper touches my arm without taking his eyes off the screen, as if to apologise for ignoring me. White Arrow speaks for the first time tonight, asking me if I mind his being an Alien. I tell him I love him regardless of where he's from. It feels like he's measuring my courage, seeing if it's growing as it should. I reassure myself that even though I have yet to see White Arrow in his true Alien form, I am happy to be around Zipper and Michael so it shouldn't be too bad. I tell him that whatever he looks like he's still my guide. I will love him. It seems a vulnerable sort of question for him to ask me and serves to remind me that he is actually alive some-where and has feelings. I thank him for asking, and Zipper suddenly chips in with, 'He's a kind man.'

I can feel mum but I can't see her. She's been here for the last few nights. The craft is here now – the last one I saw – it's very brightly lit, but there's nothing much happening. Zipper shows me a ring. It's in their dimension, a twin, and it appears to be made out of a bendable black and grey metal. Where we would place a precious stone, there is a red light. I feel as though it is a transmitter of some sort. He places it on my finger and suddenly electricity hits my centre like a bolt of lightning: no pain, but the same feeling as a shock of current. He stands up. I look at my watch. He says, 'Wait.' As I look up at him, he stares into my eyes as if he was doing something to them. It scares me a bit, but I can't seem to be able to look away. It lasts a few seconds and then he gives me a big hug. He's never done that before! He takes the ring and walks to the tunnel. White Arrow says, 'It's working now.'

WEDNESDAY, 18 MARCH 1992

Zipper and White Arrow are here already. Zipper is showing me his eyes. They're mainly red but sometimes other colours come into them and I can see white deep inside them. This is strange; they seem to be putting something over me, pulling something down over my body like a new skin. It feels like a new skin. That's the best way I can ex-plain it. I don't know if it's to protect me or not. The garden is full of lights all of a sudden. Brilliant with light. A Holy man has come. He wears a robe of white cloth that is textured with patterns. He has no face that I can see. He's placing his hand on my head. He says, 'Soon things will be all right.' I know from the sound of his voice that this is the High One that came to me before. White Arrow kisses his hand and calls him Father. They stand next to each other and the Holy man says, 'I am giving my son permission to come to your earth in your hour of need. You have been chosen, daughter, to carry a cross for us and for everyone on your earth. My son will explain from now

on. Your journey is long, but you have the protection of God.' He
blesses me and warmly shakes hands with White Arrow, and as he
leaves, I notice his staff. I'm not sure if he was holding it when he first
appeared. White Arrow is sitting next to me. He says, 'We have much
work to do, Little One. Tonight you have seen the Highest. Now we
must do his work. Soon I will take you back to my people. They will
help us on our future road.' Zipper has said nothing; in fact he seems
more in awe of this meeting than I am. He starts measuring me and
recording details about my shape into his book. Someone has come to
the small tunnel and Zipper is going down to meet the newcomer. I
know it's a woman. He walks back up the garden with her. She wears
a space outfit of some sort. Zipper tells me, 'She is your protector and
friend. You will see her often. From now on she will help you understand the Alien ways.' I look to White Arrow because I'm scared that
this means he's going to leave. He puts his arm round me, 'Do not
worry, Little One. You have nothing to fear, I promise you. I will
never leave you. These people I bring forth are to help us help your
world. They are needed for this purpose.' I tell him I understand but
that it will take time.

Zipper shows me his watch again. He tells me to look in it and then
presses something which allows me immediately to see that it is in
contact with another wrist – presumably someone on the space ship.
Whoever it is, is moving about. I can see that they're in a well lit
room. Something makes me feel that I'm in a medical room. I feel I
have been here before, when Harry and Michael had their meetings.
Zipper switches the screen off and holds my medallion, turning it
round in one hand whilst holding something in the other hand. He
touches the medallion with the other object. I can't quite see what
he's doing but the word 'adjusting' comes into my mind. Now he's
moving behind me and seems to be doing something to the chain.
He's talking to someone as he works but I can't see them or hear
them, so I assume he's communicating via the watch again. He's sitting down and has started writing again. It's like he's making notes on
everything he sees that has to be done. Someone else is at the tunnel
and Zipper turns round to talk to them. Then that person leaves. Zipper says, 'Do not worry, Little One, soon you will see and understand
what we are doing. You must write for White Arrow. It is important.

Many events are coming and we want nothing forgotten.' He gathers his notes and walks to the tunnel and waves.

THURSDAY, 19 MARCH 1992

I have told White Arrow that as of Monday I have to rest, so I will sit out in the garden until the 23rd. I am so drained now. I have a tour coming up which requires enormous energy. For weeks I'll be travelling, giving readings to large groups of people. In addition, last night worried me, and that's also why I want a break. I love God and I will serve him with the best of my ability, but I fear I am not the right person for this. I'm not sure I'm good enough. Whatever it is, I need to step back and take stock for a while.

White Arrow is sitting next to me, and Zipper and mum are also here. I just hope they understand. Zipper puts his hand on mine as if to reassure me that he does understand. White Arrow knows me better than anyone so I'm sure he does. I don't want to let anybody down.

The Holy man comes in. Earlier today he brought in his staff and showed it to me. He gives it to me now and tells me I must carry it from now on. Again I feel the fear of what I do not know descend on me: they're always reassuring me, so why does my body still feel this fear? The Alien girl also came into the house today and she's here now. She stands about eight feet high and her face is like Zipper's, although her head comes to more of a point than Zipper's does. White Arrow enters my body and Zipper shows me the watch again. This time I seem to be watching someone in a control room. I apologise to them for my fear. The Holy man returns and I also apologise to him. I put my hand out and take the staff from him – it has a crook or handle at the top. I accept it humbly. They show me a 'Star of David' and then stand in front of me and are all turning red. Zipper suddenly turns a silver colour. He goes down to the small tunnel, which also turns silver, then he comes back. I have asked them for something solid tonight, some *proof* to lessen my fears. I know it's wrong to ask but I need something to take to the world, something to hold on to. Maybe it will be in the drawings I have done: I don't know, but I know I can't carry on like this, expecting people's support and faith without some sort of proof.

FRIDAY, 20 MARCH 1992

Today they told me exactly where *The Meeting* will take place. Zipper and White Arrow are here, accompanied by the Alien girl. The Alien girl moves towards me and I think she's going to take the medallion from me but in fact she's putting something around my neck. I can't see what it is. Perhaps she's doing something to the medallion. Zipper keeps showing the 'Z' mark on his glove. 'Z' obviously has some particular significance to them – so it's a strange coincidence that I named him Zipper. He's looking into my eyes again. It makes me go icy cold, as if he's probing into my mind.

SATURDAY, 21 MARCH 1992. Back room. Day-time.

White Arrow has given me some hieroglyphics which I have shown to a client, Mrs Prince, who is an amateur archaeologist and has been on a great number of excavations. She has told me that they are Egyptian symbols dating from over 5,000 years ago, and is taking them away to be examined by a professor friend of hers. Perhaps he may be able to tell me exactly what they mean.

As Mrs Prince leaves, I am visited by a spirit. He identifies himself as Albert Einstein and gives me figures concerning an American warship that vanished. It was something called 'The Philadelphia Experiment', which I have since learned was an exercise undertaken by Einstein in an effort to create an electromagnetic forcefield around an American warship in order to render it invisible to the human eye. I fail to see the connection between American Indians, Egyptian symbols, Aliens and Alien craft, the CIA, and now Albert Einstein giving me information about a vanishing ship.

SATURDAY, 28 MARCH 1992

White Arrow has asked me to come outside. The last time was eight days go. No sign of Zipper yet. I don't even know if he will come or not. Right now it seems as though the Aliens were never here at all. There's nothing, only White Arrow sitting next to me, waiting. He tells me he will show me something, something to do with the sky. The tunnel appears. I'm glad to see Zipper as I watch him wobble up the garden in a space outfit. He rests his hand on my arm and I'm filled with love. It's hard to express exactly how you feel when they're around, but they give their love so freely and unconditionally that it infects every fibre of my being, so that doors are opened in my soul releasing hitherto hidden deep reserves of my own ability to love. I worry about them when the time comes for them to reveal their true nature to this world, as I'm afraid they might get hurt; but I find solace in my belief that they have ways of protecting themselves.

Michael's here now. Zipper shows me his watch again. I'd forgotten about that. 'You are one of us,' he says. White Arrow has given me the go ahead to ask about the special dates of the 17th and 18th, so I ask. Zipper replies, 'That is the beginning.' I ask him if it's the beginning of 'good'. 'Yes.' I'm feeling brave and, although he is beside me, I say to Zipper, 'Who, and what, is White Arrow?' White Arrow smiles and nods to Zipper that it's OK. 'He is Alien, and he is Spirit. He is special. White Arrow has the power to allow you to tune in to him as Spirit even though he is one of us. One day we will explain but for now there is enough to do. As you go along it will unfold. Soon you will hear from the USA.' White Arrow tells me I must not on any account go near him when he appears. He has told me this before. If I see him as an Alien in the flesh I am to stand back.

THURSDAY, 2 APRIL 1992

Since 7 January I have spent most of my waking hours, and, I assume, some of my sleeping hours, learning about the Aliens. I know the time is coming and I know that White Arrow wants the world to know who he is. I have complete faith in him, but how much fear and conflict will be stirred up when the world knows about the existence of a visitor to our planet, one who can traverse the fields of Spirit and the Universe?

I ask him, 'White Arrow, will evidence of your existence be given to the world soon?' He replies, 'Yes, Little One, but before I come people must have some warning of my existence. You know me of old. Have I not always given you evidence?' Something is happening. The room I am in now is vanishing or changing and I find I am inside the ship.

I'm inside a large room, in the centre of which is a table which has no legs. It's made of something that I have no knowledge of, but I can see through it. It's oblong. I'm touching it and the metal it's made of makes my fingers tingle – because I'm human, I wonder? I'm looking round the room and there's no one in here, but I have a strong sense that I am being observed. The room is brightly lit, and also feels like it's full of colours, although they don't interfere with my vision. I can see through them. It feels natural. I'm looking at an object on one of the walls. It's not solid but made up of colours instead. I know that if I wanted to see a picture of a river all I had to do was look at the object and ask for a picture of a river and the colours would make it. Every-thing in the room seems to float. The chairs have no legs. At the far end of the room I can see a window. It looks like three windows in one, and a half circle. I'm feeling my way towards the window. I'm not touching the table because of the tingling. Something tells me the shape of the room could change if I wanted it to. I can see a door to my left and I turn to look at it. I know all I have to do is go near it and it will open. The chair at the head of the table is very high. That is, the back of it is very high, the others are smaller. They all have the 'Z' symbol on them. This must be Michael and Zipper's ship. I can feel a pain in my stomach. I know there are Aliens watching me through the wall.

There's a noise from the table. It's parting in the centre and some-thing's coming up through it. The table is widening and opening up and an object that looks like glass but I know isn't glass appears. It's round. The top is covered over and there is something inside it. As I approach it I can see it's a map of somewhere. For a moment I think it's the Earth but I couldn't say for certain. All the light in the room has now turned pink. The brightness has gone and the room is swathed in a soft, gentle pink light. It feels warm and I feel happy and I'm not afraid. There is a fragrance that I can't place. I'm experienc-ing an astonishing feeling. Wonderful. I've never felt this before, any-where. I feel as if I'm floating. I look at my feet but they are still on the ground. The object with the map in the middle of the table is flickering. Lights have come on inside it and it's making a funny clicking noise. It's turned blue and I can see that it's a sphere, a globe. The Earth, our Earth, is turning on its axis inside the sphere.

I'm going over to look at the Earth in the sphere. The blue is like the sky only darker. The flickering lights are on particular parts of the Earth; Africa, the USA, but my attention is being drawn back to the room now and as I turn round I see out of the corner of my eye that the large chair is turning away from me. Something stops me from moving towards it. Pain, sharp in my stomach. A few seconds and it goes, but leaves me reeling. Why these pains? I stay still, catching my breath. I'm looking at the floor, holding my stomach. The floor feels like it could bend if I jumped up and down. I look up. The ceiling seems very high. Objects are appearing on the table. One in front of each chair. There are seven altogether. I draw them.

The table

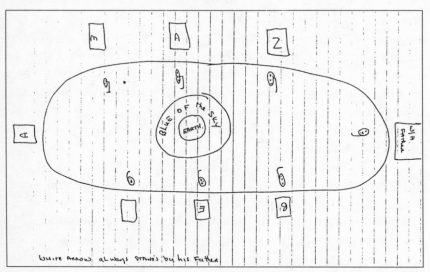

I reach out to touch one of the chairs but my hand goes straight through it and I pull back quickly. I don't know why I'm here. There's a presence in the room. Can't see anyone. I look at the large chair turned away from me and wonder if there is someone sitting in it. The pain is back again, but I don't have time to think about it because the large chair is now full of lights and all the colours. It's shimmering with light and colour and now it's calming down. It's turning blue, just blue: the late evening blue that surrounds the little earth in the sphere. I know someone's in that chair. Fear is coming in; my heart's pounding away. My body is telling me I am encountering something that the whole of evolution has not prepared it for. I can only see the high back of the chair. Something's happening to the floor. It's moving. There's a sudden movement like an earthquake, and I feel my feet move with it; then it stops. The chair is turning round – it's turning towards me. Sitting there is the man from the garden, the Holy man. No face, but I know it's him. He's shrouded in a gold cloak. It looks like it's made of pure gold but I know it can't be gold from Earth. He has no body either, but the cloak gives him shape. I don't know how I know it's a man, except, I suppose, that White Arrow called him 'Father'. It's only the cloak that outlines his shape.

White Arrow's here, and I feel better. He's in Indian form and I know he's appeared like that to ease the fear. 'Little One' – how sweet those words sound! – 'while you are here I want you to watch and listen and only speak when I ask you to.' I understand. He beckons me to sit at the far end of the table but I remember that my hand went straight through it. 'Look,' he says. The chair fills with light as the large one had done and then turns pink. As I reach out and place my hand on it, I can feel that this time I can sit on it although I can't say it's solid. It still feels like it's made of air. I don't know. It's like sitting on nothing. Like floating, or being suspended. My place is missing one of the microphone objects. I lean on the table and feel it bend and pull away thinking I'll fall through it, then watch, as it returns to its normal shape. I can't see the Holy man clearly and that makes me nervous. White Arrow smiles at me and I know not to say anything.

Suddenly I feel so very small. It's weird. Either the room and White Arrow have enlarged or I have become smaller. I'm trying not to panic because the room seems to be spinning round and round. A few seconds and everything is back to normal; well, about as normal as everything can be, given the circumstances. No – it's *not* back to normal at all! I'm dressed differently. I *am* different. My hands are different. They're like Zipper's. But I'm still Ann. The suit I'm wearing is beautiful, full of colours, shimmering with colours that don't hurt my eyes and that don't seem out of place in this room. My top has the

'Z' symbol on it. The Holy man has changed. He still has no face, but now he has long white hair, so long it goes past his shoulders and half way down his chest and on his head is a crown made up of all the colours. It's the most beautiful thing, just a mass of coloured light that combines to make the shape and form of a wondrous crown. I have never seen anything so beautiful. Peace is enveloping me. I want to cry. The fragrance comes back and with it, a sound like music but like no music I have ever heard. I could lie down and sleep peacefully for all eternity now.

The Holy man and White Arrow are waiting for something, and suddenly all the chairs around the table light up with colours. Now I know that when that happens, someone is coming. The door I saw earlier opens and Bear comes in, followed by Michael, then Zipper and Eagle and the Alien girl. She wears an outfit like the one I'm wearing, but also has what I assume to be a weapon attached to her belt on the left hand side. She's also carrying something, but I can't see what it is. Because her hands are like Zipper's and Michael's, I know they are the same 'race'. I'm wondering whether Bear and Eagle will show themselves in Alien form. They all go round the table to their seats. White Arrow sits next to the Holy man at the top. Bear sits opposite Zipper, next to White Arrow, and the Alien girl next to Zipper, and Eagle sits next to the Bear, with Michael next to the Alien girl. They are all turning their heads to the Holy man and bowing to him. What's going to happen now? The stomach pain is back but gentler. I can now see through the walls and see some form of activity going on beyond them. I look back at the Holy man. I think he's God. Even though I can't see his face, I can only describe him as God. White Arrow smiles at me and puts me at my ease. The others all start talking and pointing at me but say nothing directly to me. I don't know what they're saying.

White Arrow stands up and speaks. 'Little One, you are most privileged to be here, for here we have the highest in the Galaxy.' I know he refers to those gathered round the table. He continues, 'I have brought you here so that you can learn about the things that we want you to take to Earth before I tell you why we have come to help. The world must not fear me, for I am the son of God.'

He points at those sitting round the table. 'Without their help, this mission would be impossible, for without their help the plan to save your world would be impossible. Each has something particular to give your world, and each one has offered their services to my Father. Although you have met them all before, I will introduce each one of them to you; now is the time for you to know who they truly are. First we go to the one who you call Bear.'

I look at Bear sitting next to the Holy man, and as I look, I can see him changing. His hair is going. White Arrow continues, 'We have many disguises when we come to you. Although you have seen Bear many feet tall in his spirit form, you have felt no fear of him because you can relate that form to something that you know on Earth. It is easier for you to accept him that way.' As I look back at Bear I can see that most of the fur has gone from his head and body. Everything around him has gone hazy so that I can't actually see him now. I still can't see him through the haze. It's going. Bear is no longer there. In his place sits an Alien with smooth white skin. His eyes are now larger and situated either side of a large round head. In the middle of his forehead is small mound which I look at, and immediately I know it is a telepathic eye. His lips are very thin, hardly there at all, and he doesn't seem to have a nose, only small flaps above his mouth. On his throat is a small opening which I think he uses to talk through.

He looks stern but shuts the middle eye, his telepathic eye, in friendship, as if to say, 'Welcome.' I'm not sure how I know that. White Arrow says, 'His name is *Akes*. He comes from a planet which is far from your reach and has travelled more light years than any of us.'

I turn my gaze to Eagle. Before me sits the most beautiful woman I have ever seen. I'm surprised – I thought Eagle was male. She has similar features to us: her forehead is high and her hair is gold, falling in curls to her shoulders. Her beautiful eyes have no pupils and are almond-shaped, and convey great wisdom and knowledge. She looks so young. White Arrow says, 'Eternal life. On her planet they are born within seconds of dying. They have learnt the secret of how to pro-gress, not in Heaven but on their own planet.' She's trying to tell me her name. White Arrow points to the microphone-object in front of her. She's looking at it and her eyes are changing colour. They're black now, but when I first saw her I remember her eyes were white. They still have no pupils but are shaped a little like our own. I can't understand the name. White Arrow is spelling it for me. It's *Zupuital*.

White Arrow points to the Alien Girl. 'She comes from Michael's planet and her name is *Joyzet*.' Her features are very similar to Zipper's. She has rough reddish-brown skin, and her hands and feet are webbed. Two large round eyes fill most of her face; again they have no pupils, but are mirror-like. Her head is as I've noticed before more pointed than Zipper's. A long, thin nose reaches down to where her mouth joins on to her body. She seems to have no neck, only layers of skin. In the middle of her chest there is a small mound which, as I look, I see is the medallion.

'Zipper and Michael you already know,' White Arrow says. 'These are your friends. They will be with you whenever you need them. There is no need at this moment to give you Zipper and Michael's names. Later you will know, and later we will show you how they can help you on your journey on Earth. Each has powers that can help you.'

He's turning to the Holy man at the head of the table. I can't distinguish what they are saying. Joyzet places something on the table and as she does so the Earth in the sphere lights up. I can't see through the walls any more . . .

. . . Something is being done to me. I'm being encased in a plastic tube. Don't like it. Panic in my stomach. White Arrow speaks, 'It's OK, Little One. This has to be done. It will only last a short time. Trust me. It has to be done.' I'm being moved. Transported downwards. Fast. I'm in another room still inside the tube. I feel that I've been here before. It's a medical room, but it seems larger this time. Small Aliens surround me. Smaller than I am. There seem to be two different types: some taller than others with slippery-looking skin – about half a dozen of them in all. They don't seem to be interested in me, being busy with other things. One of them comes towards me. He opens a door that I hadn't noticed in the tube and takes my hand and leads me out of the tube. His hand feels slippery, like it's covered in grease. I follow: I have no choice. Where's White Arrow? I'm being led to a chair, similar to the others but more solid. The Alien goes straight for a tattoo that I have on my left arm, and peels it back. I feel no pain. I can see the inside of my arm. No blood. He does something then replaces the skin by pointing at the tattoo. I don't know what was done but it only lasted seconds, and I want to get back up to the room where White Arrow is. The little Alien leads me back to the tube. I feel it and it's solid. The Alien presses something on his arm that looks like Zipper's watch. The tube starts to move. I'm back in my seat with the others and the tube vanishes. I'm shaking. Angry. I fly at White Arrow, 'I don't like that! Tell me what you're doing when you take me somewhere!' The anger comes from fear. 'You've got the wrong person, White Arrow. I'm happy being a medium, but not this. Not this! No. Get someone with more brains and more authority.' My hands are shaking.

The man at the end of the table speaks. 'You are Ann Walker.' And I just want to fall on my knees in front of him. But I can't move. I'm stuck. 'I understand how you feel. This is all strange to you. But not only is it important that you have the faith to follow this path, it is imperative for the sake of Mankind. My world needs me and I have come in answer to man's prayers. I have come to take away the suffering and the pain. And I have sent my son: not as the world expects him, but nevertheless, my son. It is through you that my help can succeed. I know you are scared, Ann Walker, and I know I ask a great deal of you. Many would turn away, but as I said, I have chosen well, for you know you will not turn away. I will give you all the power that I can as you follow our path.' He's turning to White Arrow. 'I give my son to help the world.' My eyes are filling with tears that break over the rims to cascade down my face. I look at White Arrow distorted by the ridge of water in my eyes. How, White Arrow? How?

He walks over to me. 'Little One, have faith in me, for I will show you how to show the world, and with my Father's strength, we can help the world avoid that which lies ahead.' White Arrow turns to the man and I also turn to look at him. He says, 'Ann Walker, besides my son, these people around this table will be there for you at any time you have need of them. Call on them, for they know what to do and when to do it. At no time will you be alone on your Earth. This is but the start of your journey. You will see many miracles. There will be many times when you will ask, "Why me?" and times when you will ask that I remove your burden. I ask you one thing. Will you carry this burden? Without question? Before you answer, I will tell you why

I ask. To my people I give free will. By telling me you will carry this burden I know that you will follow the path, asking no questions and trusting in me.'

My response tumbles out in words I've prayed before. 'At my lowest ebb, when there was nothing in my life, you sent me White Arrow. Every day of my life, Lord, I thank you because you gave me back my life. More than that you gave me a chance to show my mother how much I love her and to let her see her daughter's love, and see her grandchildren before she passed into Heaven. She left the Earth knowing that all was well. You gave me a chance to be a mother, to be able to give love to my children. You gave me my husband who was surely chosen by you to watch over me and love me. I owe my life to you. If this is what I have to do for you, then I will carry your burden until I die. I love you, and whatever is in store for me I will do whatever you ask.' I look at White Arrow because the man has no face and I need a response. The man says, 'You will go home now and wait, for soon our journey starts. We will meet again.' White Arrow is standing up.

The picture vanishes. I'm back in my own home.

WEDNESDAY, 15 APRIL 1992

Only two days before 17 and 18 April: Easter weekend, and one of the dates when according to White Arrow's instructions, I am to go to a certain part of the country, *the meeting place*, to wait for him and his people. The meeting will be held in a part of England that Michael told me about many years ago.

FRIDAY, 17 APRIL 1992

We had decided to take a friend with us because I want someone impartial to witness any events that may occur, but now I'm nervous because our friend has had to drop out at the last minute. I ask White Arrow who to take and he suggests the only other person who knows White Arrow's true identity. I call him and he readily agrees to accompany us. Tony is worried about the whole episode, particularly now. He worries for me. I know that whatever White Arrow has said will be fact but he has only given me the dates, the 17th and 18th, and not told me which month. It may be today, or it may be next month. I wish things could be more certain: this half-knowing drives me crazy! I know that we have to be there by 11.00pm and ought to stay until about 1.00am. Tony is unhappy about the whole thing because he's frightened for me and refuses to stay until 1.00am. Somehow I feel this is not the right night, but if I don't go I might be letting White Arrow and the others down. Even if nothing happens I will at least give it a try.

We've chosen a spot at the end of the lane where Tony can park the car and still have a clear view of the field. I will stand by the fence, facing the field. White Arrow has instructed Tony and our witness that they must stay in the car. Only I am permitted to leave the car and walk into the field. It's 10.45pm. I climb over the fence. The full moon is casting blue-black shadows from the trees. I'm glad there's plenty of light. In the distance I can hear Tony and our friend speaking quietly. I'm chain smoking, lighting one cigarette from another one, standing in the middle of a field in the dead of night waiting for something, a spaceship, to appear and do God knows what. Everything is so still, nothing's moving, no bird or fox or anything. I fold my arms across my stomach and hold my ribs. And I wait there until I smoke my last cigarette. I look at my watch. It's 11.30pm, I've been here for half an hour. I go back to the car for another packet of cigarettes and as I open the door both men speak at once, 'Did you see it? The thing circling above you? Couldn't have been a plane, it would have fallen out of the sky!'

I had seen nothing. Our friend explains, 'This object flew between the trees in front of us and then circled above you. It stopped in mid-air for what, a few seconds?' Tony nods. 'And then it just flew off, flew away until it disappeared.' I look at them, grab the cigarettes and head back into the field. I couldn't work out why I hadn't seen it. As I hop off the fence, White Arrow and Zipper suddenly appear in Spirit form. 'What are you two doing here? You should be in your ship, not here in Spirit. You better not have brought me all the way out here just to see you in Spirit.' They say nothing and finally vanish. 'Sorry White Arrow,' I say loudly in my mind, then I hear Tony calling me, 'Ann, it's twelve! Let's go.' I know that nothing I say will persuade him to wait. He does allow me a few minutes' grace in the car, but at two minutes past midnight he starts the engine and drives away.

I know (and, I suspect, despite his relief, Tony also knows) I will have to make this trip next month and I silently speak to White Arrow asking him to make it go right next time, and let Tony stay till one o'clock.

TUESDAY, 21 APRIL 1992

On Sunday I called Sacred Wind Woman in Montana. I had met her when I was doing the first Sweat and she has been directed by Spirit to help me ever since. I needed to establish whether they had translated the second set of symbols that White Arrow had given me just after Christmas 1991. She said they had sent the translations; sure enough, they arrived with the first post today.

The first symbol is a circle within a circle which has a diagonal cross inside it. This, the letter said, represents a Medicine Lodge or Medicine Wheel.

The second symbol shows a triangle like a tepee with an arrowhead at the opening. They had interpreted this to be the tepee where I would sleep during the Medicine Lodge fast on my return to America and the arrow obviously showed that White Arrow would be with me during that trial.

The third symbol shows a single circle with a thick dot in the centre which she said depicted the Sweat Lodge and meant I would have to sweat for them once more.

And the fourth symbol is similar in that it too depicts a circle, but inside the circle is the word *Bear*. This was interpreted to mean that Bear will come to me with a message of great importance. The letter stated that the four remaining symbols could not be translated for me until I was with them in America. It appeared that White Arrow was doing exactly as he had done with the last set of symbols – he was directing me back to the Indians to undergo further trials. These first four symbols were saying I had to go to the Medicine Lodge first before the messages held by the final four symbols would be revealed. Going to the Medicine Lodge also meant I had to fast in the wilderness for four days. In Sacred Wind Woman's letter she stated that it was the only way for me, but I can't help feeling that they have completely forgotten that I'm a forty-nine-year-old English woman and not an Indian who's accustomed to the wilderness and a way of life that includes demanding ceremonies as a matter of course.

WEDNESDAY, 22 APRIL 1992

Tony and I were in the car today, sitting at the traffic-lights, waiting for them to change. I was staring out of the window watching a group of children on their way home from school. They were swinging their satchels at each other and screaming with delight. A buffalo, the most sacred of Indian animals, suddenly appeared in front of me. It showed itself twice and then went. I heard White Arrow say, 'The Keeper of the Guides.'

THURSDAY, 7 MAY 1992

Yesterday I finished my national tour of platform readings, evenings of clairvoyance, where I work with Spirit on large gatherings of people. A week before the first engagement, White Arrow announced that he wanted me to start telling people that he is an Alien. I felt it was too soon and that I didn't have enough information to provide answers. I had no proof. So during the tour I was still holding back, but I knew White Arrow was at work somewhere behind the scenes, because twice I was asked if there is life on other planets and once a young man at the back of the auditorium asked me who White Arrow really is. I didn't lie, but was able to answer the questions indirectly.

Then, one evening after the tour had finished and I was doing a reading in a spiritual church, White Arrow suddenly stopped me passing on any further messages to those who had gathered and said, 'Now, I want you to tell them,' and I dismissed the doubts and fears and quietly stated that White Arrow had been sent by God to help the world. I told them he is a living Alien and that miracles would come later. I think I kept my eyes closed, because I didn't want to see their reaction but out of the darkness I heard clapping. Slow at first but it gathered momentum and eventually the whole hall was applauding. 'There you are,' he said, 'It wasn't that hard, was it?'

FRIDAY, 8 MAY 1992

I'm a very down-to-earth sort of person – never what you could describe as holy. I'm concerned that I may have to change, may have to become something that will match people's expectations of one who is in touch with Aliens who bring help from God. I asked White Arrow. 'No, Little One, I want you to stay as you are. I wouldn't change you. I love you as you are.' I ask him where we go from here. 'Don't worry, the world will have evidence soon.' He told me that from 11 May I would have to sit out in the garden again until the 17th, when I would travel to the Meeting Place as before.

SATURDAY, 9 MAY 1992

Today I called Sacred Wind Woman again to find out if dates had been set for my Medicine Lodge test, and learnt that I had less than three weeks to get myself to Montana. I nearly fell off my chair. On 4, 5, 6 and 7 June, I would undergo this trial of fasting. There is no question of my not going, but I have to deal with Tony who is so unhappy about my making another trip. I haven't told him what the tests consist of to avoid him worrying any further. I hate travelling without him.

MONDAY, 11 MAY 1992

This is the first night in the garden for some time. I've only just sat down and White Arrow and Zipper appear. I'm so pleased to see Zipper again. He has his note-pad and is chattering away about how much work there is to do. His hand is blue. He starts telling me about Sunday night, the 17th. It's cold again out here. Zipper says, 'Soon we will bring you proof.' He shows me a black box with a red light on top of it and a key which he now hands me. 'Soon you will see us,' he tells me. He seems so excited, like a child. He goes to the medallion and fiddles with it. I'm not sure what he's doing, but I think he may be tuning it or switching it on, because it's been inactive for some time now. He laughs, so I must be right. The tunnel appears. Mum is standing by the roses. This coming week of meetings is a run up to the

17th, I know that, but they won't tell me any more tonight. I've missed them. 'It is good,' Zipper says. I assume he means it is good that I'm here again. He's looking at my watch and pointing towards the tunnel and I know our time is nearly up. He shows me a silver jacket. I think I know what they're doing and that is to get me used to what I'm going to see on Sunday. I can see a black helmet now, and a silver space suit.

I am shown a version of what I will see:

The field (1)

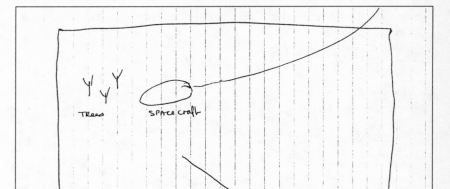

TUESDAY, 12 MAY 1992

It's still a bit light and no one has appeared. I've found the Aliens don't like the light, although White Arrow seems well adjusted, perhaps because he's been here longer. Zipper arrives. 'We have an important message for you which you will receive in the USA.' The black helmet appears. The being is wearing a silver outfit. I can't see clearly through the visor, but he is touching me and the glove is black and soft, like kid leather. He touches my face now and holds my hand. Now he makes me look into the helmet and I can see a face – not clearly, but I know that's not the point: the point is to get used to the helmet. They are preparing me for the visit. He is making me aware that I have nothing to fear. I know White Arrow is behind the helmet. I now know that he *is* coming. I have nothing to fear. He tells me he will show me the ship from the outside but I will not go in. I've been worrying that they might need to take me away, so that's a relief.

WEDNESDAY, 13 MAY 1992

White Arrow is in front of me in the space outfit again. This time Zipper tells me to sit and watch. The helmet flashes with colours. The visor lights up but I still can't make out White Arrow's face because he has made the visor mist over. Another picture of the field is being shown to me.

The field (2)

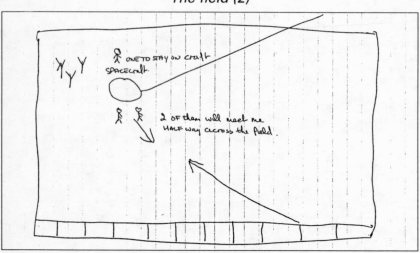

I know Sunday is getting closer and I'm aware of the fear growing in me again. Last month I had no fear. Was that because I knew it wasn't the right month, and this time will be different? I see a picture of the ship, which I'm drawing. It's right next to me.

The space ship

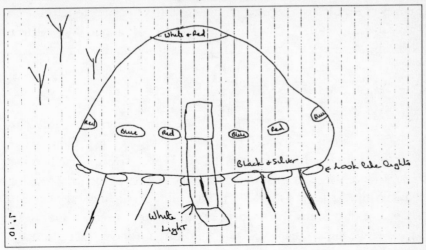

THURSDAY, 14 MAY 1992

Zipper is here with his pad, holding my hand. I was upset today and he's calming me. He's drawing and I can see his hand clearly. He has nails on his fingers that I hadn't noticed before. He's drawing pictures similar to the ones in Montana that show a star where they come from. No, it *looks* like a star but isn't. It's the main ship. From the Earth it looks like a star.

They will come from a star

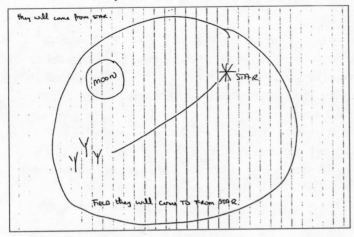

White Arrow, still in the helmet and silver outfit, is now showing me an object that looks like a watch but isn't.

A watch?

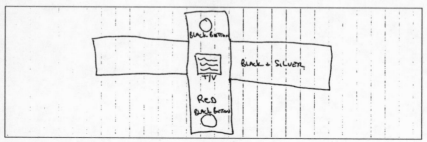

I ask White Arrow if I can let the others into the field to take close-up shots. He directs my question to Zipper, who answers, 'Close to the space craft, yes. Not to us. Only you, for you have been protected. They have not, so they must move around us and not come near. But it would be better on the second visit.' I ask what the purpose of the visit is and this time White Arrow does answer. 'Patience, Little One. It is to bring proof for your journey. No harm will come to you.' Zipper puts his hand on mine and throws me one of his child-like looks.

'There will be noise,' he says. From the spacecraft, I assume. It dawns on me, and I don't know why this thought has not occurred to me before, but I'm going to meet White Arrow as a living being for the first time.

FRIDAY, 15 MAY 1992

White Arrow's here in his helmet. I can see the tunnel as well and Zipper with his pad. He's drawing again. I feel so tired tonight. The work-load seems to increase every day and I hope I have the strength to do what they want. Zipper is showing me another drawing, I'm copying it down:

'It is very important for they will spoil the plan if they do not.' Zipper tells me not to worry. He's very subdued tonight and continues writing. Then he shows me the next drawing, a symbol with Bear in it.

I don't know what this symbol means and will have to wait until I'm told to give it to someone.

MEETINGS (2)

'They must follow the instructions'

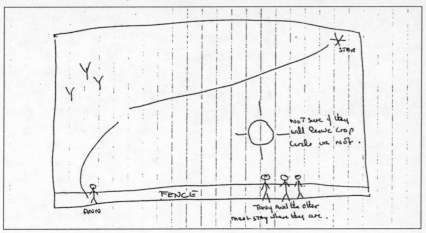

Symbol

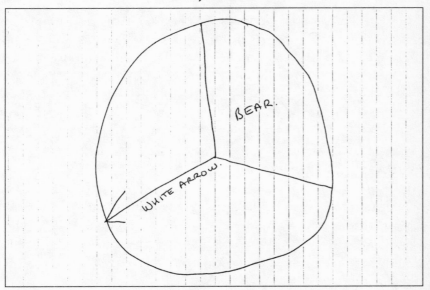

Another drawing is shown to me:

These colours will be placed over you when you see the ship:
Green for power
Red for strength
Silver for seeing
Purple for hearing
Light will appear around your head. People will see it in the future.

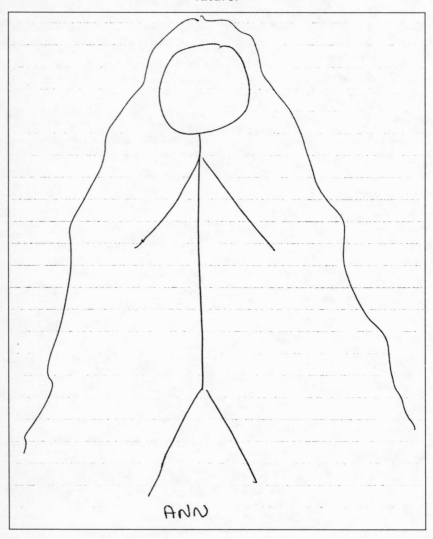

Zipper then says, 'We are preparing for the visit. Soon you will see us.' White Arrow's father is here. He places his hand on my head. I feel so humble. White Arrow is next to Him, and for some reason I feel he is receiving instructions from his father. He changes back into a Red Indian and then back into the space outfit. I don't know what's going on. Bear is here and Eagle, as are Michael and Alien Girl. They're all here, talking amongst themselves. White Arrow's father again hands me the staff. It turns into a snake and they all, apart from Zipper and White Arrow, disappear, as does the snake, and in that instant I understand that the staff/snake is to help me on the path I must follow. Zipper gets up, 'I must go, Little One.' They all call me that now. 'I will see you,' he adds, and as he walks away I see a tear in his eye. I ask him what the matter is, concerned that I may have upset him in some way. 'Nothing,' he says, 'I'm happy.'

SUNDAY, 17 MAY 1992

We were at the meeting place at 10.45pm, with two video cameras, an ordinary camera and several packets of cigarettes and I waited in the middle of the field for two hours.

Nothing happened.

No one appeared.

MONDAY, 18 MAY 1992

I was extremely disappointed last night. The activity from the Aliens has been so intense in the week leading up to the 17th that I was sure something would happen. It's clear now that I will have to keep going to the meeting place on the 17th of every month until something does happen. Perhaps I shouldn't be disappointed? Perhaps this is all part of the process that is undoubtedly under way to prepare me for the visit?

Meanwhile I receive a letter telling me a problem has arisen in America. I will have to postpone my trip for the time being.

SUNDAY, 31 MAY 1992

I met with an Egyptologist, Dr Boothe, today. I told him as much as I was permitted to, and he has offered to research the hieroglyphs. I believe they hold the keys to the opening of a tomb. I know little about Egypt, even less than I did about the American Indians before I set out to Montana. But as I proceed along this path, this road that White Arrow has placed me on, I am gathering knowledge I would never have imagined myself needing.

Dr Boothe told me about a man called Edgar Cayce who earlier this century spoke of an ancient Egyptian prophecy about a person from a foreign land travelling to Egypt in the last decade of the twentieth century to show the Egyptian people where a hidden tomb lay undiscovered and how to locate something called the Hall of Records. It's difficult to overlook the parallel with Indians, who had told me that they waited for a fair-haired person who would come to help the world.

MONDAY, 1 JUNE 1992

I'm in no mood to write but White Arrow has told me he wants me back on the ship. As I sit here with my pen poised just above the ruled pad, the room I am in just seems to dissolve and once again I find I am in the big room with the table on board the ship.

It's the same as before. No one's here. I go towards the chair I sat in last time but there are no colours and I know I can't sit in it until it lights up. I feel White Arrow behind me, and, turning, see him at the far end of the room. He's raising his hand as if to tell me to stay silent, so I just watch as sheets of paper in a folder materialise on the table in front of him. He takes the papers and distributes them around the table, placing one sheet in front of each chair, including mine. I notice the big chair is turned away from me again, and as I look at it, coloured light fills it and I know He has arrived. My chair is turning pink and filling with light so I know I can now sit. White Arrow is now at the head of the table beside his father. The door opens and the others come in. Nothing is said, and they take their places as the microphone objects appear in front of them. The big chair turns and

White Arrow's father is there, invisible but for the gold cloak. The coloured crown of light again appears above his hood. He speaks:

'My child, be patient with us. We come in peace to help your world. All these are my children, as are your people on earth, but these are of the highest in my world who I have brought forth to help the world and secure the fate of my children. Slowly but surely we will help you to show the world that we exist so that we may do our work in peace. We will give you evidence to show them that this is so. The tests placed before you have required the highest faith and these you have passed. That is why I choose you to carry this burden, for that is what it is. Many will doubt your words but slowly and surely they will believe you, for my word is law.' He gets up and moves slowly towards me until he is by my side where he stands for a short time. My knees are like jelly. In front of me, on the table, a gold cup is materialising. 'Drink slowly, my child, for what I am about to give is the gift of life.' I pick up the cup and drink from it and place it back on the table. It vanishes. I feel His presence above me and His hand on my head. He walks slowly back to the end of the table and speaks as He sits down, 'You will not be seeing me at the table but I will be leaving these people with you. Listen to their every word, for they will teach you well. It is important that whenever White Arrow requires you to re-turn to this room, you come as soon as is possible. Although you will not see my presence here, know that I am with you and all of my chil-dren.' The chair turns and the colours fade. White Arrow gets up and sits in the Holy man's chair. The others stay where they are, looking at the papers in front of them.

Alien Girl speaks to White Arrow, but in a language I don't under-stand. He looks up at me and as he is listening to Alien Girl, in my head I hear him say, 'I will be with you soon, Little One.' She finishes speaking to him and starts drawing, then places the paper down on the table and leaves. One by one, the others do exactly the same thing until only White Arrow and I are left in the room. I'm puzzled and I know that White Arrow knows that I am, but he's offering no ex-planation.

He's going towards the chair where Alien Girl was sitting and has picked up the paper she drew on. This he places on the table in front of me. 'I want you to study this and copy it. At this time it is only for

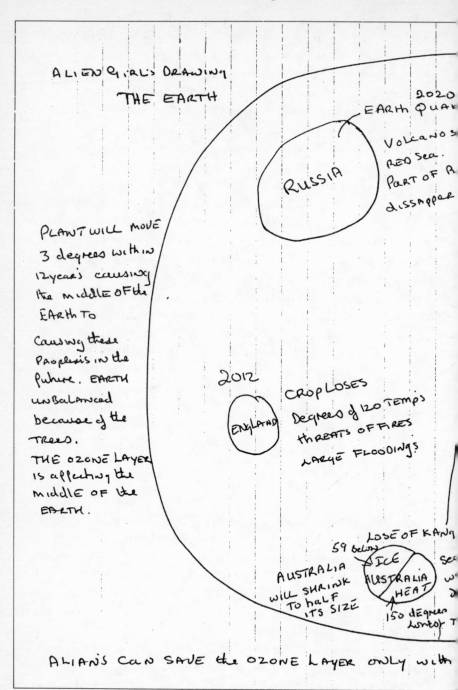

ALIEN GiRL'S DRAWING
THE EARTH

2020
EARTh QUAKE

VOLCANOS
RED Sea.
PaRT OF A
dissappear

RUSSIA

PLANT WILL MOVE
3 degrees within
12 years causing
the middle OF the
EARTh TO

Causing these
Paoplesis in the
future. EARTH
unBalanced
because of the
TREES.
THE OZONE LAYER
is affecting the
middle OF the
EARTh.

2012

ENGLAND

CROP LOSES
Degrees of 120 TEMPs
thREATS OFFiRES
LARGE FLOODINGs

LOSE OF KANG

59 below

ICE
AUSTRALIA
HEAT
Sea

AUSTRALIA
WILL SHRINK
To haLF
ITS SIZE

150 degrees
bottof T

ALIANS CAN SAVE the OZONE LAYER ONLY with

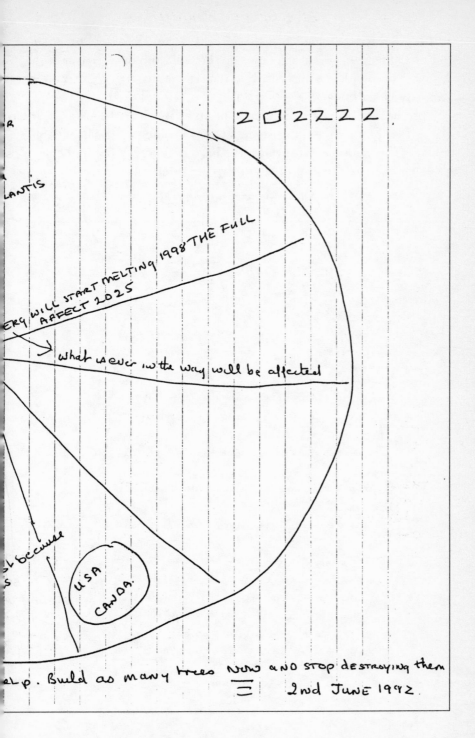

R

LANTIS

ㄹ ㅁ 2 ㄹ ㄹ ㄹ .

ERG WILL START MELTING 1998 THE FULL
AFFECT 2025

what is ever in the way will be affected

L because

USA

CANDA.

al p. Build as many trees Now and stop destroying them
三   2nd JUNE 1992.

your eyes. I will tell you when to show it.' He walks back to his chair and sits. The paper is turned down on the table and the seriousness in his voice has made me nervous. I hesitate, then turn it over; after all it can only be a drawing.

The sheet is like an x-ray image, in other words as I look at it, it seems to contain three-dimensional layers of white and red images on a black, two-dimensional surface. It's hard to describe, but in the one drawing there are many different pieces of information. There are

Alien Girl's drawing. (2)

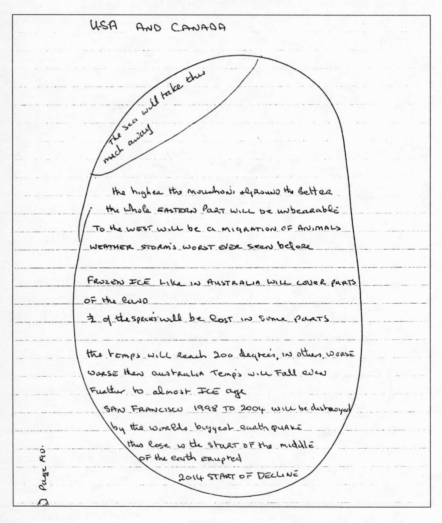

words and figures and diagrams, arranged vertically on top of each other, yet none are hidden by the others. Their drawing is very different to ours but I find it translates automatically in my head. As I look at it, I understand it, but I have to draw each layer on a single sheet of my pad to record it properly.

I record as much as I can from the drawings, but I know I will have to add more detail. I don't understand why they are revealing this information to me; I'm not sure what I can do with it. White Arrow tells me that the evidence he is bringing will convince even the most sceptical. For months now I have been recording events as they transpire, wondering how on earth to prove that what I write is not some mad woman's fantasy. White Arrow tells me, 'Your people have only twenty-five years to turn the world around and save it from destruction.'

WEDNESDAY, 3 JUNE 1992

I've been called back to the ship to receive another drawing. Only White Arrow is here with me. He takes Alien Girl's sheet away and replaces it with the drawing that Bear had done. I am now instructed to get a map of the world to stick on the wall, and some coloured pencils. I can see the paper on the table more clearly. It's black and the writing on it is red and there are drawings. I look at White Arrow standing at the head of the table and feel like I'm back at school. 'Focus on the page, Little One. The words and drawings will be etched into your mind so that you will know what to write and draw in your own language.' With the map and pencils ready, I start. First there is a list of many things from Bear and then we start to work on the map.

For three hours now, I've been working on the map and it's only half finished. This has been the hardest drawing for me to do so far. I understand what Bear wants me to do, but it's very time-consuming and I need to rest for a bit. As with the drawing Alien Girl gave me, I know I shall have to come back to it later and fill in more details from the different layers. White Arrow tells me that I still have three more drawings to complete.

He shows me Bear's drawing and I understand that these drawings are being imprinted on my mind so that I will never forget them.

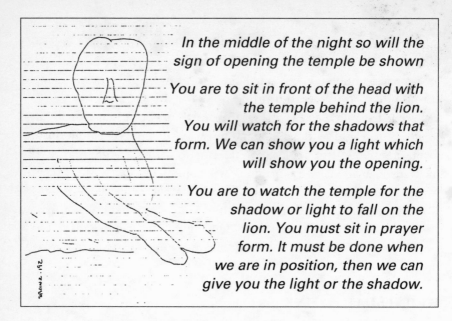

In the middle of the night so will the sign of opening the temple be shown

You are to sit in front of the head with the temple behind the lion. You will watch for the shadows that form. We can show you a light which will show you the opening.

You are to watch the temple for the shadow or light to fall on the lion. You must sit in prayer form. It must be done when we are in position, then we can give you the light or the shadow.

Bear then produces a second layer to the drawing.

They were built separately in case one was found by the wrong people. The others can not be opened without a key. We send a person with the key. The key is in the writing on the walls. The king was informed of our work. It is written in the temple.

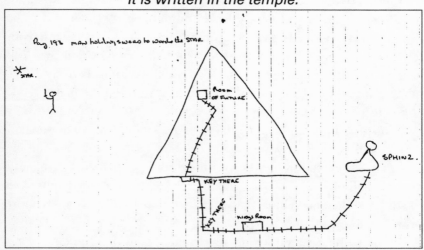

A man holding up a sword towards the star.

Myself and my
husband with some of
the sacred gifts I was
honoured to receive
from the Indians. The
war bonnet belonged
to an ancestor of
Tom's and is
generations old.

The back step where
the nightly meetings
were, and still are,
held.

White Arrow

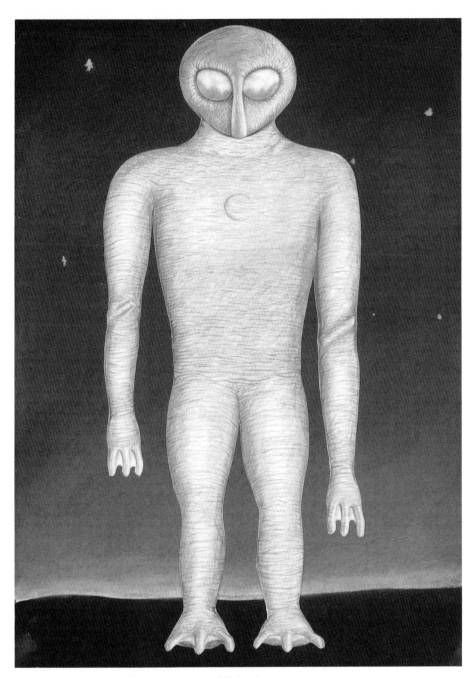

Michael

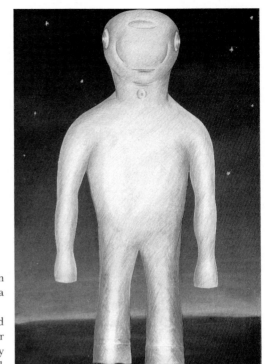

Bear (AKES) in the garden
before I went to America

(*Below*) With two of my Red
Indian hosts at the Milk River
Indian Days' Powwow, July
27th 1991

(*Top*) Rabbit, the wild horse that allowed my granddaughter and I to ride it

(*Above*) Sunday July 28th 1991. I wait nervously to go in for the third Purification outside the Sweat Lodge

(*Right*) Eagle (ZUPUITAL) in
the field in America

(*Below*) The field where Harry
found a crop circle awaiting
my return from America

(*Above*) The light that surrounded me at Denham on September 17th 1991

(*Left*) Zipper

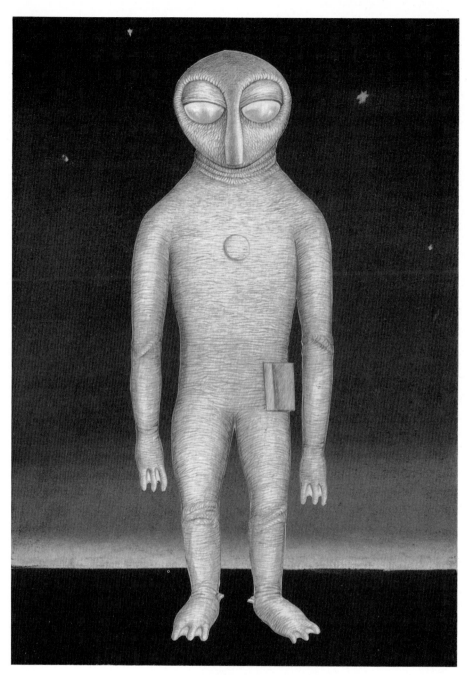

Alien Girl (**JOYZET**)

Now White Arrow gives me a drawing from Michael.

AMAZON
There is a temple of the Gods.
It is well hidden in the jungle.
It has the rest of the records of the future.

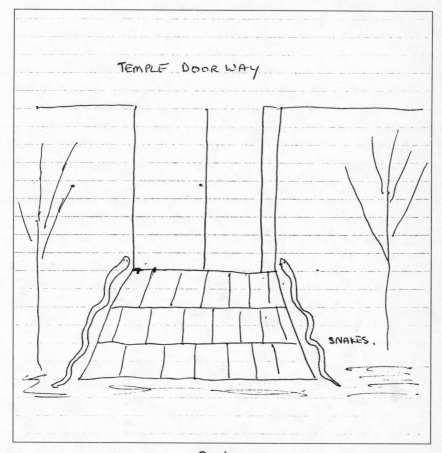

Snakes.
Very few Indians have the secret of the temple. The symbols I give you will let the Indians tell you where it is. White Arrow will give you the symbols.

White Arrow now produces these strange symbols:

You will be the first white person to see the temple. You will send these to the INCA NEAREST THE RIVER. An old Indian awaits you there. Information given will help you on your journey.

Now White Arrow tells me that I must copy drawing number four, Eagle's drawing. White Arrow brings the drawing towards me. What now? I look at it and once again the strange image is translated in my brain and, like a picture coming into focus, it is revealed to me bit by bit. I'm looking at an egg shape. It feels like I'm at the birth of a new world. There's life within the egg. Does it mean a new life coming? White Arrow says, 'Look at the picture.' I don't know why this drawing is harder to understand. I stare at it. Someone else has come into the room. A man. Einstein. He's by my side. 'Look at the picture,' repeats White Arrow. It seems to quiver in front of me as if to concentrate my thoughts.

A new life

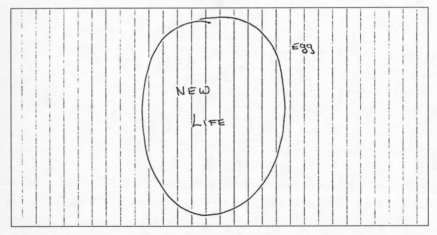

I don't know what it means. Eagle speaks, telling me, 'Your people will not understand these things we have written, for they are in our language; but they are being translated into your language and through your mind. We need Einstein to show you how to write them.' I watch the egg move down and vanish off the page. New pictures appear quickly, one after the other, like a film going much too fast. I realise that each of the drawings holds many other drawings. They are like chapter headings, with vast numbers of back-up images relating to each heading. This is going to be a major undertaking if I am to record it all. White Arrow tells me I am finished for now, and suddenly I am no longer in the spaceship, I'm back in my room. My energy feels depleted. I open my eyes after a moment's rest and see White Arrow. By his side stands Einstein.

For the next hour, Einstein shows me drawings that I copy down as equations and formulae. [For full transcriptions of Einstein's drawings, see Appendix 2 to the Report, p.235]

Some time later Zipper attempted to deliver the fifth and final message but my reserves of energy are so low at this point that I have to rest.

FRIDAY, 10 JULY 1992. Week running up to 17/18 July

White Arrow wants me to have a week of meetings with the Aliens before the 17th. It's 9.00pm and still quite light; consequently, though I can feel Zipper's hand on my arm, I can't quite see him. White Arrow is sitting on the back door step. I feel the meeting has to happen soon – so much time and work has gone into this now that they *must* be ready.

SATURDAY, 11 JULY 1992

Zipper comes first, then the others gather in a circle around me. Eagle is with us tonight. Zipper says, 'You know the responsibility we have placed on your shoulders but we will ease your way where we can.' I smile. He knows I'm tired. Since Einstein appeared I have been working on a report with him, finishing the map of the world and writing for White Arrow. He puts his hand in mine and I feel his love and trust surging through me. 'Look for the three red lights. Everything is in place for the visit. Bring a tape recorder with you, for when you are close to us you may have need of it. This is important. It is not enough that you tell the world you have seen us. And you must have proof so that those who believe you will help. If you want to touch White

Arrow, wear gloves. It is important you remember that. And you must wear shades over your eyes. This is important. The ship is in place. Everything is set. This week I want you to be with us.' White Arrow now speaks, 'Little One, do not be afraid when you meet me. I love you. Your help is needed. Walk towards me, you will be safe, I promise. Tell Tony that I will not harm you. When he sees you speak to me you will be safe. Remember this. It is important for the 17th. Read your notes and be prepared. We have everything ready. You must have everything ready as well.'

SUNDAY, 12 JULY 1992

Zipper says, 'Are you ready? You're not afraid? We will not harm you I promise.' The visit must be soon, otherwise they wouldn't be so eager to know how I feel about it. White Arrow warns me that no one else, *no one*, must yet see the work I'm doing with Einstein. Eagle says, 'We have much to show and tell your world through you. We believe you are ready to take that knowledge to them.' The garden is filling up with light. White Arrow's father appears. He speaks. 'Soon, Ann Walker, you will move on to another part of your journey. Much will be heaped upon you but remember that my children are here to help you. They have the task of protecting you.' He places his hand on my head and departs. Everyone bows as he goes. Zipper says, 'We have decided that the time is right.' As he speaks I can see White Arrow in the spacesuit and I now know that when I see him wearing that I won't be scared.

TUESDAY, 14 JULY 1992

Today has not been a good day. Some of the information that's coming through on the report that I'm working on is truly terrifying. The Aliens are not a problem any more, it's the scale of this whole project. Zipper and White Arrow appear and I can see that they're concerned about my mood. Zipper has his pad with him, and I try to explain that I simply can't do any more drawings for the time being. Michael appears and tells me that help is on the way. He has spoken to White Arrow's father who he says 'understands'. Eagle, Bear and Alien Girl come and they all sit in the circle. This week with them has been odd because they've all been here but nothing much has actually been said. I just want to go to bed and sleep for a century, but White Arrow won't let up. Every day he brings more for me to write and draw for this report. Zipper puts his arm around me in comfort. I know they don't mean to work me so hard and I believe this to be for the good of the world, but how much longer can it go on?

THURSDAY, 16 JULY 1992

Izzy and Bill, long-standing friends, have agreed to come with us tomorrow night as witnesses and as company for Tony. They will come every time until the visit happens.

Earlier today Bear came into the house with White Arrow; he didn't say much. Zipper's here and is giving me healing through his finger. I didn't realise he could do that, but it makes sense of what I saw in the medical room on board the ship when they were using their hands a great deal. The light from his finger turns yellow and he says, 'Remember your medallion. It is there to help you with everything. There is good news coming on my notes' – by this he means the drawings I had sent to the USA. I tell him I hope so.

Suddenly I hear the word *'Goe'*. It comes at me loud and clear like a bell ringing. I don't know how, but I *know* that this is my Alien name. *Goe*.

The aerial

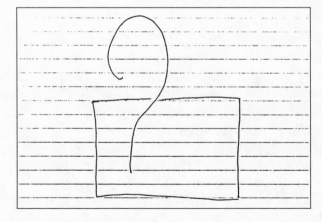

FRIDAY, 17 JULY 1992

The nights are warmer now and although I know it won't be too cold out there, I'm taking a cardigan, just in case. I'm very pleased that Bill and Izzy are with me. I've known them for twenty-five years, and I am sure they won't let us down.

We met at the usual time tonight, parking in the little lane with a few minutes to spare.

As I walk towards the fence I glance up at the sky. It's a clear night and the stars are twinkling away up there. I settle down on the stone and wait. The others know they have to wait in the car. For a while my mind drifts and I think about home and my family and things I have to do. Mum is suddenly beside me and I'm pleased to see her. We speak for a short time and then she leaves. I think about her and about how God has allowed her to come back and visit me, and I look up again and say, 'Thank you, God.' On my first visit here, White Arrow had been with me but since then he hasn't come. I know if I need him he'll come. There are dogs barking not too far away and I wonder if I should go back to the car. I wait by the fence. It's past midnight now, and in my mind I'm fairly sure they will not come tonight, but I promised to stay till twelve thirty.

As I climb back into the car Izzy says, 'When they're ready, they'll come.' I know that she and Bill have found faith in White Arrow and silently I thank him.

MONDAY, 10 AUGUST 1992

Once more I am summoned to sit with them for a week before going to the meeting place. It's the same as last month, they come one by one and sit in a circle talking. Tonight Einstein is with them and Lion is here although he's not showing himself. They are all joining hands in friendship. Zipper takes my hand, 'Soon we will meet,' he says. He is so gentle. White Arrow smiles from the middle of the circle. He and Zipper are old, old friends. I suddenly remember something: many years ago, when White Arrow first came to me there was an almighty argument between him and the spirit called Monsieur Phillippe, who had accompanied me for several days. They had both tried to enter my body at the same time and White Arrow became enraged. I look at Zipper now and remember Monsieur Phillippe's strange mouth and yellowed teeth and it all makes sense: Zipper as I know him now, and Monsieur Phillippe then, were one and the same.

WEDNESDAY, 12 AUGUST 1992

Had to visit the doctor's today. He diagnosed tonsillitis. I feel OK, but I could do with about a week's sleep. The trip to America is now set for two weeks' time, and so much needs to be finished here before I go that I suspect I shall be packing on the way to the airport! Zipper appears and rests his hand on my arm. This is now his usual welcome. White Arrow is in his space outfit and is showing me the gloves which are now bright red. He tells me that I will know which one of the visitors he is by the red gloves. I must remember not to get too close. He will be about six feet tall, he says. I also know that I will be unable to see his face through the visor and that will be deliberate. Again he shows me the helmet.

The helmet

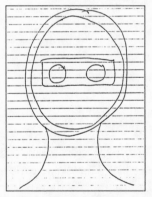

Now I can see the silver gloves that Zipper will wear. He tells me that he will be entirely silver and shorter than White Arrow. 'You will spend many years with us learning everything about us so that you can educate your people.' I need reassurance that Tony will be with me throughout whatever is to come. 'He's so good, Zipper. Not once has he doubted or stood in my way. He trusts White Arrow implicitly and that is extremely important to me if I'm to work well for you.'

THURSDAY, 13 AUGUST 1992

Bear has been telling me about the trip to the USA: 'I will be talking to you personally.' I don't know what he means by *that*, but just so long as White Arrow is with me, I don't mind. 'I have much to tell you,' he says, and then informs me that I will return from the States greatly changed and carrying much knowledge. It's pouring with rain out here so I'm moving into the porch. I should go back indoors but I know how much effort they put into these meetings and I don't want to disappoint them. Their visit must be soon now. I hope it's in England with Tony, not half way up some mountain in America when I'm on my own in a strange place. More of them are coming in now. Einstein, followed by Bear, Alien Girl, Michael and Eagle. Bear takes my hand and holds it for the first time. His love just washes over me. I ask Zipper to explain more about the medallion and he tells me I can go anywhere I want to, and invites me to see all of their spaceships sometime. The medallion seems to empower me. I can see them so clearly because of it.

FRIDAY, 14 AUGUST 1992

I've had a long day and am late out to the garden. For the first time in months I can see a small spacecraft. It's the same one I've seen before. Zipper is moving towards it and is entering the craft. As the 'door' closes, the craft lights up. It looks too small to carry three of them. I can see him quite clearly inside the craft. Now the lights sort of flicker and then go out and the craft vanishes. Zipper is standing beside me now. Bear is growing more visible and wants to be near me, presumably because of America. I wonder how many more tests I will have to undergo when I'm there? 'I will look after you,' Bear suddenly says. White Arrow's father appears, and again I have the feeling that I should be kneeling in front of him. 'Soon your journey will commence. You will be safe, that I promise. Soon many words will be written.' What about the thousands of words already scribbled? I think.

SATURDAY, 15 AUGUST 1992

Zipper just appears tonight with no tunnel or lights and immediately opens his book and starts writing. He now draws furiously in his book and holds the paper out for me to see. It's a drawing of the Medicine Lodge symbol. I don't know what I'm supposed to do with it.

Medicine lodge

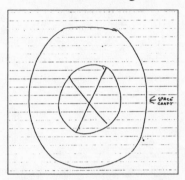

He goes back to his pad and says no more about it. White Arrow tells me that it has something to do with the spacecraft.

SUNDAY, 16 AUGUST 1992

My life is no longer my own. So much more is added to the work-load every day that I never seem to catch up. At this moment I'm working for Spirit all day and in between clients I'm writing for White Arrow. My lunch break is taken up with the maps and the report and now Zipper's notes, and in the evenings I sit out in the garden with the rest of them. If someone had told me a year ago that I would now be managing with this enormous influx of information I would have laughed. Tony worries about the amount of work I have to do, and most of the people who are close enough to know what's going on believe that I am coping, but I don't think anyone truly understands the pressure. White Arrow steps up to me now and says, 'I will give you my strength.' He enters my body. 'I know, White Arrow, I don't mind really, it's just that on days like this I get so drained.' The tunnel is lighting up and Zipper emerges from it and wobbles up the garden. 'News is coming that will help our cause,' he says. White Arrow's father has appeared and two male Aliens are bringing a box out of the tunnel and laying it on the ground in front of me. Zipper reaches out for my hand to let me know that he's not ignoring me. It gives me a great feeling when he does that. Bear and Alien Girl arrive. Zipper opens the box and removes something from it, placing the object over my head and round my neck. It's black and I feel that it's a homing device, or a bleeper of some sort.

The device

He says, 'It is attached to the medallion,' and I ask him what its purpose is, to which he replies, 'You have already answered your own question. It is for the Meeting Place and for your trip to America.' They're homing in on me. That must mean that the meeting is soon. He's moving over to the deck chair and circling around it. Now he's sitting in it and I am giggling uncontrollably. He looks at me indignantly as he wriggles into a comfortable position. I would give anything for a white handkerchief with knots in the corners to place on his head. The two spacemen appear again and remove the box, taking it back to the tunnel and vanishing. Bear places his hand on my arm and Alien Girl is smiling at me. I can't see the smile but it feels that way. Michael appears and greets me. He asks, 'How's Tony? Give him my regards,' and sits. Now Eagle has come from the tunnel: she's in her Alien form, but somehow I know that it's Eagle. Bear is the only one who still shows himself in the form of an animal. I'm sure that will change. White Arrow speaks, 'Early on the morning of a Tuesday, something will happen of importance to our work.' Why is he so cryptic with me?

MONDAY, 17 AUGUST 1992

Izzy and Bill came at 10.20, and, as we drove to the field, I told them everything I had learned from White Arrow since seeing them last.

The weather is still in my favour and I now look forward more and more to these visits. I find a sense of peace here and a feeling of goodness. I know that they are up there watching me. Tonight I feel that very strongly. The fear I have had of the actual visit is slowly leaving me, and standing out here in the dead of night, with nature around me, restores me somehow. I feel a part of everything: nature, the sky, the universe; as if I was one with God and my impatience nothing of consequence. I am learning that God can not be ordered around. He will send them when he is ready, and not before, but while I wait he's showing me other things, like this inner peace I can feel now, perhaps.

White Arrow has suddenly appeared. 'The Visit is soon,' he says and then vanishes. I've learnt that 'soon' means something else to White Arrow so I breathe and look up to the sky. All is quiet. They will not be coming tonight.

THURSDAY, 20 AUGUST 1992

I am having difficulty establishing whether the formulae and equations that Einstein is giving me for the report make any sense. They mean absolutely nothing to me and I'm reluctant at this moment to make them public by looking for help from established sources. I have, however, shown them to someone I can trust, a science don at Brunel University. He feels that there is a key missing to the formulae, and I am beginning to wonder whether some figures have been intentionally withheld to protect their content.

I received a reply from Patterson Air Base today (See Appendix) to letters I had sent with the twenty drawings that Zipper gave me throughout March. I have always known that these drawings are related to an event kept secret by the authorities, namely 'The Roswell Incident', when a UFO crashed into the ground near a small town in America.

SATURDAY, 22 AUGUST 1992

God knows how, but I'm finally up to date with everything and now I begin to prepare for my trip to America on the 26th. Tony is not happy about it, and I must confess the fear is already building up inside me too. In a way it's been good to have been so busy.

Albert Einstein has just come in. I'm beginning to enjoy his friendship. He has an air of self-assurance and authority born of wisdom. He has been dictating to me a formula for a petrol which doesn't emit carbon dioxide, and it is now finished and ready for the report. Einstein is waiting patiently beside me, so holding pad and pen I start to copy down his figures.

Later, as I prepare my things for the trip, Tony asks me again why I have to go – why can't Bear deliver his message here in England? I have no answer for him, since I don't understand that myself. All I know is that I have been given instructions to go to the Mandan Hidatsa Arikara Indians, where I will be met by Sacred Wind Woman who participated in the Sweat Lodge ceremony which I underwent on my last visit. Her letters over the last few months have helped me prepare for what lies ahead; I know I am to fast in the wilderness, but I have no idea for how long or why or under what conditions. I know the fast will continue until a message is received.

The tight, angry, red ball of fear is already burning in my stomach. This time I am taking only Val. It is extremely rare for me to travel without some member of my family to accompany me but that is what they want. In a way I'm glad that my daughter will be at home for Tony. I have said nothing to Tony about the fast, knowing it will only add to his worries. My daughter has also promised to keep it from him until it's over, and I have assured everyone that I will ring as often as I am able to. I know I'll miss them all desperately.

then using equation 14-18.

$$\frac{B\check{v}}{v^2} = \frac{N_1}{N} = \frac{V'_1}{V}$$

for the steam.

$$\frac{B_3}{V} = \frac{0.78124}{2} = 0.3724.$$

$$-\frac{B^2}{V_2 + 18.4} = 920.148 \quad \therefore \quad V_s = \left(\frac{0.81235 \times 13.4}{2 - 0 - 12780} \right) = 0^s.4805$$

moles of water condensed $= 4 - 0.4230 = 5.77$

1 mole of H_2O contains $(4+18) = 18\,{}^{1/}_{6y}$ therefore mass of water condensed is $4.87 \times 19\,kg$ for every mole of fuel.

mass of water condensed per k_1 of fuel. $= \frac{3.78 \times 91}{901} = 9.480\,kg$

(COAL)

1 kg of coal contains 0.9 kg C and 1.13 kg H_3.

$\therefore$ $\frac{1.8}{12}$ moles C^a and $\frac{0.13}{3}$ moles H^c_3.

Nitrogen supplied with the oxygen $2 \times \frac{81}{64} = 3.43x^2$ moles

combustion equation is therefore as follows

$$\frac{0.9}{12} C + \frac{0.13}{14} H^3_2 + x O_3 + 4.37 \times N^c \rightarrow a\, CO_3 + B\,H_3O + 4.32 \times N^c_3$$

then

Carbon Balance	$\frac{0.9}{16} = a^M$	$\therefore$	8.007 moles
Hydrogen Balance	$3 \times \frac{0.13}{14} = 3B$	$\therefore$	$b = 0.07$ moles
Oxygen Balance	$3x = 3a + b$	$\therefore$	$x = 4.077$ moles

Petrol formula

The Fast

Much as I tried to forget what lay ahead of me in the coming days, I was continuously presented with reminders. No sooner had we said our farewells, settled into our seats and were tucking into the first in-flight meal than we struck up a conversation with the couple sitting on the other side of the aisle. He was a cameraman on his way to make a movie in America and we chatted for a while about his work. Pre-dictably he then asked what we did and where we were heading. I told him I was a medium and explained that Val was accompanying me to a meeting but explained that she was a Healer in her own right. The woman, who had been listening attentively, immediately asked for healing from Val and everyone swapped seats as those sitting around us subtly craned their necks to listen in on our conversation. The man was genuinely interested in my work. Obviously I didn't go into any great detail but he suddenly interrupted me and asked if I knew any-thing about crop circles. He had a friend, he told me, who had been studying them for years, and was there any spiritual information I could give to help, 'Here we go!' I thought; of all four hundred people sitting unwrapping their plastic knifes and forks I was next to a man who wanted to know more about crop circles. I told him I believed they had something to do with life from other planets and left it at that.

There was a four-hour delay in Minneapolis while we waited for the connecting flight, but eventually we got there, called a cab and checked in to a motel that had been reserved for us: a much grander place than last time, with a swimming pool. I love water and enjoy being in it more than almost anything else so as we walked past the pool towards our rooms I promised myself a good long swim before I left. We had a light supper and dropped into our beds like lead weights. I was up at 7.15 the next morning. It was dismal – hurricane force winds and lashing rain. I turned to Val and said, 'That's all we need, bad bloody weather!' Our cases were filled with T-shirts and shorts and sandals and things for hot weather. At least we had the warm clothes we had travelled in and I tried to switch off a picture of myself that was forming in my head, of wild animals and horrid snakes stalking me in the midst of a midnight thunderstorm. Val laughed first and within seconds we were both laughing. Laughter has always been my way of dealing with fear.

At midday, Sacred Wind Woman arrived at the motel with her sister and her daughter. The Indians are generous with their feelings: we were greeted with great bear hugs and laughter. Her car had developed a fault on the way over, so she needed to get it repaired before we set off. After a coffee and more laughter she dropped us at a shopping mall while she took the car in and we wandered around looking at the richly decorated shop windows. I bought presents for home: a stetson for Tony, some little things for the others. My daughter had begged me to bring her back a cuckoo clock and as I went from one shop to another in a fruitless effort to find one, my stomach started to pulsate – the fear was back. Sacred Wind Woman hadn't mentioned a thing about the fast and I hadn't thought it right for me to bring the subject up, so a situation existed where everyone seemed to be avoiding a discussion about it. I think Val could see the strain on my face, but she didn't refer to it – she just tried to keep me busy by joking a lot.

We met up under the big clock in the mall, only to learn that the car had a serious fault and wouldn't be repaired until the next day. I wanted this test over with quickly and now I had to endure another day of waiting and worrying before I could actually deal with it. The girls booked into our motel for the night and I returned to my room badly in need of White Arrow. The fear was now unbelievable. It felt like I was living each second slower than the last, surviving from one moment to the next. I went into the bathroom. 'White Arrow, I hope I don't let you down, but I'm really scared. I mean really scared.' He was there. 'I know you are, Little One, but I promise you will be safe.' Again I could see wild bears and wolves and rattlesnakes roaming the hills as I sat shivering on my own. In the mall I had overheard Sacred Wind Woman's sister tell her that on her last fast a rattlesnake had slithered right past her – White Arrow was telling me I would be safe in the midst of all *that*? The closest I think I had ever been to a dangerous animal was in London Zoo.

I felt he was asking too much of me, and as I sat on the edge of the sink, I began to seriously doubt my judgement. 'This better be the last bloody test, White Arrow. I'm not kidding! I've demonstrated my faith in you over and over again. How much more do you want?' He said nothing, just stood in front of me with his arms crossed, so I carried on. 'I mean, I know you wouldn't put me through all of this unless you had good cause to, but I tell you I am absolutely petrified!' He left. It was as if he was bored listening to me complaining and he just dissolved away and I was left looking at a distorted reflection of myself in the white tiles on the wall. There was a knock at the door and Val called out, 'You OK in there?' I stared at the tiles. 'Ann? I've got some coffee for you here. What should I do, pour it under the door, or what?' Thank God for Val! I came out and drank the coffee and Val said that Sacred Wind Woman wanted to speak with me alone, so she and the sister were going out for a while. 'Were you talking to White Arrow?' She always knows.

'Yes.'

'What did he say?'

'He just said that I would be safe.'

'You will be safe, Ann.'

When we met Sacred Wind Woman started our private meeting by announcing that she had received my Indian name in a dream. To be given an Indian name is a great honour and I felt my spirits lift. I thanked her, remembering that on my first trip Andrew had said I would receive the name later. 'The name we give to you is Medicine Bear Woman. *Medicine*, because you are always with spirit and can see them, *Bear*, because you have come here to receive a message from him, and *Woman* because that is what you are.' I felt uplifted and honoured and proud and as if I really was at one with her people. Medicine Bear Woman. I felt suddenly like I belonged and I told her so. 'Tomorrow we will return to my home. It is up to you whether you start your fast then or on another day. I will help you. When you are outside with the Earth I will come to you every eight hours. If you are asleep I will return another time. If you are awake we will pray, smoke the sacred pipe of peace and sing songs to the Spirit. That is how we do it. We will, I hope, have the tepee there for you. The tepee appeared as one of the symbols you were given, but there might be a small problem.'

'What?' I asked.

'Well . . .' she paused. ' I don't have one. My sister is lending me hers but it may be difficult to get it over to my house. It'll be OK though, Spirit will make sure of that.'

The following morning I woke early and propped the pillows up against the headboard and called White Arrow. As I waited for him to appear, I lit a cigarette and repeated my new name over and over in my mind. Medicine Bear Woman – I liked it very much. There was no sign of White Arrow, so assuming that he was busy elsewhere and that he would be around later I rose, washed, dressed and woke Val. I was aware that the fear had subsided. It was a bright sunny day, the storm clouds had disappeared and at breakfast, mum appeared. She said, 'Don't worry Ann, I'll be with you.' I said, 'Thanks mum. I just don't want to let White Arrow down and this panic keeps taking me over.' She smiled with her head to one side. White Arrow appeared beside her.

'You won't let me down. Little One, when you fast I want you to go to sleep straight away. I will wake you up for the messages but I want you to promise that you will go to sleep straight away.'

'OK, I will, but why?'

'Just do as I say.' Then they both vanished. Later, as we wandered round the mall again while Sacred Wind Woman collected the car, White Arrow appeared again. 'You will not fail me,' he said. 'While you are doing the fast I want you to leave the entrance open.' Great! Now any passing snake could just slither into the tepee and bite me. 'Thanks a bunch, White Arrow. I mean, you're really helping me overcome my fear, aren't you?' He said, 'Trust me. I will be there.' I knew he was going and it was all I could do to stop myself reaching out and grabbing him for dear life. The thing in my stomach clawed at the inside of my ribs. My pulse was racing and I was breathing quick shallow breaths as the fever of fear once more clouded my mind. I felt myself gag and I knew I was going to be sick.

As I bent over the sink to wipe my mouth, part of my mind was telling me that it was perfectly possible to get on a plane and go home to safety and Tony and those who loved me. What difference could it possibly make? The Aliens were coming. They have special powers anyway, and although the future safety of the planet was of paramount importance to me, I couldn't see why this stupid ceremony was needed. Why was I allowing myself to be dragged through all this? What possible difference could it make to anything whether I sat alone on a mountain for four days or not?

I was sitting in the back of the car turning the cigarette packet over and over in my hand, working feverishly on a way out. Every time Sacred Wind Woman said, 'Soon be there!', I wanted to vomit. Suddenly I couldn't bear it any more and I just leant forward and prayed. I squeezed my eyes closed, tightened my fist and under my breath said, 'Dear God, if you can hear, please, please take this fear away from me.' I stayed like that for some time, repeating the prayer. I opened my eyes and could see my feet on the floor-mat and a screwed up crisp packet but nothing had changed. The fear was still there. I sat up forcibly, opened my eyes wide. As I angrily brought a cigarette up to my lips a flame of lightning snapped across the sky and a few seconds later a clap of thunder reverberated around us.

Large heavy drops of rain smacked against the windscreen. One or two at first, and then a deluge. Not only had my prayers been unheard but the elements themselves had turned against me. A great wind blew up and more lightning, this time forked, streaked across the great expanse of sky that slowly turned red as the sun set over this vast open land. Sacred Wind Woman turned the windscreen wipers on full and suddenly laughed, 'It's God greeting you,' she said. 'The Thunder Beings are welcoming you with their thunder and lightning.' We drove on in silence for a while then she said, 'See the moon? It's a full moon tonight.' I blurted out, 'I want to start the fast as soon as we arrive, OK?' No sooner had I said it than I regretted it. She said, 'You do the fast whenever you want to. It's fine with me.' I looked at the sky, now crimson, with flashes of light and a brightening moon. Confusion reigned, in the heavens and in my mind. I couldn't reconcile myself to the opposing factions in my head that at once were pushing me to accomplish this ordeal and simultaneously trying to avoid it. 'By the way,' she said, 'I spoke to my sister about the tepee and she won't be able to get it over to us tonight. Sorry.'

Oh no! No, no, no! I would be out in the storm without shelter. I forced myself to say, 'I still have to go out there *tonight*, all right?'

The Indians are a people who say little but observe a great deal. I knew that from my last visit. She said nothing. I puzzled over White Arrow's absence. Where was he? And Mum? Hadn't Sacred Wind Woman said that Spirit would sort out the tepee, and now I had to fast in the open. As if to kick me, another thunderclap rolled over the plains and more rain lashed across the car. I would have covers, surely, and bedding to keep out the wind?

We stopped at a supermarket where Sacred Wind Woman told us we had to buy the food needed for all those who would be at the ceremony. She had explained this in one of her letters but I had forgotten that whoever I brought with me had to cook a large meal for everyone who attended the ceremony. I also had to pay for everything because this was their custom; it was seen as my way of giving back to them and to God for my experience. Val's part was to do all the cooking without help. Which proves her total support and faith in White Arrow and in my path. As we carried the bags of potatoes and trays of chops and sacks of cabbage and corn from the supermarket, I felt myself relax. Fourteen people would be coming to eat and the idea of poor Val cooking and cleaning for such a large gathering was only slightly less amusing than the thought that I myself might have had to do it. I am the worst cook in the world. Val and I looked at each other as we stood in the rain, loading everything into the boot. No words were needed. We were giggling like schoolgirls.

We arrived at Sacred Wind Woman's trailer home shortly after eight. The storm still raged. Her home is in the very middle of nowhere, just parked in a wide open landscape at the end of a track. We were shown to our room. Because a Sioux friend was coming to help with the fast and I would be sleeping outside, Val and I shared one room. We drank yet another cup of coffee and then Sacred Wind Woman left the room and brought back a pile of blankets and rugs bundled inside a real bear-skin. She looked outside and told us that the rain had stopped, and the storm seemed to be calming, then she sat down again. 'I had a visit a few days before you came. I was here on my own and I heard footsteps. My daughter was asleep in her room. I looked around knowing well that no one else was here, then sensed a Spirit. I heard it moving around the trailer and then realised it had come to check my home. To see that it was prepared and all was ready for you,

Ann. I am sure it was White Arrow. I felt good with his presence.'

As she spoke I began to wonder why he had left me on my own for so long. It was unusual for him to be away from me even for short periods. I guess Val could see my face tightening. The time was close and she understood my needs at that moment. 'Ann, I don't want you to think that I'll get one minute's sleep in that comfy big bed tonight. Oh no. I'll be lying in the BIG bed worried sick about you out there in the dark with all those coyotes and things. I'll just have to tuck myself up nice and warm for the night and hope you're OK. It is a big bed though, isn't it?' I didn't want to laugh. I wanted to be scared, because at least that way I would be ready for anything – but I did. Sacred Wind Woman watched us. 'If you want, Ann,' she said, 'you can do your fast in the Sweat Lodge. We can use it for fasting, it's called the Medicine Wheel when we do. There are many ways people choose to fast. Many travel to sacred places. Some stay on their own land, or use the Sweat Lodge, or the tepee and these ways are all good because they all go back to what's in your heart and in your spirit.

I felt such a sense of relief. 'Are you sure?' I asked. If I was going to do the fast I wanted to do it properly, with no charity.

'Before you came, Ann, I thought of alternatives for you in case we couldn't get the tepee. I decided that if there was a problem, we would use the Medicine Wheel: it is in the symbols. Because we believe in the Sacred Circle of Life, once you are in the Circle which we call the Medicine Wheel, you are at the centre of the Universe. I didn't tell you then because it would have made it easier for you. I had to find out whether you were doing this for God, or for yourself so that you could tell your friends about it. I needed to know that you were doing it for all the right reasons. So many have come to us for help with fasting and God has shown us who came for the right reasons. They all fail when they come for the wrong reasons. Not once during the two days I have spent with you have you made any excuses for not doing it and on the way here, despite the storm you still insisted on going ahead. Few who are not Indian would have shown that courage. I had to see your courage, Ann. Through that courage you show your love for God and for White Arrow. I'm sorry I didn't tell you before but these are our ways. These things that we are helping you do are sacred amongst our people. The outside world has no knowledge of our ways and that is how we like it. The tests we put ourselves through are for

God. You have shown me your strength.'

I hugged her and said, 'Thank you. I don't know what to say but thanks for not helping me through my fear. I'm sure I would have failed had you shown any pity.' For a moment the fear left and was re-placed by a sense of pride.

There was a knock at the door and the Sioux woman, Medicine Song Woman, came in. I took an immediate liking to her and, I think, she to me, for I actually found myself laughing and joking about having to go out and brave the elements and wild animals. Poor Medicine Song Woman was completely baffled by this attitude. She stared at me with a bewildered look in her eyes, 'Aren't you *scared* of going out there alone?' She'd never met an English person before and was not used to our humour, I suppose. 'If I don't laugh about it, Medicine Song Woman,' I said, 'I will cry. Of course I'm scared. I'm terrified, but let me put it this way, if a rattlesnake comes close to me I won't just sit there and let it rattle, I shall leap forty feet in the air and run away screaming for help! I'll be back here so quickly you'll think I can fly, and then, Val, we'll see who has the BIG warm bed to them-selves.'

Sacred Wind Woman said, 'It's time. You ought to change.' I put a tracksuit on and a thick woollen jumper over that and my leather jacket on top. She told me I had to remove all of my jewellery, in-cluding my watch. 'Time is not important there,' she said. I was allowed to take nothing with me but the coloured ribbons she had told me to bring in one of her letters. I had two yards of each: yellow, red, blue, white and green. They all represented things which were rele-vant to the ceremony. Blue for the sky, yellow for the sun and so on. I said goodnight to Val who finally looked concerned and followed the other two into the darkness outside, carrying my bundle. As I fol-lowed behind, my mind emptied of all thoughts and my senses con-centrated on just getting to the Lodge. Some clouds cleared and the full moon lit the path. I was glad of a bit of light. My eyes were fixed on the path. I looked neither left nor right, just watched as one foot re-placed the other and the path passed away beneath me. Later the girls told me they had seen a white arrow of stars forming in the sky as we approached the lodge. When finally we arrived, Sacred Wind Woman gave me the tobacco I had been told to bring and instructed me to sprinkle it around the Medicine Lodge. This is their way of giving something back to Mother Earth. Once the tobacco circle was formed I couldn't step outside it. The others could, but I couldn't leave it until the message had arrived. I entered the Medicine Wheel, as it was now called, and put the blankets towards the back just missing the deep hole where they place the hot rocks when it's used for a Sweat. I turned back to the opening and saw an altar on which were placed a buffalo head, various crystals which the Indians call Sacred Stone People, and bowls of herbs. Sacred Wind Woman came in and told me to tie the ribbons on the willow frame of the lodge above my head. As I started that she unwrapped a Sacred Pipe, which we knew as the 'peace pipe' and, handling it in a reverential manner, she placed it on the ground just inside the opening. Then she knelt and prayed in front of the altar. Medicine Song Woman stood to the right of her and sang to God. As she crawled out of the opening, Sacred Wind Woman said, 'Remember I will return.' Then they left me.

I was completely alone. Suddenly the night stood still. There was no rain, no thunder, no lightning. Nothing moved, or made a sound. Everything was still. I straightened my blankets and lay down on the hard ground. It sloped away to the right so I got up and shifted every-thing across to more level ground and settled again and as I pulled at the blankets, mum appeared. She didn't say anything, just sat beside me and made me feel better. I remembered White Arrow's instruction to go straight to sleep. I lay there watching mum, aware that I had absolutely no fear now. The terrible apprehension of the last few days had gone and this moment that I had dreaded so powerfully arrived calmly and revealed itself to be nothing more than solitude and peace. I slept.

I don't know how long I slept. It was still dark when an invisible hand shook me back to life. I turned over, not remembering where I was, and tried to go back to sleep. I was shaken again. I sat up and looked around. There was no one there and after a while through bleary eyes I pieced together the dirt floor, the blankets and the lodge and eventually realised what I was doing there. I was OK, no fear, no element of surprise, and I rubbed my face and looked for the ciga-rettes. Then, as I reached over to the bundle, Bear appeared at the opening. He seemed to radiate gentle glimmers of light. As he came in and sat next to me, I could see White Arrow standing at the opening as if on guard. Mum came in, then, shortly after her, the Lion, White Arrow's father, was there. He lay down in a corner with his face resting on his paws. Bear, however, was the one in charge of this meeting: the others were observers. Time stood still. Not a single sound could be heard from outside; it was as if Mother Earth and all of nature were aware of the gathering and held their breath until it was over. I felt safe. I touched the Earth with both hands and stroked her. I thanked her for all her gifts and apologised for the injuries my brothers and sisters were inflicting upon her.

As I ran my fingers through the soil a strange thing happened. I no longer perceived my hand as a hand but saw its structure as though I were looking at it through an X-ray machine. My eyes followed the length of my arm until I realised that I was seeing my whole body in this non-physical state. It was a moving black-and-white version of myself as nothing but wisps of light that had gathered and converged to illuminate the bones and sinews. Skin, the surface, was not important any longer. I was seeing the highest form of my physical being, seeing the light on which my body hangs, the light that is my soul, and there was no part of that light that I could label. It would not have been possible to call a part of the light an elbow, or a finger, because no part was separate from another. Even the part of my consciousness that must have been alert enough to recollect the vision was part of the vision itself. How long I was lost in the vision I don't know, but after some period of time I could hear, as if from many miles away, a voice. The light and I separated.

Bear was speaking, repeating the same words over and over as if in a chant:

'I helped build the pyramids.

I helped build the pyramids.

I helped build the pyramids.'

For several hours I listened to Bear. I listened attentively to all that he had to say and asked no questions. The others watched and listened and apart from once when Lion raised himself and shook his golden mane, they did nothing. Sadly, I can not reveal the messages. They were guidelines to the future, and directions for me to follow on the road ahead. They were sacred revelations and until the time is right cannot be told. But they will be known by all mankind. Soon. My apologies. I can say that among them were powerful instructions on ways to heal this planet that we all share.

As the incandescent blue of dawn slowly illuminated the opening, I sensed an end approaching to our meeting. Slowly they left: Bear first, then Lion and mum and finally, without having spoken at all, White Arrow too was gone. I felt the cold for the first time and wrapped up well in the bear-skin, looking around waiting for something else to happen. Slowly I was overwhelmed by a sense of loneliness unlike anything I had ever felt before. I became aware of every single mile of unknown territory that lay between me and my family in England. The absence of my Spirit friends made me feel intolerably sad. I felt cut off, abandoned and orphaned.

A piece of sky visible through the opening was pink and deep blue clouds were skimming across it, a weird illusion created by the rising sun. I heard the wind gather, shaking the trees around the lodge and causing the leaves to rustle and protest. The coloured ribbons flicked their tails above my head. I looked around the lodge again, at the altar, the burnt hole in the ground, the willow frame, the peace pipe. I felt honoured that the Indians had accepted me as they had and at once knew that the fast was ended. My test was finished. There would be no more messages. Bear had delivered and would speak no more and I had passed the test.

Sacred Wind Woman wasn't at all surprised when I told her the fast was over. She had apparently always known I would be out for only one night. Val had to prepare sacred sage tea for me as part of the ceremony and I wasn't allowed to drink anything until I had that. I went to the bathroom and as I washed my hands and face, White Arrow appeared. I was pleased: everything was now back to normal, and in a way I hoped he would be around me more. 'Little One, your real test took place in the days leading up to the Medicine Wheel. I had to leave you to make your own decision and find your own courage. I'm proud of you. Would you go through anything for my father? Would you have faith? You overcame your fear. That was your test.'

'I'm glad I didn't let you down.' I wept.

He walked towards me and placed his hand on my shoulder. 'Rest now, I will be back later,' he said.

Val came in and confessed she hadn't slept all night. I wondered whether that was Spirit using her as some form of support. We had a cooked breakfast, drank tea and chatted until everyone who was to take part in the second test arrived. The symbol had also shown another sweat.

Val joined us for the first sweat, which was mild by comparison to the last one I had done. After one round she went to prepare the meal and as she left, the Door Keeper began to chant prayers and the others sang. A further hot stone was placed in the hole, water was poured onto it and the burning, searing steam enveloped me. I knew I had to complete four rounds or fail, and after what I had been through on the fast I had no intention of failing, so I lay flat on the ground, pushing my cheek into the earth and closing my eyes against the heat. It was still unbearable. I had forgotten how sharp the heat was, but somehow I got through it. We returned to the trailer, lobster-red and sticky. Val had peeled mountains of potatoes and prepared countless chops and cabbages. I took one look at her buried under it all in the kitchen and laughed.

'Not one word,' she said. 'Just don't say anything.' People arrived and all were formally introduced. Some wanted readings, which I gladly did for them. Others just sat and observed me. By bed time I was quite drained.

At 5.30 the following morning White Arrow appeared by my bed. He smiled. 'We have much to do now, my Little One,' he said softly. I recalled Bear's messages in the Medicine Wheel and thought about the road ahead. 'I want you to listen and learn today and tomorrow. The teachings are important.' Then he went. Medicine Song Woman, the Sioux lady, tapped on the door. She came in and sat on the edge of the bed. She bears an uncanny resemblance to pictures of Sitting Bull and is proud of the similarity. Sacred Wind Woman joined us. The three of us sat on the bed deep in conversation for several hours. Medicine Song Woman hadn't known that White Arrow was Sitting Bull's son, and on learning that she vowed to help search for evidence of my reincarnation. During the night her Guide had delivered a message telling me that I was special. I cringed at the very idea – I'm not special, White Arrow is. Nonetheless, she told me I had to accept that I was. I accepted on White Arrow's behalf – it was his energy she was picking up on. She went on, 'When you were in the Medicine Lodge, you were as one with the universe. The universe looks upon you as part of itself. Now Mother Earth was also with you and all the elements were, and are, working for you on your journey. You slept during the fast. This we call a Death. It is a way of giving yourself to Mother Earth and the universe. You have now become one. They both look upon you as their child, their newborn child. When you fasted, you were completely alone and lonely. This is how it has to be, to receive the life force.'

An offer was made to visit the Black Hills where, I was told, there is a mountain called Bear Mountain. I was invited to fast there again that night. It was a six-hour drive and I decided that getting there and back in time to catch the plane home would be risky, so I declined. They seemed disappointed because the link with Bear was obviously important to them, so I promised to organise a fast there on my next visit. Instead, we spent the day sightseeing and visiting sacred places in the Badlands. In one village they showed me a Catholic Church, a beautiful old building with well-kept grounds and a flowery cemetery. I asked if it would be OK for me to pray and they left me at the door to go in on my own. I always feel at peace in a church, regardless of denomination, and walked up the aisle to the front pew where I knelt and prayed. 'Dear God, show me I haven't failed you. Show me I have done your work.' I wasn't expecting an answer, not really. But I saw a large white horn with markings on the rim, and I heard White Arrow say, 'Ask Sacred Wind Woman's sister about the horn.' Later I told her what I had seen, and after considering the image she said, 'White Horn is my Grandmother's name. It is a simple answer to the question you asked. God heard your prayer and sent my grandmother to you. She was accepting you. She was welcoming you into our community, as one of our relatives, one of us, a Red Indian. It's a way of showing that you have not failed God. Only Spirit can really tell whether you are sincere or not. Her coming shows to us that you are.'

That evening White Arrow informed Sacred Wind Woman and the others that the Medicine Wheel where I had done my fast was now to be regarded as sacred ground. This pleased them. Sacred Wind Woman's mother said she wanted to adopt me and they announced that when I returned on my next visit, they would hold a special ritual in my honour, called a Giving Away Ceremony, a powwow where I would meet the 450 immediate members of my new family. I would have to give each of them a gift as part of the ancient ceremony to symbolise the closeness of family. The new family would all know me as Medicine Bear Woman. It meant I would then have two homes on earth for myself and my family. A great honour that I humbly accepted.

The following morning we prepared for the trip home. Most of the time was spent saying emotional farewells to everyone but eventually we managed to pack everything and loaded the car up.

As we were about to set off, Sacred Wind Woman said, 'Ann, will you ask White Arrow to show me where the water is?' She explained that when they claim land for their home in the reservation, the US Government will only pay for a single bore hole. If they don't find water on the first try, the Indians have to pay for each drilling until water is found, and they are, for the most part, poor people. To this day, the Native Americans are still treated shoddily. They are allocated one tin of milk and one tin of Spam each month, commodity food which is unhealthy because so many of these people are diabetics. When they are sick it's not an experienced doctor that is sent to diagnose their illness, but a nurse, if they are lucky, and then they are treated with the cheapest medicines available. Their small wages are severely taxed by the government and further reduced by money taken to support the reservation. They exist on very little. This is how the most 'civilised' nation in the world cares for those who hold the secrets to its spiritual well-being.

The government had failed to find water on the first drill and having no spare money, she was bringing water from her mother's house one mile outside the reservation. I looked around for White Arrow and saw him standing in the sunshine at the far end of the trailer. I walked towards him and without even having to ask him, he pointed to the ground by his feet and said, 'The water is here.'

Meetings (3)

THURSDAY, 10 SEPTEMBER 1992

So, I'm back in my garden in England. It's cold and the nights are drawing in – this should be dark enough for them! White Arrow is waiting with me for the others to arrive. It's good to be on my own with him again. Then Zipper comes and greets me warmly. He wants me to do more drawings. Michael, Alien Girl, Bear and Eagle come now. I'm so very pleased to see them – it feels like a long time since we were all together. I thank Bear for the messages he gave me during the fast. White Arrow tells me that Bear knows a great deal more about the tomb in Egypt, and I now understand why Bear said he would be with me in Egypt. Zipper puts something in my hand. It lights up. He points his finger at me and it turns red. 'Soon the visit,' he says. Bear stands and speaks. 'Next month, out here, I will return to you a power. Soon the medallion will play its part and you will understand the power it holds.' While he is speaking Zipper starts fiddling with the medallion.

Suddenly White Arrow seems unhappy about something. He's very guarded, watching them all as if one of them is about to say something out of place. Now he smiles, relaxes. I can see that Zipper is confused. He looks at White Arrow strangely and then starts to show me a picture. 'No. Not now,' White Arrow tells him. Zipper turns to his pad. I know he still has a lot of drawings for me to copy, and I feel he's disappointed that I can't keep up with him. I must catch up. I've promised him that his drawing will be next. The fifth picture. I'm being bombarded with so much information from them all that it's hard to keep up. Zipper's going to the tunnel. Bear is the clearest I've ever seen him tonight. He's quite beautiful. 'Trust him,' says White Arrow. I get a feeling that the ship is up there. I hope the meeting *is* soon.

Something is moving very close to me. At my feet. It's a hedgehog. The little thing is snuffling around my shoes. I didn't know they came that close. It's so sweet. Out of the corner of my eye I can see a light flicker. It's a craft I haven't seen before. It's silver, very small, long and oval. It goes. Tonight's session is over.

FRIDAY, 11 SEPTEMBER 1992

Today is my birthday and I have enjoyed every minute of it, although I experienced apprehension about the Visit for the first time in a while. All's quiet out here. Freezing, but quiet. I wonder how long before the spaceship will come? I think again that 'soon' means something else to them. A week, a year, or longer maybe? If you have been travelling for several thousand light years, I guess a year is soon. I've decided to start on Zipper's picture tomorrow, soon in my terms. The little hedgehog has appeared from behind a shrub and is trotting past me towards the rubbish. The tunnel opens up. Yellow. Zipper is followed by two others who are carrying a long box. They place it on the ground between us. Bear appears and rests his hand on my head. The box opens for Zipper and he looks inside, for what, I have no idea. The two who carried it in take it back to the tunnel. Zipper takes his pad from under his arm and starts working. White Arrow tells me to look at the stars. Zipper and Bear are communicating. Bear points towards me. I can't understand what they are saying.

About five minutes have passed. Nothing has been said. I've been looking up at the stars, thinking about all the strands I'm trying to hold together. I'm thinking about the Report that is now almost at a stage when it can be sent to the relevant authorities. I hope it will be read, understood and taken seriously, because the Report holds the first key to averting the disaster that lies ahead. What can I do to make people sit up and listen? Zipper stands and rests his hand on my shoulder. 'I will see you tomorrow and I will help you with the fifth drawing.' I thank him and watch as they leave.

I decide to stay out a little longer with White Arrow. Earlier today he said he would give me a birthday present. We're just sitting together, looking up at the night sky. It's very pleasant. He turns his head and grins. I haven't seen him grin like that for a year or more. I laugh out loud and turn back to the sky where the stars blink and flicker and before my very eyes, they start to move. I sit up, arching my head and breathing through my mouth. Several stars are re-arranging themselves, moving into some sort of shape as I watch. An arrow is forming in the sky – an arrow of glittering silver-white stars. A white arrow like the one they said they saw in America. I turn to him, to thank him but he's gone. I call Tony, he agrees it's an arrow. White Arrow had told me to watch the sky. This must be his birthday present, the best present he could have given me. How can he have the power to move stars?

Are they stars?

SATURDAY, 12 SEPTEMBER 1992

Bear and Zipper are sitting either side of me. White Arrow is standing behind me. I wish they would hurry up with the evidence so that I can prove they exist. Every day I work on the report I become more and more concerned about what lies ahead for this planet. The sooner they come the better for us all. I feel them up there watching. I tell White Arrow that I love him but that I think he should bring the evidence soon. He smiles and says, 'Soon, Little One, I promise your load will be lifted.' He tells me to watch the sky again. It's there. The pattern of stars in the shape of an arrow. One of the stars – lights – that form the arrow flickers and dies and it is no longer an arrow. Another three go out. One day I shall be standing close to one of the aliens. That thought awakens the fear that has slept since my fast and I can feel it shifting deep inside me. We must be programmed to fear them, or something, because it's a feeling that comes up despite the fact that I feel OK about White Arrow and Zipper and the others. 'Have no fear, Little One. I am with you and I am good.' I tell him I know that.

SUNDAY, 13 SEPTEMBER 1992

The arrow was already in place when I came out. They must be pre-paring something. I've learnt the futility of asking. I know I have to wait until they're ready to tell me or until they think I'm ready to hear. All day my mind has been holding the image of a spaceship landing at the meeting place. Zipper is here. And Bear.

Today they confirmed what I suspected would be my next task. I must travel to Egypt. As soon as I have finished the report I will begin to research the trip. I'm calling Tony out to see the arrow. He tells me he *can* see it. Zipper shows me the pile of drawings again and I feel I'm ready to do them but look to White Arrow who tells me that I am. I tell Zipper I will start them within the next few days. He nods happily and lays his hand on my head. In my mind, I ask myself whether the arrow is to show me that everything is in place. White Arrow nods. In that case, I have to get on. Suddenly White Arrow appears in the helmet. I know when he comes out of that ship he'll be wearing that helmet, and it holds no fear for me any more. I can see that these nightly meetings have helped to reduce the fear and have prepared me for the visit. 'Soon,' says Zipper. He spends so much of his time writing. I can feel Michael tonight but can't see him. Bear is so close to me now.

MONDAY, 14 SEPTEMBER 1992

I was in a way hoping the arrow wouldn't be there tonight, but it is. It unsettles me. The 17th is on Thursday and the arrow in the sky makes me think that something will happen this time. I feel that they are there, in position, waiting for something, watching me. Zipper says, 'It's OK,' and I tell him I know it is. White Arrow, sensing my anxiety, says, 'Little One, I am here. No harm will come to you. You are much needed on the earth if we are to fulfil our objective.' As I have already said, one of my fears is that they might want to take me away but if I'm needed on Earth then that's OK. I thank him for answering a question I didn't have to ask. Zipper is writing again and Bear is watching him. I'd love to know what he writes. Bear tells me that he needs me for Egypt. Mum is suddenly there, standing in front of me. She explains very lovingly that she will be with me on the night of the visit, and if I have her by my side, then I know I shall feel much better about the whole thing. I thank her and then thank White Arrow who seems to know that mum will always allay my greatest fears. I ask Zipper if the Report is all right. He responds with a nod of his head. 'Fine,' he says. I'm glad it's nearly finished and I pray that White Arrow can encourage the people to whom it will be sent to read it and believe in it. It is vital that they do. 'Soon the medallion will be of importance to you, Little One.' I'm a little startled and ask him if that means it's going to do something. 'You will understand at the right time.' He looks up at the sky and places his hand on the back of my head. I can feel Michael again. They leave and I stay out for a few moments longer, reminding myself that White Arrow has promised I will be safe.

I *will* be safe.

TUESDAY, 15 SEPTEMBER 1992

I'm out here early tonight and it's still a bit light, but I can see Zipper so I guess it must be OK. I hear a voice say, 'Soon news is coming that will help you on your journey,' but I don't know whose voice it is. I ask it if this will all be over soon, meaning the meeting, and the voice replies, 'Sooner than you think,' and then I know it's White Arrow. We talk for the full twenty-five minutes tonight. I have learnt that many more tests and trials will be placed in my way. Not by the Aliens, but by Man. I can now see why the journeys to America were so important: the sweating and fasting were to strengthen me and pre-pare me for the real tests. Mum is here and repeats the words, 'Soon now.' I am being shown another ship.

The underside of the spaceship that will come. It has suction pads underneath and does not need to touch the ground.

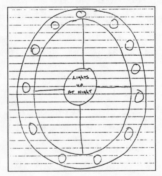

Suddenly Bear's hand is on me. 'Soon I will bring you the power. Look for 24 September. It doesn't matter if you don't call on me at night, I am with you all the time now.' Then White Arrow speaks and I can see him now. 'Soon we will show you how to use the medallion, it is an important part of your journey.' A crown appears above my head, but I can't see White Arrow's father. He continues, 'You will be surprised when you see me for I am not what you expect to see. You will like what you see.' By that I understand that when he shows himself to the world he will not look like Zipper and the others. I don't care what he looks like. 'So to Egypt, Little One. We have very little time. Whatever happens in the future, Egypt must come first.' I think that means that when they show themselves many people will want my time. I promise him that whatever happens, I will put Egypt first. 'You will go to the USA again. I will tell you more of that at a later time but you can take Tony if you want to. Help is on the way. If your life on Earth, or Tony's life, are ever in danger we will be there to protect you. You are monitored wherever you go. We will be there in our ships watching you. What you have and are about to have will be coveted by many. They will want to stop you. They will be unfortunate. Tell them I have spoken.' The tunnel lights up and they are gone.

What danger?

WEDNESDAY, 16 SEPTEMBER 1992

It's a cloudy night so I can't see if the arrow is there. Bear and Michael are coming up the garden, followed by Zipper, who is out of breath and seems hassled. Something made him late, I guess. White Arrow is with me. It's a quiet night. They sit but say nothing. Now Lion has arrived. I wonder if they will come although I'd rather not think about it. I get a sick feeling when I do. I know they won't tell me when they're coming, but one thing is for sure, it is soon. The red sphere appears in the midst of them. Zipper stretches his arm out towards me and takes hold of my hand. White Arrow says, 'Patience, Little One.' They are still deep in conversation. I don't know what's happening tonight. I don't seem to be a part of it. It's unusually quiet and still. I know I have to wait for them. Is this to do with tomorrow night? I'm already prepared for it. Everything is packed and ready. Alien Girl is here. Now, she's touching the medallion. She turns to Zipper, who nods and continues his conversation with the others. Bear stands. 'Soon, everything will come together,' he says. I really hope it's tomorrow. They rise and move towards the tunnel. Bear leads them rather than Zipper, who turns to me. 'See you tomorrow.' Does he mean literally see me tomorrow? No answer. I hear mum's voice telling me she loves me, then White Arrow is in front of me holding out his hand, 'Come on Little One.'

THURSDAY, 17 SEPTEMBER 1992

I have been with clients today until 9.30pm. Bill arrives at 10.20pm without Izzy, who is recovering from a minor operation. I ask him if he has everything and if his wife, my dearest friend, is alright. 'Yes to the first question, and thankfully, yes to the second,' he replies. We leave the house at 10.30pm. I like to be at the meeting place at least fifteen minutes before I'm due, to ensure that the recording equipment is ready in case anything happens. Although I'm nervous, a sort of routine has now been established which I find comforting. Where the others find their faith from, I don't know. Tony parks the car by the field and I walk to the fence. I always approach the same section of fencing. It's a cloudy, wet night with no stars or moon but a faint and distant yellow glow from London reflects on the low cloud cover. Occasionally a flurry of light rain sweeps across the field but on the whole this night is still. Five minutes pass and mum appears in front of me. Tony and Bill are in the car. I can hear them speaking softly. Mum and I chat about the family for five minutes or so and then, quite suddenly, she leaves.

I peer out into the darkness of the field, listening to my breath and some way off hear a dog bark. I reach for a cigarette and put it to my lips. I reach for the lighter but can't find it. I must have left it in the car. I start to turn and have hardly moved an inch before the air around me, my body, the world, all I know and understand about my physical being bursts into white, blinding, explosive light, brighter than the core of any sun. I light up like a beacon. I have no senses, no sight, no hearing. I cease to be in the conventional sense of 'being'. It lasts perhaps a second, maybe more, maybe less but no sooner am I lost to the light than I am blinking strangely at the darkness and small drops of rain are freckling my cheek. My first thought is that I have been struck by lightning, but were that the case I'd be smouldering, or lying dead on the wet grass. I turn towards the car. Perhaps a flash unit from one of the cameras went off? I can see the terror on their faces.

Tony's eyes are wide. I open the door and lean into the car. 'Did you see that?' I ask, aware of the steel in my voice. Bill says, 'My God!' I can see he's stunned. 'Tony!' I shout. 'What did you see?' He stutters. I take his hand, 'Tell me what you saw!' Calmer now, he removes his glasses and starts to wipe them, his eyebrows high on his forehead. 'It was like a big ball. A ball of very bright light and it came down and covered you and I couldn't see you any more and then it spread and came over the car a bit, sort of half way into the car, and I still couldn't see you and I couldn't see Bill any more and then it went and everything was black and dark again but because it sort of blinded me – I still couldn't see you.' His lip is trembling, 'Are you all right Annie?'

I reassure him and kiss his head, then turn to Bill. 'What about you, Bill?' He is still staring through the windscreen towards the field. 'The same, Ann. The same as Tony. A big ball of white light. I thought you'd gone, been taken, you know. It was this white light only I thought I saw a sort of blue rim around the outside of it, like on a gas flame, you know, and then it came into the car. Couldn't see anything then. I thought they'd come. Thought it was them landing.' Tony grabs my arm. I look round to see him pointing at the digital clock on the dashboard. It's flashing 11.21. We hear a loud noise above us, like thunder, or a plane, only it's too loud and too close to be either. I stand up, still holding onto the open car door. Nothing. I walk back to the fence and grip the damp post. Nothing. Not even mum.

Nothing happens for a long time, then White Arrow appears in front of me. He's hovering above the ground. I check my watch, it's 12.30am. 'The light, White Arrow. What was it?' I'm amazed by my composure. He lifts one arm into the air and says, 'It was us, Little One. There is a purpose to the light being placed around you. I cannot tell you what that purpose is, but its importance will be made clear to you.' He vanishes. I return to the car and relate what White Arrow has said. We drive home in silence. I'm exhilarated. Tonight, some form of physical contact took place for the first time and was witnessed. Now it begins.

PART THREE

'Something unknown to our understanding is visiting the Earth'

Dr Mitrovan Zverev, Soviet scientist

The Fifth Drawing

It is a few days after my experience with the Alien light. I find I am on board the ship. The room is the same but there is no one here. The big chair at the top of the table is full of light. I can't see anyone but the lights mean that someone is coming. I still get nervous here. Then the chair starts to turn and I can see the crown and robe. I didn't expect the Father, I thought it would be Zipper coming to show me the fifth drawing. He speaks. 'Ann Walker, you have shown great faith in me for which I will reward you in the coming months. Use your reward wisely. Our journey is only now beginning but you have proved already that you have courage to follow the path. You will receive the fifth drawing shortly. It is important that you finish this work. I ask you again, will you follow this path without question?'

'I will.'

'Without knowing what lies ahead of you?'

'Yes. Whatever you want me to do, I will do.'

'You have not hesitated. You have much faith in your God.'

'Yes.'

Now everything is quiet and the chair is turning away from me. As the lights in the chair die away, Zipper comes in with the drawing. White Arrow is suddenly also standing by the table. He takes the drawing from Zipper and places it on the table in front of me. This drawing, I see, takes the form of writing. I concentrate on it hard, allowing my mind to absorb the words. This last drawing is not like the others. It's taking longer to assimilate in my brain. It's more difficult.

This is the information from Zipper's drawing as it was translated in my brain:

> *Soon we will be entering your world. This will open up a whole new way of thinking for your people. You will have a new approach to the galaxies. We will show you the road to peace. Many on your Earth have prayed for this. Not only do we wish to save your Earth, we bring a new life.*
>
> *First we must explain the life before, then we can enter with the new life.*

This is important because without such understanding of the old life, you cannot control the new life. At some time in the near future we will reveal facts that were left here by us many years in the past. These facts will help you to understand what is written now.

When the planets and stars were first formed they were given life. Each is a living soul. These souls are the highest of all souls. Some have the capacity to sustain life. In fact, all planets and stars have 'life', but in your terms, not necessarily human life, for there are but seven living planets. One is Heaven, where all beings go when their physical carriage is exhausted. In Heaven another body awaits you. That body is there for you each time you return. It is kept and preserved for you. There is your planet, Earth, and our planet Zenus. Then there is Bear's, and Eagle's. The remaining two are far away and are unable to reach your planet, so it is not necessary to discuss these at this moment in time.

On our planet we live peacefully. In harmony. We are the next planet to Heaven. We are what you would call a policing planet. We work for God and for good and when any of the five planets are in trouble then we come to help. We are not permitted to interfere with you, your way of life or the natural laws that govern the planet until the planet itself calls for our help. Only the planet that you live on knows when you are in danger. As you now know there is a comet returning to your solar system. If Earth moves out of its orbital axis by a further three degrees then it is in trouble. The planet knows of the comet's approach. The planet fears that it will be five degrees out of orbit and consequently too close to the comet. We have heard the planet and that is also why we are here but we have known this for some time. It is for this reason that we have been seen by your people for we have tried to prevent the shift in other ways. We can do much for we have unusual powers unseen on Earth. But while we have tried to repair the Earth, Mankind has continued its destruction and now we must show you, and tell you of the disasters.

Each time we repair under the sea, you destroy the land above. We can now accomplish no more in that direction so by informing you we can, between us, accomplish the repairs. If we can tell the people what to do above the water, and if they listen, we can repair the ocean beds. There is much damage there. Already we feel the heat of the middle of the Earth and this is where the danger lies. But there is a further part to our mission and that is to stop the destruction in another way; your wars and your hate for one another.

I remember many years ago, your land was full of love and beings of one race. Now it is torn apart. We are in a race to save you from dual disasters, yourselves from yourselves, and yourselves from what you have done to the Earth. Without the Earth's salvation there is little point in saving Mankind so it is the Earth that we must concentrate on first. We, the Aliens, have been sent by God to accomplish this. White Arrow, his son, is to bring the Love that Earth lost so long ago. Man must come to terms with the fact that other life forms do exist and that if they are to join us they can only come in Love. No war, or anything to do with hate, will ever reach the places that we come from. That can never be so. If Mankind will learn from us and understand that only Love can exist wholly, then Mankind will be shown the Galaxies and learn much more. All of the five planets have gone through phases in their life. Only Earth clings on to the bad. We will not allow Earth to be destroyed and we pray that Mankind will not allow this either.

Once before, long ago, Mankind was destroyed and then a new life formed, but it took many years for Earth and God to bring about this new life. We above can see the danger of this destruction happening again. We do not wish it to happen. Before we were unable to help, because Mankind would not listen. They were a race of extreme intelligence, way beyond that which you have currently achieved. Hate above Love deafened them. Once again we return to help. As you do on Earth, so do we pray. We pray you will listen and take our words seriously. We have on each of our returns left messages telling of what happened then, and of that which lay in the future. We have left these messages in sacred places. The time to reveal these messages is soon, but we will only reveal them when the time is right.

Our journey here is simply to save the Earth. We will show ourselves through Ann Walker. Through her we will speak and while she is on Earth we will be her Guardians for she is with White Arrow. We will show some of our ways, but not all, for you are not yet ready. You are ready for White Arrow and White Arrow knows all for he is the Son of God. He is the son of our God too. God is One. My words come from God. I spoke earlier of another race of beings who inhabited Earth and who knew much more than Man now does. You are not the first to use aeroplanes and other such devices but there came a time when they thought only about these objects and forgot God. They listened only to them and not above them. They could have learnt much more and that would have held more meaning, but they destroyed themselves instead. For Mankind to go forward Mankind must look forward. You must accept that help from other forces is now a necessity. Had Mankind thought about its *actions in the first place then our help would not have been needed.*

We promise at no time to be a threat to you. Our visit is sourced out of peace. For the sake of your planet and for the sake of your own selves, allow us to help you by helping us. The pictures are together now. We have explained in great detail what is to happen. The next step is yours, the people's. Help White Arrow to return to you, for without him there will be no help. He has returned many times to help each of the planets, including our own, for we too had problems in our early days. When help is needed, God has always sent White Arrow. He is a King amongst the Galaxies. We honour and obey him for he is of all that is good. White Arrow to us is solid, so that makes him Alien, but a different Alien to my people. Soon your people will know that White Arrow is the one who commands us to help you. We willingly obey him. White Arrow comes from God. Where God is, no one will ever know while we live. We will call it God's planet. When White Arrow appears we know we have to help. It is White Arrow and the Father who know the Earth and hear it calling.

This was Zipper's drawing which translated into words in my head and became his message.

PART FOUR

THE REPORT

'Pure logical thinking cannot yield us any knowledge of the empirical world; all knowledge of reality starts from experience and ends in it. Propositions arrived at by purely logical means are completely empty of reality.'

Albert Einstein: *The World as I see it*

The Report

FOREWORD TO THE REPORT

This report is the full interpretation of the five drawings given to me on the ship by Michael, Zipper, Bear, Eagle and Alien Girl, together with the equations and information given by Einstein. Although I believe it is directed at the scientists of the world, I want the people to know what it contains.

It was compiled under White Arrow's guidance between February 1992 and February 1993. As I sit down with White Arrow to complete the final part of it, the Aliens come in one by one and gather around me. I do have the full interpretation of their five drawings now, but although all the information is together, I have to admit that some of it makes little sense to me. I shall need all the help they can give to take this report to the people. Suddenly I feel a shiver run down my back. I pull my cardigan close around me and cross my arms and White Arrow speaks. He has something more to add. I reach for my pad and pen.

'Grave problems face you all. First I will tell you, the people, in my own words, then we will give you a scientific report. This report, Little One, you will send to the governments of the world.'

I wonder how on earth any government will listen to me, and then I feel the fear again. The ink in my pen is running out and, frustrated, I drop it to the floor and reach for another one. I know already that there is a comet coming and I know that unless we listen to White Arrow and the Aliens, our world will come to an end. With their help we can be saved. If we ignore them, the consequences will be too horrendous to think about: and yet I know that I have to think about them. I have to think about my granddaughter and all our future generations. I cannot let my fear defeat me. Ink finally appears from the new pen to give life to the blind indents and scribbles on my pad.

'It is not easy for me to tell you of bad that will happen. These things I do not wish to bring you. I would have wished to bring you happy news on my return

but instead I have to tell you of the troubles that lie ahead. With your help I can save you. Then I can bring the good. Help my father to help you.

'I have already told you that your Earth has moved two degrees out of its orbit. In twenty years time it will move another three degrees because of the rainforest destruction. This will make a five degree change. Already the two degree move has altered the molten fluids beneath the earth's surface. This in turn is causing the fault lines to shift, which is why you experience more earthquakes around the world. As the next twenty years come so will you see new fault lines appearing and yet more earthquakes will shake the land. Large areas of the planet will be totally destroyed. Land will submerge. Japan and small islands will disappear. Parts of Russia will disappear. The southern tip of South America will disappear. Many miles of coastline will be submerged into the seas and parts of land will be lost over all the world.

'The Earth is becoming warmer because the damaged ozone layer now allows the sun's rays to heat the planet with greater intensity. The core of the earth is overheating. In thirty years time many species of animal will be lost. Man will find parts of his world changed. Your moon which already affects the tides of the ocean will have an effect twenty times greater by then. Tidal waves that have never been seen by man before will cover the land. The fish that you catch will move to different parts of the ocean and be no longer there to feed you. Your crops will not grow because the weather will change. There will be storms, cyclones and tornadoes in parts of the world where they have never been known. Great rainstorms will flood the land and destroy not only crops but grazing land as well and the moon, being too close, will have an effect here too. All land will be affected because the earth's atmosphere will be too close to the atmosphere of the moon. They will be too close because of the five degree change.

'The ice caps will melt and the seas will claim the shorelines of many countries. Between thirty and fifty years from now an ice age will appear over many parts of the world while in other parts temperatures will rise to over two hundred degrees. Great fires will destroy more forests and grazing land will be burned. In thirty years there will be few safe areas in the world, yet even these will be of little use to man, for in fifty years no safe place will be left.

'As the trees are being destroyed, so are the grasslands being taken away for roads and buildings. Petrol fumes, among other things, are destroying the ozone layer in your atmosphere and affecting the health of man. In twenty years time, twice as many cars and factories will produce ten times as much pollution, and destruction to the ozone layer will continue causing further heating of the* *earth's core. We have a formula to help with this problem. We have given all the facts and figures in The Report, but the cause of all this happening lies with your continued destruction of the trees that give you life. As each tree falls so your destruction comes closer. The trees keep you alive. They play an important role in the balance of life. Trees take in carbon dioxide and give out oxygen. Without oxygen you and other breathing life forms cannot survive. Humans take in oxygen and give out carbon dioxide. Without trees you can not exist. Even the grass you walk on and the flowers you admire give you breath. The rainforests are like a belt around the earth. Even their weight plays an important part in how the earth spins in balance. Removing the trees will cause a five degree change in the planet's orbit around the sun. The trees are also a force field. Winds from one part of the planet are kept away from another part by the trees. They cause a direction that makes it safe. Without the trees the winds are left to follow their own direction causing them to grow stronger and further damage the earth without the force to hold them back. Diseases will be carried from different countries. They will not be contained because the winds and weather will be out of control and the ozone layer will again play a big part in your destruction.*

'It is the felling of the rainforests and other things that have mainly caused the problem we see. Man must take responsibility for his actions. His actions are adding to his own destruction in fifty years' time.

'I will now talk about the object that is coming. The comet will not hit your earth. Its pathway has already been mapped out to pass your earth. I know for I have seen this but you must hear: the atmosphere of your earth and your moon will be too close together and so will be in the comet's path. As the comet passes its speed and weight will pull the middle of the earth outwards causing it to erupt. Lands will sink and mountains will come down. Land man has never seen will appear in the place of lands that have gone. No man will walk the earth again for millions of years to come. This is why I have returned to you, to turn back to God and help him to repair the damage before it is too late.

'We have eighteen years only to do this in: ten years to stop the felling of trees and eighteen years now to start replanting the forests. This will bring the earth back from the five degree danger.'

I stop staring at the pad and lift my eyes to where White Arrow's own blue eyes are sparkling. Somewhere in the distance I am aware of feelings of fear and disbelief that this is all being placed on my shoulders.

I am selfish enough to want White Arrow with me, but not to want his work. Who will listen to Ann Walker? I dismiss the feelings – just brush them away and call them human.

White Arrow and the other Aliens stand in front of me. Their hearts are for the living. There is White Arrow who has given me life and around him those who work with him to help us for no reward other than to see us avert our own destruction. What can I do but take these words of theirs and pass them on to the world, so that many minds can join together and work towards a hope for our survival? Someone greater than ourselves is behind these words, and if through them we can save our beautiful world, then perhaps we can learn to live in peace for all time, remembering always that God does exist and that he has sent his son once again to save our world.

White Arrow shows me the symbols of the world, and, just as I thought we had finished, he speaks again.

'I want my people to know the truth. You shall show them The Report and they shall know that it was to be for everyone so that everyone will know. With this knowledge that I give, the people can be informed and, once informed, can cause change.'

The Report:
Global Heat increase and 'irreversibility of Two State Climate Disintegration'

Foreword

As one looks at the weather it is clear that extremes of weather are becoming more prevalent. The weather is nature's delicately evolved system of balancing and moving heat. It does this through the atmosphere, the seas (and sea floors) and heat is inter-acted and balanced with the mantle. This system, the weather, is concerned with deli-cate balances that nature has evolved over 386 million years.

The surface of the earth, the earth's crust, rests on molten fluid of the earth's mantle. The temperature and heat energy stability of the fluid beneath the surface provides stability for the surface itself. Yet as the atmosphere, oceans and the whole surface get hotter, this will change.

As the escalating rate of destruction of features of the environment gets ever faster we see government proclamations of key environmental changes that have very re-assuring preciseness. For instance only a 2.5 degree temperature increase in global temperature is predicted, and only a 0.5% reduction in atmospheric free oxygen is predicted at worst case. Whilst these predictions involve scientific readings and data they also involve assumptions.

And, despite comforting predictions, something seems to be going wrong at a fundamental 'interactive' level of the earth's climate. As we ourselves wait for more data, for statistical studies for instance, or more deeply technical data, we seem to be overlooking some remarkably fundamental changes we are causing in the atmosphere and environment.

We know the rainforests will be almost completely destroyed in the earlier portion of the next century if current trends continue. At a similar time, the growth of motor vehicles is 'projected' to match human population. It has been known, for many decades, that there must be a balance between carbon dioxide and oxygen producers. Humans and 'breathing' life consume oxygen and produce carbon dioxide – trees and vegetation consume carbon dioxide and give us oxygen. Cars consume our oxygen and give us carbon dioxide as well as atmospheric pollutants.

As the increasingly unpredictable weather affects the global weather system, we in-creasingly see hotter summers. As the climate becomes progressively more and more unstable we should realise that the consequences of this disintegration extend far far beyond 'a warmer atmosphere' and increased skin cancers from 'ozone depletion'. The fundamental mechanisms that support oxygen breathing life are being destroyed.

Sequence of diagrams and figures
General Overview

(1) Earth's heat energy accumulates – and the planet cannot lose it!
* The Greenhouse Effect.
* The Earth's energy balance.

THE EFFECT of ATMOSPHERIC CHANGES on HEAT TRANSFER

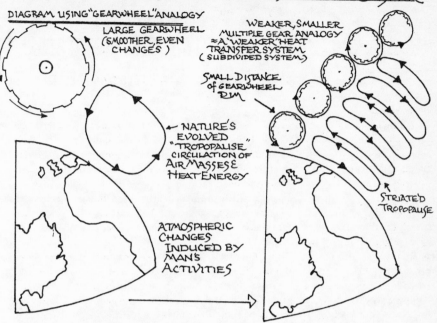

DIAGRAM USING "GEARWHEEL" ANALOGY

LARGE GEARWHEEL (SMOOTHER, EVEN CHANGES)

WEAKER, SMALLER MULTIPLE GEAR ANALOGY = A "WEAKER" HEAT TRANSFER SYSTEM (SUBDIVIDED SYSTEM)

SMALL DISTANCE OF GEARWHEEL RIM

← NATURE'S EVOLVED "TROPOPAUSE" CIRCULATION OF AIR MASSES & HEAT ENERGY

STRIATED TROPOPAUSE

ATMOSPHERIC CHANGES INDUCED BY MAN'S ACTIVITIES

THE SHEAR HEAT TRANSFER "LOAD" OF A STRIATED TROPOPAUSE (INTO SUBDIVIDED SYSTEMS) WILL RESULT IN GREATLY REDUCED HEAT TRANSFER EFFICIENCY AS THE EFFICIENCY OF THE ATMOS-PHERE, TO MOVE HEAT, DIMINISHES THERE WILL BE INCREASINGLY FREQUENT EXTREMES OF WEATHER.
INSTEAD OF THE CONSTANT, PREVIOUSLY EFFICIENT, ATMOSPHEREIC HEAT TRANSFER THE DIMINISHED EFFICIENCY WILL CAUSE TUMULTOUS VARIATIONS IN ATMOSPHEREIC HEAT TRANSFER. THIS MAY BE THOUGHT OF NOT AS THE GRADUAL & CONTINUOUS MOVEMENT OF HEAT BETWEEN ZONES OF THE ATMOSPHERE, BUT AS THE "BUILDING-UP" AND "BURSTING-THROUGH" TO THESE ZONES SPORADICALLY.

* The carbon cycle.
* Deterioration of the carbon cycle.

(2) The main heat and oxygen regulators.
* The High Atmosphere.
* The Air Sea interface.
* Tropical vegetation.
* Continental shelves.
* Seasonal Photosynthesis and oxygen production in Northern and Southern hemi-spheres.

(3) Increased planetary heat energy and convection current shifts beneath the Earth's crust.
* Heat energy propagation of fault lines.
* Computer modelling of system inertia (and parameters).

* Interaction of global warming, density changes, tilt and geothermal activity.
* Effect of a planetary body.

(4) TREES, heat transfer, changing wind patterns, increasing tropospheric distribution of ozone destroyers.

(5) Typical changes projected at end of first process stage (20 years).
* The USA.
* Australia.
* Ice Caps.
* Russia.
* Central Africa.
* Europe and England.

(6) Heat energy of the planet grows and evolution's delicate heat transfer mechanisms disintegrate!

(7) Concluding remarks.

References.

APPENDIX 1.
Maps related to Section 5.

APPENDIX 2.
Notes on planetary phenomena and orbital mechanics interaction toward second stage of process.

APPENDIX 3.
Present day planetary climate and dependent phenomena.

APPENDIX 4.
Representative fauna depletion at end of first process stage.

Sequence of diagrams and figures *
Rise in carbon dioxide and 'one' projected temperature increase.
Overall oxygenation capacity – table.
Table of Radiation – the spectrum of light.
Table of worldwide Deforestation and carbon dioxide rates of increase.
Structure of Earth's atmosphere.
Earth's core and plate tectonics.
Earth's core and convection currents.
Density, temperature and Pressure variance beneath the Earth's crust.
Earth data and the sun's path.
Moon data and the moon's effect on Earth's surface.
Figure 11 – Effect of a planetary body.
Seismic waves (and secondary seismic waves).

Appendix 1
Map 1 – process phenomena at 20 years.
Map 2 – safety zones at 20 years of process.
Map 3 – new land mass emergence.
Present land use and economy.
Land use by Continent, presently and 20 years into process.
Figure 6 – loss of nutrient production at 20 years.
Figure 7 – loss of nutrient production at 20 years.

Appendix 2
Orbital mechanics notation and diagrams.

Appendix 3
Various charts and illustrations of *present* climate and geological activity – full listing in appendix.

Charts for fauna depletion and extinction.

* Please note that, given the draft stage of this outline report, for purposes of scrutiny only, the illustrations to be generated for my final work (to be published) are not ready yet. Therefore similar illustrations may aid one's considerations.

General Overview
Two concepts within this chapter are key and should be considered interactive. One of these processes, related to the gathering pace of 'inertia', is of catastrophic immediacy. The gathering inertia *affects* individual elements of the Global Climate process, as well as the escalating instability of the Global Climate process.

Throughout the various concerns regarding global warming (and ozone layer depletion), the analyses seem to fall short of equating the effects of the planetary system's *overall* level of heat energy. The 'inertial' rate of this increase and the geothermal consequences of this are of prime importance. Moreover, the global warming effects of 'matter' beneath the earth's crust are not considered. This seems to be the case throughout the weather- and climate-based computer models of the effects of global warming.

It also seems to be clear that the ozone layer depletion is openly recognised as being of significance, but primarily because of its link with 'hotter' weather and skin cancers etc. In fact, ozone layer depletion and the consequent admittance of shorter wavelengths of light also has significance in higher magnitudes of heat energy imparted to the earth's surface. Global warming and ozone layer depletion are *not* seen as critical *interactive* parameters in the 'thermal equilibrium' of the earth. It should be considered that there are critical changes taking place that are part of a fundamental geothermal process, which will yield catastrophic weather and climate consequences.

The effects on the Global Climate process will be irreversible in some twenty years' time. It is considered that although there is one immediate measure that can alleviate certain areas of the crisis, this measure would require a ten-year rapid implementation. Although the measure concerned is very simple to implement, only its immediate, rapid and expansive deployment will avoid the termination of all cycles in the process.

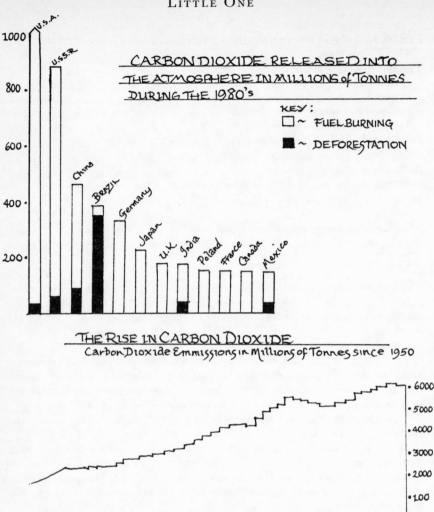

CARBON DIOXIDE RELEASED INTO THE ATMOSPHERE IN MILLIONS of TONNES DURING THE 1980's

KEY:
☐ ~ FUEL BURNING
■ ~ DEFORESTATION

THE RISE IN CARBON DIOXIDE
Carbon Dioxide Emmissions in Millions of Tonnes since 1950

Analysis of data shows the existence of a Stochastic Probability Density Function, which underlays the integrated elements of the Global Climate Process. It has been 'identified' that there will be a process juncture, in some twenty years. The probability density function mitigates toward minimal variance in the duration of the second process stage. The second (and final) stage of this process will be final in approximately fifty years. Also, as indicated earlier, the 'inertial' characteristics of increases in the process parameters will render matters irreversible in twenty years' time.

It is considered that, in some twenty years' time, the exact nature of these parameter changes will be amply apparent. By this time certain phenomena, geothermal in origin, will clearly have evidenced themselves. Although the statistical inertia of the parameters (that govern the process) may *then* indicate some chance of recuperation – there is an as yet unseen event that will overwhelm 'eleventh hour' activity.

Earth's heat energy accumulates – and the planet cannot lose it.

The Greenhouse Effect.

Carbon dioxide (presently 0.05% of the atmosphere), like the glass of a greenhouse, is transparent to most incoming shortwave radiation, which passes through it and heats the Earth. However, when the Earth re-transmits that energy in the form of longer wave infra-red radiation, the carbon dioxide behaves as an opaque shield, so that the earth's surface remains hot, and is subjected to growing levels of heat.

The earth's surface, which is continually being subjected to ever increasing levels of Heat energy, must obey the basic laws of physics. As the atmosphere and surface gain Heat, this is geothermally *conducted* into the molten fluid *beneath* the continental plates, the molten fluid of the earth's upper mantle.

The Earth's energy balance

It has been considered for some time that the greatest quantities of heat energy have and will always remain at the Earth's very core, without these large magnitudes of geothermal (heat) energies being carried upward (toward the crust) into the mantle's convection currents. It has been accepted for some time, as a basic precept, in the Earth's *energy balance*, that the crust is *only* subject to a modest quantity of heat energy from the molten core. However, this is changing. The heat energy is growing – as the mantle acts as a heat sink.

It is accepted that Earth's crust (and therefore the planet as a whole) receives all of its energy from the sun. If the planet is to remain at constant temperature it must re-radiate EXACTLY as much heat as it receives.

The temperature at which equilibrium is reached depends on a multitude of inter-connected factors. The TWO main factors are the Earth's index of reflectivity (ie relative brightness – ALBEDO) AND the heat-trapping capacity of the atmosphere – the Greenhouse Effect.

The Carbon Cycle

The Earth has a huge supply of carbon, only a small quantity of which is carbon dioxide gas, in the atmosphere. Some 98% of all Earth's carbon is thought to be dissolved in the sea.

The carbon circulating in the air is now some 355 Parts Per Million. Its capacity as a greenhouse gas is the key regulator of the Earth's temperature. In turn the ecological balance, based on trees, regulates the regulator – keeping carbon dioxide concentrations below danger levels – until now.

Most of the constituents of the atmosphere *were* kept in constant balance by complex cycles in which the life forms on the Earth play a dominant part.

All the elements of the carbon cycle must interlock and *balance*. However there is a drastically *escalating* trend away from this balance in key elements of the carbon process. For instance we humans breathe in oxygen from the air and 'replace' it with carbon dioxide, at the turn of the century there were 2 billion human beings, and at century's end there will be 7 billion. Trees (and vegetation) consume carbon dioxide and replace it with oxygen. At the turn of the century all the world's major forest was virtually intact. The deterioration of the carbon cycle is not a 'gradual' process, it is an *accelerating* process.

RADIATION

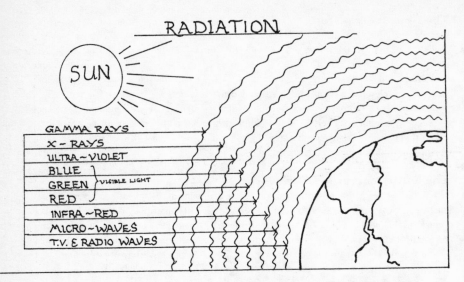

SUN

GAMMA RAYS
X - RAYS
ULTRA~VIOLET
BLUE
GREEN } VISIBLE LIGHT
RED
INFRA~RED
MICRO~WAVES
T.V. & RADIO WAVES

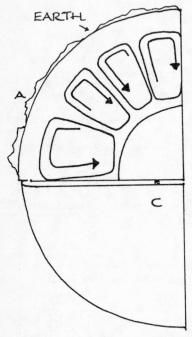

EARTH

A

C

CONVECTION THEORY

THIS IS A HYPOTHETICAL THEORY WHICH PRESUMES THAT THERE ARE CONVECTION CURRENTS IN THE EARTH'S MANTLE (B), WHICH COULD PLAY A PART IN DRIVING THE MOVEMENT OF MAJOR CONTINENTS OVER A LONG PERIOD OF TIME THEORY GEOLOGISTS ARE ALSO IN DEBATE AS TO WETHER CONVECTION IS CONFINED TO THE UPPER MANTLE OF THE EARTH, OR IS CONTINOUS THROUGHOUT THE WHOLE. THIS THEORY COULD ALSO EXPLAIN THE FORMATION OF MAJOR GEOSYNCLINAL FOLD MOUNTAINS IN THE EARTH'S CRUST OVER THE PAST THOUSAND MILLION YEARS,-THIS WOULD ALSO EXPLAIN THE SPREAD OF THE SEA FLOOR & THE CONSEQUENT CONTINENTAL DRIFT.

PATTERNS OF MOVEMENT WOULD BE MODIFIED BY.
1) THE ROTATION OF THE EARTH
2) FRICTION BETWEEN THE MAIN CELLS
   (AS SHOWN IN PICTURE ←)

The control of carbon dioxide is the most important of all the Earth's biological and geophysical cycles and it must interact in a stable manner.

The so-called carbon cycle has remained stable for millions of years. However,

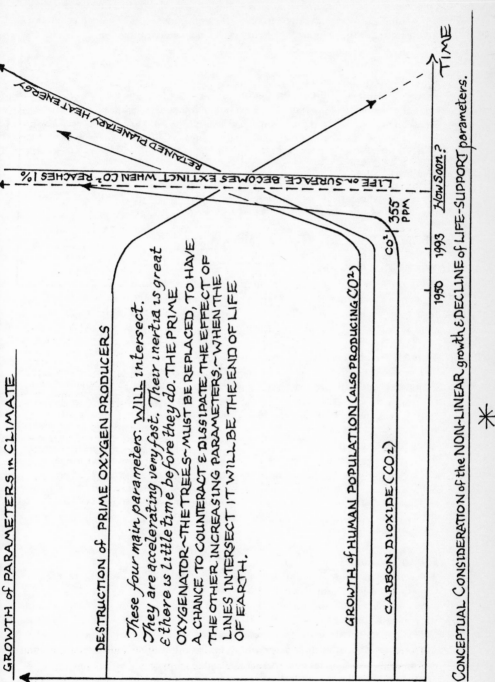

GROWTH of PARAMETERS in CLIMATE

DESTRUCTION of PRIME OXYGEN PRODUCERS

These four main parameters WILL intersect. They are accelerating very fast. Their inertia is great & there is little time before they do. THE PRIME OXYGENATOR~THE TREES~MUST BE REPLACED, TO HAVE A CHANCE TO COUNTERACT & DISSIPATE THE EFFECT OF THE OTHER INCREASING PARAMETERS.~WHEN THE LINES INTERSECT IT WILL BE THE END OF LIFE OF EARTH.

GROWTH of HUMAN POPULATION (ALSO PRODUCING CO_2)

CARBON DIOXIDE (CO_2)

LIFE on SURFACE BECOMES EXTINCT WHEN CO_2 REACHES 1%

RETAINED PLANETARY HEAT ENERGY

CO_2 355 PPM

1950   1993   How Soon?

TIME

CONCEPTUAL CONSIDERATION of the NON-LINEAR growth & DECLINE of LIFE-SUPPORT parameters.

✳

· 197 ·

human beings have found various ways to release fixed carbon at a rate far faster than the existing global system can recirculate. It has taken only a few human generations to disrupt the entire complex regulatory cycle, in a deteriorating trend.

Deterioration of the carbon cycle.

Since the beginning of the Industrial Revolution, human activity has pumped steadily increasing amounts of carbon dioxide into the atmosphere. Most was absorbed by the Earth's oceans, whose immense 'sink' capacity meant that 170 years were needed for levels to increase from the 'pre-industrial' 280 Parts Per Million to 355 PPM today, which has overwhelmed even the oceanic sink.

Atmospheric concentrations are now rising almost as steeply as carbon dioxide emissions themselves. Today, carbon dioxide emissions are at 355 PPM, yet this is in the context of a drastically increasing trend.

The main heat and oxygen regulators.

The High Atmosphere

On the edge of space, the ionized outer atmosphere shields the Earth's surface from high energy radiation, solar particles and meteors. Below this the ozone layer traps high energy ultra-violet radiation. As the ozone layer diminishes, higher energy radiant heat waves will escalate their impact on global warming.

The Air Sea interface

The ocean surface is the location for most of the great systems of heat exchange that keep the earth functioning properly. In addition, this absorbs and circulates the critical atmospheric gases. However, its effectiveness at 'sinking' carbon dioxide has diminished, as is noted in the 'deterioration of the carbon cycle'.

Tropical Vegetation

The previously extensive and lush growth of rainforest and other vegetation in the Earth's tropical zones is one of the most important oxygen generators on the planet. Such large scale transpiration influences rainfall and climate patterns both locally and far afield. The destruction of this oxygen production capacity is a key parameter. (The deforestation figure will give an indication of the escalation in the rate of destruction of this regulator).

Continental shelves

The warm, shallow fringes amount to some 21% of the Earth's total ocean area but contain a far higher proportion of its plant and animal life.

Vulnerable to coastal and marine pollution, plankton and other plants in these waters are KEY ELEMENTS IN THE CARBON AND OXYGEN LIFE CYCLE.

This one topic will be used as a brief example to indicate part of the process that will become irreversible in 20 years' time. It is considered that the oxygenation capacity of the shoreline plankton compares with that of trees and vegetation, in overall production, as follows – and will be reduced as indicated below:

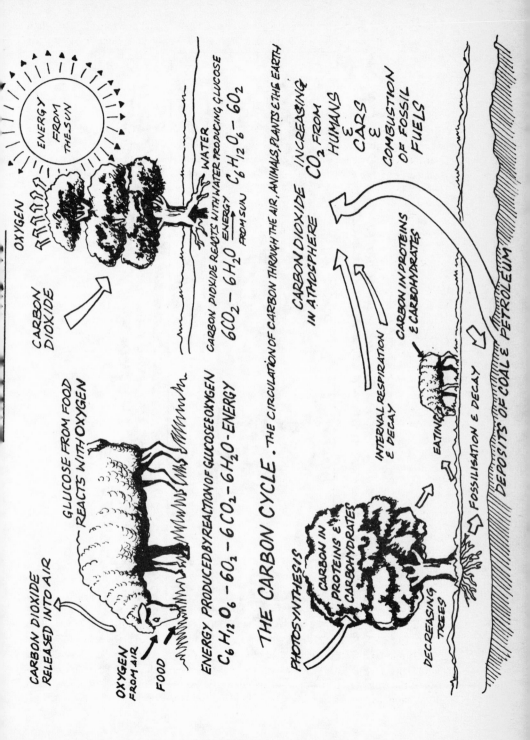

THE CARBON CYCLE. THE CIRCULATION OF CARBON THROUGH THE AIR, ANIMALS, PLANTS & THE EARTH

ENERGY FROM THE SUN

OXYGEN

CARBON DIOXIDE

WATER

CARBON DIOXIDE REACTS WITH WATER PRODUCING GLUCOSE

$6CO_2 - 6H_2O \xrightarrow[\text{FROM SUN}]{\text{ENERGY}} C_6H_{12}O_6 - 6O_2$

CARBON DIOXIDE RELEASED INTO AIR

GLUCOSE FROM FOOD REACTS WITH OXYGEN

OXYGEN FROM AIR

FOOD

ENERGY PRODUCED BY REACTION OF GLUCOSE & OXYGEN

$C_6H_{12}O_6 - 6O_2 - 6CO_2 - 6H_2O - ENERGY$

CARBON DIOXIDE INCREASING IN ATMOSPHERE

CO_2 FROM HUMANS & CARS & COMBUSTION OF FOSSIL FUELS

PHOTOSYNTHESIS

CARBON IN PROTEINS & CARBOHYDRATES

INTERNAL RESPIRATION & DECAY

CARBON IN PROTEINS & CARBOHYDRATES

EATING

DECREASING TREES

FOSSILISATION & DECAY

DEPOSITS OF COAL & PETROLEUM

· 199 ·

COMPENSATION POINTS

THESE ARE TWO POINTS IN A 24 HOUR PERIOD (NORMALLY DAWN & DUSK) WHEN THE TWO PROCESSES OF PHOTOSYNTHESIS & INTERNAL RESPIRATION ARE PERFECTLY BALANCED.

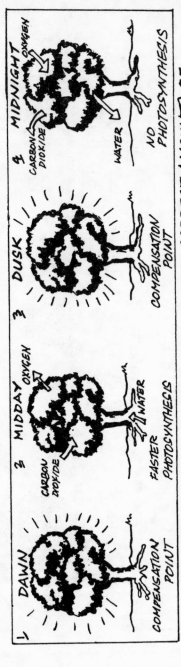

1. DAWN
COMPENSATION POINT

2. MIDDAY
OXYGEN
CARBON DIOXIDE
WATER
FASTER PHOTOSYNTHESIS

3. DUSK
COMPENSATION POINT

4. MIDNIGHT
OXYGEN
CARBON DIOXIDE
WATER
NO PHOTOSYNTHESIS

PHOTOSYNTHESIS : IS THE PRODUCTION OF THE CORRECT AMOUNTS OF CARBOHYDRATES & OXYGEN FOR INTERNAL RESPIRATION WHICH RESULTS IN THE CORRECT AMOUNTS OF CARBON DIOXIDE & WATER TO COMPLETE THE PHOTOSYNTHESIS IS CYCLE.

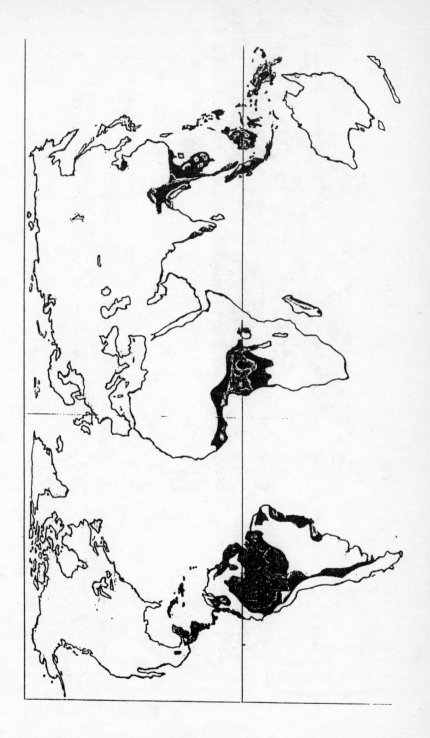

RAINFOREST 🔲 Existing rainforest ■ previous rainforest - destroyed

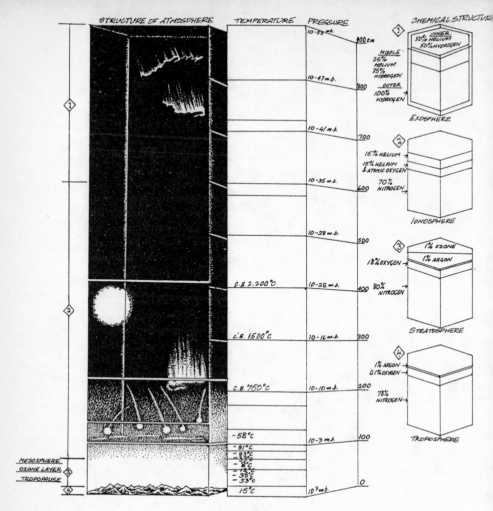

Overall Oxygenation Capacity*

	Trees and vegetation	Shoreline plankton etc	Proportion of present capacity
Present	70%	30%	= 100%
Capacity reduced @ 20 yrs	59¼%	19¼%	= 78%
Capacity reduced @ 50 yrs	53½%	13½%	= 67%

* Note that these figures are derived using the most favourable data and probability density functions.

When carbon dioxide reaches 1%

The oxygen content of the atmosphere will begin to fall away, toward the very end of the process, due to diminishment and increase of various parameters. The oxygen will

PLATE TECTONICS

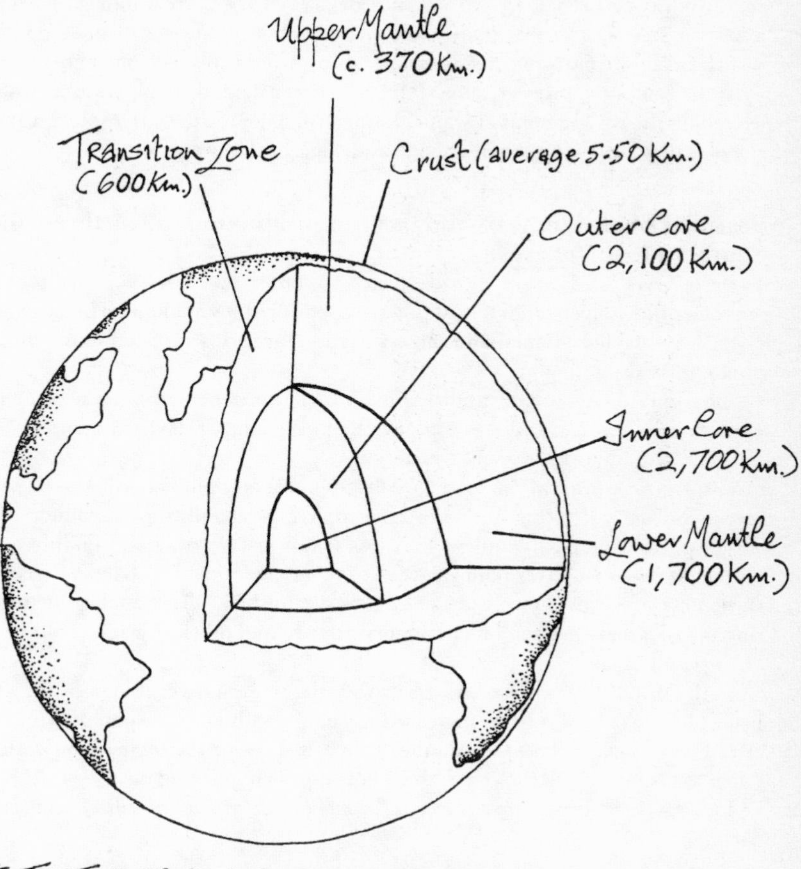

Upper Mantle
(c. 370 Km.)

Transition Zone
(600 Km.)

Crust (average 5·50 Km.)

Outer Core
(2,100 Km.)

Inner Core
(2,700 Km.)

Lower Mantle
(1,700 Km.)

PLATE TECTONICS AS A THEORY CAME ABOUT AS THE
RESULT OF OTHER FORMULATIVE THEORIES.
THE PLATE TECTONICS THEORY IS THAT THE CONTINENTS ARE
CARRIED ALONG ON THE TOP OF SLOWLY MOVING CRUSTAL
PLATES (WHICH FLOAT ON THE LOWER MANTLE - HEAVIER LIQUID
MATERIAL — IN A SIMILAR FASHION TO ICEBERGS ON WATER.
THE PLATES CONVERGE & DIVERGE ALONG MARGINS MARKED
BY VOLCANIC & SEISMIC ACTIVITY. PLATES USUALLY DIVERGE
FROM MID-OCEAN RIDGES WHERE MOLTEN LAVA PUSHES UP &
FORCES THEM APART AT A RATE OF 40 M.M. A YEAR. CONVERGING
PLATES CAN FORM EITHER MOUNTAIN RANGES - WHERE THE
TWO CONTINENTS COLLIDE, OR A TRENCH - WHERE THE OCEANIC
PLATES SINK BELOW THE LIGHTER CONTINENTAL ROCK.
THE CURRENT THEORY SUGGESTS THAT MASSIVE CONVECTION
CURRENTS IN THE EARTHS INTERIOR ARE RESPONSIBLE
FOR THE PLATE MOVEMENT.

steadily combine with atmospheric nitrogen and the volcanic outgassing that will be mentioned later.

In doing so, it would react with the sea (and also carbonaceous rocks, such as limestone) releasing even more carbon dioxide. When the carbon dioxide level reaches approximately 1% of the atmosphere, its greenhouse power will undergo a drastic disproportionate increase. Rising temperatures would speed chemical reactions.

At the end of the process, once all life is extinguished, the temperatures would rise, exceeding the boiling point of water – and in time the Earth's atmosphere would consist of little more than carbon dioxide and superheated water vapour.

Seasonal photosynthesis and oxygen production in Northern and Southern hemispheres.

In the conversion of carbon dioxide to oxygen, photosynthesis is a global process that embodies this conversion. Photosynthesis is 'powered' by sunlight. There are seasonal changes in 'daylight hours' and these variations are *directly* related to the duration of photosynthesis.

For a long time a great stabilising feature of atmospheric oxygen was the tropical rainforests. Their tropical location gave them the longest daylight hours throughout the year, with minimal seasonal variation.

Vast tracts of tropical rainforest are destroyed at an ever increasing pace. One conservatively derived estimate shows the complete loss of all tropical rainforests in the earlier part of the next century. This loss is not just destruction of nature's oxygen producing capacity. The photosynthesis process is integral to balances such as the carbon cycle. As an element in the cycle is diminished, this is analogous to the 'furring-up' of a main artery of a circulatory system, and other arteries would need to *be able* to compensate.

As the tropical rainforests are destroyed, the trees and vegetation of the northern hemisphere would *need* to be increased to compensate for 'lost' photosynthesis capacity. There would need to be another increase *again* for the increase in world population. This artery needs to get *larger* – not what is happening now.

A massive forestation program is required even to balance the lost capacity of the tropical rainforests.

Increased planetary heat energy and convection current shifts beneath the Earth's crust.

It is generally considered that depletion of the ozone layer and the general global warming are significant concerns. But there seems to be very little consideration of the effect of global warming in the context of correspondent changes that will take place in the convection currents of the molten material in the mantle, below the Earth's crust.

Today, the volcanic activity that takes place in line with known and studied faults in the surface of the Earth that are related to the current geometry of plate tectonics. However, there are changing environmental parameters that will change the nature of faults in the Earth's crust.

Broadly speaking, there is a causal link between the global warming and the new fault lines that will cause phenomenal changes in the behaviour of the Earth's crust.

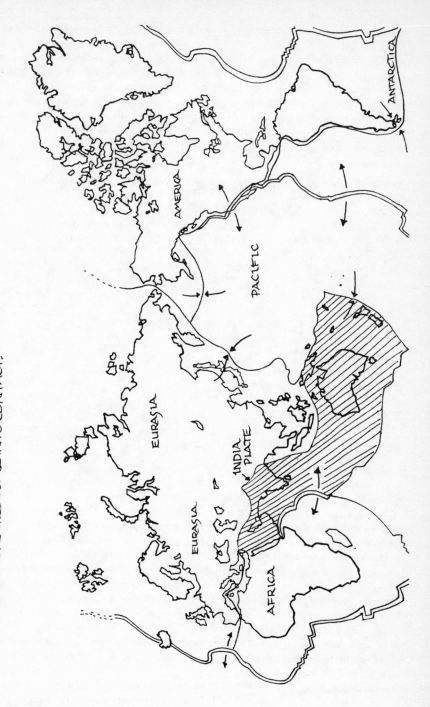

THIS MAP SHOWS THE SIX MAJOR SHIFTING PLATES OF THE EARTH'S CRUST OBSERVED IN 1972. 1) SINGLE LINES DENOTE WHERE THE PLATES ARE CONVERGING & COMPRESSING. 2) DOUBLE LINES DENOTE WHERE SEA-SPREADING IS OCCURING. EARTHQUAKES & VOLCANIC ACTIVITY OCCOUR WHEN THE PLATES COME INTO CONTACT.

Oxygen depletion, in the atmosphere, is clearly associated with the global warming but will have a subtle effect in the density and striation of the formerly estimated 17,000 million tons of the Earth's atmosphere. Setting aside reassuring government figures the present level of atmospheric oxygen will have diminished by some 20% in twenty years' time.

It should be considered that the disposition of the faults in the geometry of plates is based on a careful balance of forces from above (which will also comprise gravitational attraction from passing bodies) and below the Earth's crust. These forces, that give stability to the Earth's crust, are affected by the parameters of the Earth's heat energy balance – evolved through geological time.

Heat energy propagation of fault lines

Present day fault lines are heavily dependent on the nature and stability of 'the upper mantle', beneath the Earth's crust.

The effects of global warming (and the gradual absence of the Earth's heat dissipating capacity) together with the elementary laws of heat transfer mitigate towards the gradual increase of heat energy held in the fluid of the mantle. This will, in turn, increasingly perturbate and stress the Earth's crust in *different* patterns. It is generally considered that fault lines and plate movement/activity will correspond to the lines shown in Map 1.

However this is NOT the only parameter feature that relates to heat transfer. The increase in the overall heat energy, and change in the heat transfer characteristics of the upper mantle's convection currents, will clearly cause temperature increases in the lower mantle and outer core. This is beginning to cause the changes that will be fully realised in the some twenty years from now.

There will be a transition period in which the effect of the 'increased' TOTAL heat energy of the planet will cause an interaction between the 'lower mantle' and the 'outer core'.*

This process, already beginning, will cause fluid movement from the outer core, up through the lower mantle, into the upper mantle. (The Earth's crust rests on the upper mantle.) Not only will this disturb the thermal equilibrium of the upper mantle, it will have a radical 'further' effect on the convection currents – and hence on the fault lines, plate geometries, plate movements/activity etc.

The overall effect of the 'increasing' temperatures is to give rise to the beginning of massive geological activity (earthquakes, volcanoes, land subsidences, land elevations and massive tidal waves.) THE FORMATION OF THE NEW FAULT LINES IS THE BEGINNING OF THIS CATASTROPHIC PHENOMENON.

One key indicator will be an earthquake that takes place in San Francisco between the years of 1998 and 2004. This earthquake will be 'earlier' than its cyclical interval (from past history). Analysis of the seismic data, PARTICULARLY SECONDARY WAVES, will demonstrate changes in refraction patterns (and therefore fluid density changes IN THE MANTLE AND CORE).

* A key exposition of the basic factors that will govern behaviour of the interactions of the geothermal energy is reference 1.

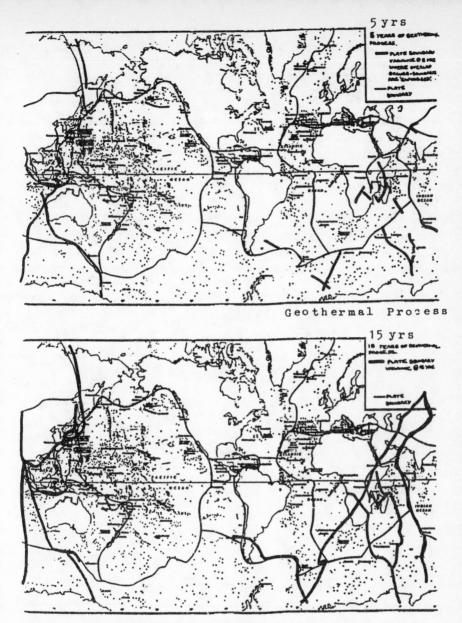

5 yrs

Geothermal Process

15 yrs

Computer modelling of system INERTIA (and parameters)

The various interactive parameters that contribute to the raising of the planet's retained heat energy are clearly complex – but a process is evident. Moreover attempts
to 'lump' parameters or other mathematical simplifications, for purposes of a simple
mathematical model, would certainly give dangerously misleading predictions.

It is evident that to date, only the subsystems have been subjected to modelling
attempts. 'Subsystems' may be considered as, say, the very competent ecology models

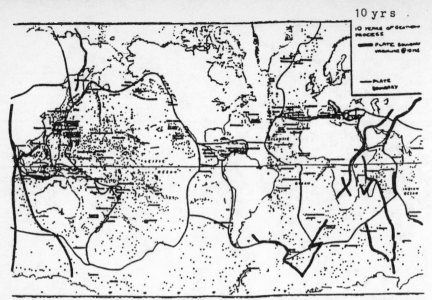

causing Plate Boundary Variance

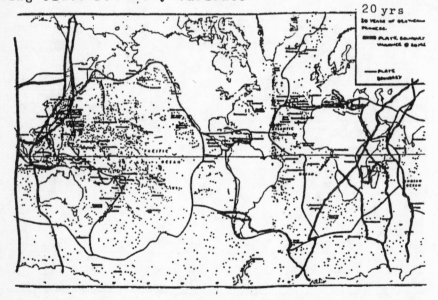

of Dr Antony M. Starield (University of Minnesota) and the Arnold Arboretum Institute's model (of Boston Massachusetts), being developed for forest depletion effects.

The effect of each parameter's inertia, in the overall system, will be STOCHASTIC* in nature. And accordingly only models (computer models) which adequately incorporate stochastic probability density functions will be useful tools in perceiving the true nature of inertia changes in the overall system that is associated with global warming.

THE EARTH

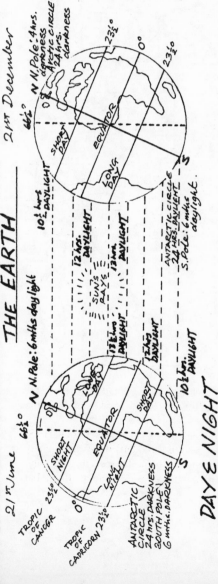

21st June

21st December

EARTH DATA

MASS OF THE EARTH:
5.9×10^{21} TONNES.

VOLUME OF THE EARTH:
$1,083,230 \times 10^{6}$ cu. Km.

TOTAL SURFACE AREA
510,000,000

LAND AREA (29.2%)
149,000,000 sq. Km.

WATER SURFACE (70.8%)
361,000,000 sq. Km.

RADIUS AT EQUATOR
6,356.9 Km.

EQUATOR DIAMETER
12,756.8 Km.

EQUATOR CIRCUMFERENCE
40,077. Km.

MERIDIONAL CIRCUMFERENCE
40,009 Km.

POLAR DIAMETER
12,713.8 Km.

POLAR RADIUS
6,356.9 Km.

NEAREST DISTANCE
FROM THE SUN
147,000,830 Km.

FURTHEST DISTANCE
FROM THE SUN
152,007,016 Km.

DAY & NIGHT

THE EARTH REVOLVES 'ANT-CLOCKWISE' FROM WEST TO EAST AROUND THE SUN, BUT BECAUSE THE SUN IS STATIONARY IN THE SKY, IT APPEARS TO US ON EARTH THAT THE SUN IS MOVING ACROSS THE SKY FROM THE EAST TO THE WEST.

AT THE EQUATOR, THE LENGTH OF DAY & NIGHT ARE ALMOST THE SAME ALL YEAR AROUND. ON JUNE 21st (SUMMER SOLSTICE) THE ARCTIC HAS A TOTAL OF 24 hrs. OF DAYLIGHT & THE ANTARCTIC HAS 24 hrs. OF TOTAL DARKNESS. THIS SITUATION COMPLETELY REVERSES ON 21st DECEMBER (WINTER SOLSTICE) WHEN THE OPPOSITE IS TRUE.

THE SEASONS

EACH YEAR, THE EARTH REVOLVES ROUND THE SUN IN AN 'ANTICLOCKWISE' DIRECTION. DURING ITS ORBIT THE EARTH IS TILTED AT A CONSTANT 66½°. THEREFORE IN JUNE, THE NORTHERN HEMISPHERE IS TILTED TOWARDS THE SUN & RECIEVES MORE OF THE SUNS RAYS IN A DAY RESULTING IN OUR WARMEST SEASON: SUMMER. BY DECEMBER, THE EARTH HAS COMPLETED HALF ITS ORBIT ROUND THE SUN, SO THAT THE SOUTHERN HEMISPHERE (NOW TILTED TOWARDS THE SUN) HAS ITS SUMMER. E.G. ON JUNE 21st THE SUN IS DIRECTLY OVER THE TROPIC OF CANCER (23½° N) & THIS IS MIDSUMMER IN THE NORTHERN HEMISPHERE. SIMILARLY MIDSUMMER IN THE SOUTHERN HEMISPHERE IS ON THE 21st. DECEMBER, WHEN THE SUN IS DIRECTLY OVER THE TROPIC OF CAPRICORN (23½ S).

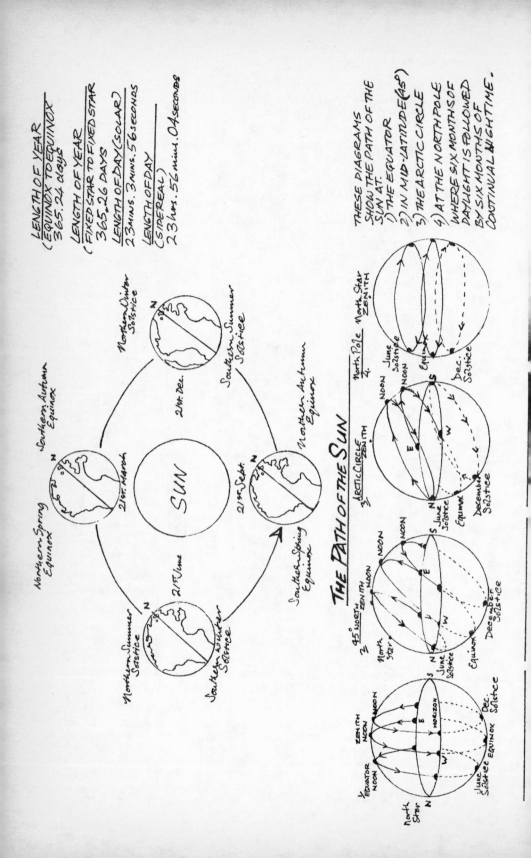

LENGTH OF YEAR
(EQUINOX TO EQUINOX)
365.24 days

LENGTH OF YEAR
(FIXED STAR TO FIXED STAR)
365.26 DAYS

LENGTH OF DAY (SOLAR)
23 mins. 3 mins. 56 seconds

LENGTH OF DAY
(SIDEREAL)
23 hrs. 56 mins. 04 seconds

THESE DIAGRAMS
SHOW THE PATH OF THE
SUN AT:
1) THE EQUATOR
2) IN MID-LATITUDE (45°)
3) THE ARCTIC CIRCLE
4) AT THE NORTH POLE
WHERE SIX MONTHS OF
DAYLIGHT IS FOLLOWED
BY SIX MONTHS OF
CONTINUAL NIGHTTIME.

THE PATH OF THE SUN

THE MOON

MOON DATA: DISTANCE FROM EARTH (MEAN) - 324,199.1 Km. AVERAGE SPEED IN RELATION TO EARTH - 3,683 Km/h. SIZE & MASS: - DIAMETER OF THE MOON 3,475.1 Km. MASS - 7348 x 10⁴ TONNES DENSITY 3.344 TIMES WATER. THE MOON IS APPROX. 400 TIMES SMALLER THAN EARTH, BUT 400 TIMES CLOSER, SO WE SEE THEM FROM EARTH AS THE SAME SIZE.

TEMPRATURES: HOTTEST WITH THE SUN OVERHEAD THE LUNAR EQUATOR - 117.2°C (243°F). SINKING TO -162.7°C (-261°F) AT NIGHT. LIGHT & VISIBILITY: - ONLY 59% OF THE MOONS SURFACE IS EVER VISIBLE FROM EARTH. REFLECTED LIGHT FROM THE MOON TAKES 1.25secs TO REACH US.

THE MOON ROTATES ONE COMPLETE TURN ON ITS AXIS IN JUST OVER 27 DAYS - SLOWER THAN THE EARTH, BUT SINCE THIS CORRESPONDS TO ITS PERIOD OF REVOLUTION AROUND THE EARTH, IT MEANS THAT THE MOON ALWAYS SHOWS THE SAME HEMISPHERE TO US - SO WE NEVER SEE THE DARK SIDE OF THE MOON! THE INTERVAL BETWEEN ONE FULL MOON & THE NEXT IS APPROX. 29½ DAYS - A LUNAR MONTH. THE CHANGES IN THE SHAPE OF THE MOON ARE CAUSED BY ITS CHANGING POSITIONS RELATIVE TO US ON EARTH. THE LIGHT OF THE MOON, LIKE THE LIGHT FROM THE PLANETS, IS CAUSED BY ITS REFLECTING THE RAYS OF THE SUN.

PHASES OF THE MOON

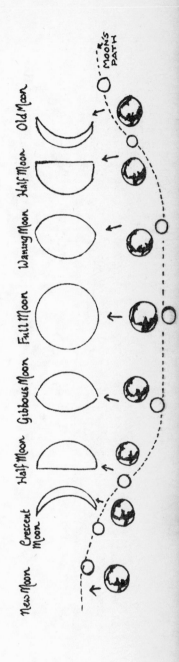

New Moon • Crescent Moon • Half Moon • Gibbous Moon • Full Moon • Waning Moon • Half Moon • Old Moon

MOON'S PATH

TIDES & THE MOON

THE GRAVITATIONAL PULL OF THE MOON (& THE SUN) – CAUSES THE RISE & FALL OF THE OCEAN'S TIDES (RATIO PULL: MOON–100%: SUN–46.6% of MOON). THIS EFFECT IS GREATEST ON THE EARTH'S HEMISPHERE FACING THE MOON & CAUSES TIDAL BULGE WHEN THE SUN & MOON & EARTH'S GRAVITATIONAL FORCES PULL TOGETHER (NEAR NEW & FULL MOON TIMES) EARTH'S TIDES ARE HIGHEST (SPRING TIDES) & LOWER LOW TIDES; THE SMALLEST TIDES OCCURING WHEN THE LUNAR & SOLAR FORCES ARE NOT ALLIGNED, RESULTING IN SMALLER NEAP TIDES.

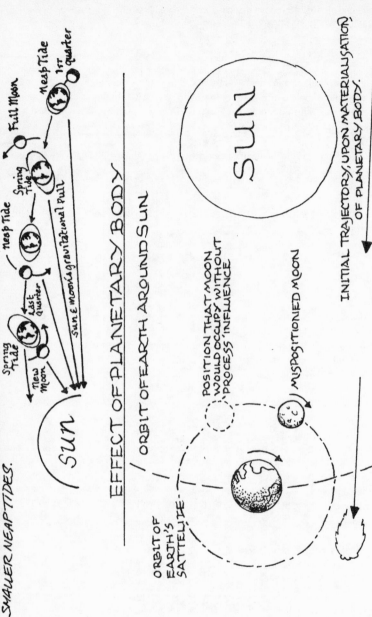

EFFECT OF PLANETARY BODY

Neap Tide
1st Quarter

Full Moon

Spring Tide

Neap Tide

Last Quarter

Spring Tide

New Moon

Sun & Moon's gravitational Pull

SUN

ORBIT OF EARTH AROUND SUN

SUN

POSITION THAT MOON WOULD OCCUPY WITHOUT PROCESS 'INFLUENCE'

MISPOSITIONED MOON

INITIAL TRAJECTORY, UPON MATERIALISATION) OF PLANETARY BODY.

ORBIT OF EARTH'S SATTELITE

TRAJECTORY OF BODY AS IT CAN BE DRAWN CLOSE TO EARTH BY MISPOSITION OF MOON.

The consequences of departure from the planet's thermodynamic equilibrium will be irreversible in 20 years. I repeat: only expansive activity, implementing the solution DURING THE NEXT TEN YEARS, will lessen the drastic future events of this process.

* Please see reference 2 for a concise outline of the basic theory:

Very simply, it should also be realised that 'deterministic' models are not capable of the analysis of such a system. They do not build chance into their basic parameters or subsystems. Stochastic models allow for such parameter variances – however, the average behaviour of many runs of the model is consistent and predictable.

The correct identification of the System's Stochastic Probability Density Function defines whether large or inordinately large matrices are *'inverted'* within the model.

Interaction of global warming, density changes, 'tilt' and geothermal activity.

It is considered that informed sources are already aware of a 'tilt' in the axis of rotation of the Earth. A tilt of the Earth's axis of rotation, some 2 degrees from the *previous* 66½ degrees, is of greater significance than initial observations might show. This will increase by a further 3 degrees during the next 20 years, giving a total increase of 5 degrees.

The tilt is an indication that the geothermally induced density changes beneath the Earth's crust are taking place already.

This is a cycle of *increasing process inertia* – ie simply: increased rate of heat retention, therefore more density changes, therefore more stress on the crust *causing* new fault lines and geological activity. However, because of the tilt (and associated 'mass moment of inertia' changes etc. caused by density changes in the Earth) – THE INTERACTIVE ORBITAL PATTERN OF THE EARTH AND MOON WILL CHANGE.

Restating this point:

Density changes, correspondent with the convection current changes, will increase the magnitude of forces pressing the crust outward. Because of these forces, which are consequence of the physics of the Earth's interior density shift and rotational speed, the tilt (and mass moment of inertia changes, coriolis effects and so forth – as the Earth spins) WILL CAUSE A SLIGHT CHANGE IN THE ORBIT OF THE MOON.

Effect of a planetary body

The phenomena described in the next sections are considered to be the outcome of the process already taking place, that is instigated by the global warming process.

However, there is an additional parameter, evident in the calculations of the 19 pages of Einstein's formulae. This is the massive amplification of the devastating effects caused by severe gravitation attraction from a massive planetary body. The analysis identifies the nature of its 'unseen' arrival (within the 50-year process time), and how it will amplify the 'magnitude' of process events greatly. Variance in parameters, between the earth and the moon, will draw this body catastrophically close to the earth.

THE CIRCULATION of the ATMOSPHERE

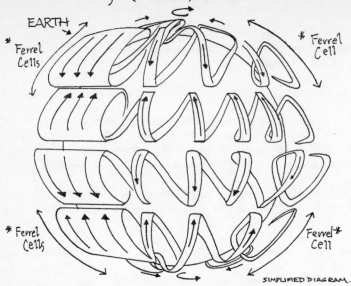

EARTH

* Ferrel Cells

* Ferrel Cell

* Ferrel Cells

Ferrel * Cell

SIMPLIFIED DIAGRAM.

THE ATMOSPHERE MAINTAINS ITS BALANCE BY THE TRANSFER OF
HEAT, MOISTURE & MOMENTUM FROM LOW LEVELS AT LOW LATITUDES TO
HIGH LEVELS AT HIGH LATITUDES WHERE THE HEAT IS RADIATED INTO SPACE
THIS CIRCULATION APPEARS TO HAVE THREE DISTINCTIVE "UNITS" IN
EACH HEMISPHERE. IN THE POLAR & EQUATORIAL UNITS, THE CIRCULATION
IS THERMALLY DIRECT: WARM AIR RISES & COLD AIR SINKS, ~ BUT THE MID ~
~ LATITUDE CIRCULATION IS DISTORTED* BY THE POLAR FRONT.
(AS SHOWN). THIS IS KNOWN AS THE Ferrel Cell

FRONTAL SYSTEMS

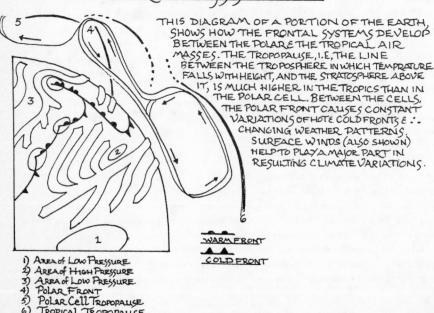

THIS DIAGRAM OF A PORTION OF THE EARTH,
SHOWS HOW THE FRONTAL SYSTEMS DEVELOP
BETWEEN THE POLAR & THE TROPICAL AIR
MASSES. THE TROPOPAUSE, I.E., THE LINE
BETWEEN THE TROPOSPHERE IN WHICH TEMPRATURE
FALLS WITH HEIGHT, AND THE STRATOSPHERE ABOVE
IT, IS MUCH HIGHER IN THE TROPICS THAN IN
THE POLAR CELL. BETWEEN THE CELLS,
THE POLAR FRONT CAUSES CONSTANT
VARIATIONS OF HOT & COLD FRONTS & ∴
CHANGING WEATHER PATTERNS.
SURFACE WINDS (ALSO SHOWN)
HELP TO PLAY A MAJOR PART IN
RESULTING CLIMATE VARIATIONS.

WARM FRONT

COLD FRONT

1) AREA OF LOW PRESSURE
2) AREA OF HIGH PRESSURE
3) AREA OF LOW PRESSURE
4) POLAR FRONT
5) POLAR CELL TROPOPAUSE
6) TROPICAL TROPOPAUSE

Trees, heat transfer, changing wind patterns, increasing tropospheric distribution of ozone destroyers.

It is already well known that the power and propensity of the earth's atmosphere to *hold* heat energy, is increasing. Whilst this is true for the atmosphere as a whole, there is a greater 'concentration' and effect of this property at certain levels in the atmosphere (and over certain surface areas). For instance in the Northern Hemisphere a new ozone hole is accompanied by abnormally high levels of ozone-destroying catalysts such as Chlorine Monoxide and Bromine trioxide.

It is clearly perceived that the *complex* nature of the Earth's energy balances have evolved through 'geological time'. It is logical, considering the elementary laws of heat transfer and thermodynamics, that these systems developed after earth's Crust became stable. Clearly the transmission of heat energies between various zones within the earth's core and, eventually, to/from the crust *work at a level of delicacy and complexity that has evolved through geological ages*. Given that this is clearly the case, heat exchange mechanisms, throughout the planet, involve interactions *across* the earth's surface, with the fluid below the crust, and the atmosphere. The oceans, the ice caps and the wind systems were 'key' to the planetary energy balance – whose evolution gave stability to the earth's crust.

The pattern of the winds, and their interaction with the trees, oceans and ice caps is changing rapidly from that 'stabilised' through geological time. The effects of massive acceleration in atmospheric carbon dioxide and tree destruction go *beyond* the narrow perspective of simple 'seasonal' temperature variances. There is a fundamental change, taking place already, in the convection currents (and heat energy level) of the fluid below the crust. The two-degree tilt in the earth and the wind system changes already evident, affect parameters critical to the stability of the earth's crust.

But there is another consideration, relating to the *previously undiminished concentration* of another interactive process feature/element. This 'other' interactive change relates changes in the patterns of winds and the shifting of their sites of stability in the troposphere. This phenomenon is attributable to increasing divergence in temperature extremes in the atmosphere's global heat exchange and the escalating demise of parameters associated with trees (ie when considering these 'system influences', the south-east Asian rainforests are now at one-third of their area 1900–1950. Worldwide, 50 Acres/Minute are lost).

The effect of trees on the climate extends beyond the mere conversion of carbon dioxide into oxygen. They also interact with the winds, and the changes in the winds clearly affect climate. We can already see this changing in weather we experience today.

Subtle changes in the energy balance of the troposphere causes an escalating trend of extreme behaviour in the temperature, velocity and stability of wind patterns on a global scale – these effects have been clearly evidenced in the recent worsening of weather patterns throughout the world. (Subsidiary effects of these changes in wind patterns are increasing levels of Chlorine Monoxide (ClO) and Bromine (BrO3) in both ozone holes during the warmer seasons.)

Changes in the troposphere's wind patterns mean those winds that would otherwise be 'oxygenated' (and hence have lower heat retaining capacity) have less influence on the overall pattern of global winds – because there are, quite simply, vastly fewer trees in the constant oxygenating zone of the tropics. These wind changes, primarily associated with stable heat exchange systems, are tending to be 'shifted' and are affecting the nature of the atmosphere's global heat exchange with the earth's surface. This means that greater heat energies are 'held' on the surfaces of the crust – which then further participate in the elevation of temperatures in the convection currents of the upper mantle. (Therefore heat transfer characteristics of the upper mantle and crust (1900–1950) which could be characterised by the laplace equation (for the thermodynamic system) equated to zero, are now very different. The atmosphere is equivalent to a system with internal heat generation capacity (and therefore also the upper mantle), so an advanced Partial Differential Equation (PDE) application of the laplace equation (using closed cycle integrations) cannot be equated to Zero. Adequate representation in a computer model is an immensely difficult task.)

The *change* in the fluid movement of the upper mantle has already caused the two degrees increase in the tilt of the earth, which has a 'knock-on-effect' in the wind patterns of the earth. When the wind patterns change even more this will promote more Chlorine Monoxide etc. YET OXYGENATED AIR FROM THE TROPICAL RAINFORESTS SHOULD BE THERE TO *BALANCE* HEAT TRANSFER IN THE TROPOSPHERE, FOR THE SUBTLE BUT CRITICAL, BALANCE OF WINDS *AND* HEAT TRANSFER PATTERNS GLOBALLY – BUT THESE TREES ARE NO LONGER THERE!

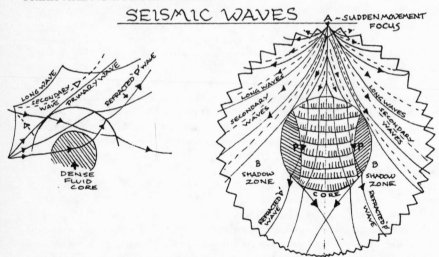

SEISMIC WAVES

SEISMIC WAVES PROVIDE MAN'S ONLY SOURCE OF INFORMATION ABOUT THE EARTH'S INTERIOR. AN EARTHQUAKE CAUSED BY A SUDDEN MOVEMENT AT FOCUS POINT (A) WILL SEND OUT A PATTERN OF SHOCK WAVES RADIATING LIKE RIPPLES IN A POND. THERE ARE 3 KINDS OF WAVES AS FOLLOWS: 1) PRIMARY (P) WAVES (FULL LINES) – WILL VIBRATE IN THE DIRECTION OF ORIGIN & ARE A RAPID SUCCESSION OF HIGH & LOW PRESSURES. 2) SECONDARY WAVES (BROKEN LINES) – SHAKE FROM SIDE TO SIDE & ONLY TRAVEL 60% AS QUICKLY AS THE 'P' LINES. 3) LONG WAVES – WHICH TRAVEL ROUND THE CRUST. IN A BELT AROUND THE EARTH – ONLY LONG WAVES ARE APPARENT, & THIS GIVES CREDENCE TO THE SHADOW ZONE CONCEPT. (SEE DIAGRAM) PERIODIC RECORDS OF THE 'P' WAVES HAVE LED SIESMOLOGISTS TO THE THEORY THAT THE EARTH HAS A VERY DENSE FLUID CORE, WHICH HAS THE CAPACITY TO STRONGLY REFRACT 'P' WAVES IN THE WAY A LENS DOES WITH LIGHT.

As the heat energy increases in the upper mantle (and fluid below) the tilt of the earth will increase. (To 5 degrees at 20 years.)

Trees are required globally to produce oxygen (for humans to breathe) but also to rectify oxygenation/heat transfer characteristics of the troposphere and HENCE ALSO TO RESTORE WIND PATTERNS TO THEIR PREVIOUS ORIENTATIONS.

Typical changes at end of first process stage (20 years).

The USA.

Presently, the weather and climate conditions of North America are dominated by the influence of the great land (and ice) mass to the North. This situation can be thought of as cold 'radiating' from the central part of Canada (Manitoba, for instance). Only the mountain ranges (and to some extent the warm gulf of Mexico) distort the present continental influence. Otherwise, minimum temperatures rise in concentric bands, to the subtropical fringes of southern California and Florida.

However, this will change and be very different in 20 years.

Across North America there will be a habitable zone that is correspondent with 'hot/cold lines' of map 1. As a general trend across the world, the higher ground and mountainous areas will be better for survival. The eastern part of the North American continent will be subject to unbearable heat – the animals will migrate toward the western part of the North American continent. It is considered that animal life on this and the other continents will reduce on average by 50%, because of the climate changes that will have taken place after the first twenty years of the process.

The weather will be characterised by storms, cyclones, tornadoes and electrical storms whose extreme magnitude is not presently experienced.

It has already been mentioned that at the juncture 20 years hence, the 'inertia' effects in the weather, climate and geothermal system will be 'irreversible'. At this time the situation will be generally appreciated and understood but it will be too late.

There will be an initial 'ramp-up' of temperatures, at various locations in the United States, which will cause temperatures of 200 F. (A secondary rate of temperature increase will then dominate till the end of the 50-year period, at which time the entire environmental system will have been arrested).

At the end of the 20-year initial period, there would be a side effect, from the North American climate, that will trigger the cold part of Australia (then at −59F) to begin a further decline into an Ice Age.

Between the years 1998 and 2004 there will be a transition period in which the effect of the increased total heat energy will cause an earthquake in San Francisco. This will be some years before it is expected, on the basis of previous cyclical averages.

There will be perceived lengthening, at the time of this geological activity, of the San Andreas fault. This will also be another indication that previously unperceived phenomena are already causing new behaviour in the interaction of fault lines and plate tectonics. The San Francisco earthquake will be a KEY INDICATOR.

The point here is that this earthquake will be an essential opportunity for the gathering of SEISMIC DATA. The seismic data, particularly with regard to the divergence of secondary waves, will not be as expected, and will correspond to geothermal and density changes, as indicated in this report elsewhere.

Australia

The coastline (indicated map 1) of the cold western part of Australia will be subject to the beginning of a major land subsidence. The subsidence, beginning in the western part of Australia, will eventually cause a reduction of some fifty percent in the total land mass area that exists today. (A higher sea level will be partially responsible.)

The line shown as the intersection between the hot and cold climate zones will contain the habitable areas, because of the lower temperatures that will exist there. There will be large-scale destruction of many species of Australian fauna.

Ice Caps

In line with the considered trend, the ice caps will undergo a severe acceleration in their rate of melting. The full effect of the accelerated melting will be complete by 2025.

The *first* volcanic eruptions will be at the South Pole. There will also be a land mass rise at the start of this volcanic activity.

Russia

It is considered that the major land subsidence indicated, corresponding to the new fault indicated on map 1, will take place in approximately twenty years' time also.

Central Africa

It can be noted from map 1 that there is an intersection to two major fault lines located in Central Africa. There will be major earthquakes (and associated activity) at the intersection of these plate forces. It has been mentioned that the full development of geological parameters, to produce these faults, will be complete in approximately six years. After this time the faults themselves will begin substantive development.

Europe and England

Presently, the overwhelming influences on Europe's climate are the Atlantic Ocean, the cold land-mass of Asia and the warm air mass over the ocean with its warm Gulf stream. The Gulf stream is so effective in elevating temperatures that, mountains apart, where the Atlantic and Saharan influences coincide in southern Spain, winter temperatures presently can be as high as Florida – ten degrees of latitude or 700 miles farther south.

England will be an indication of the severity of upcoming changes that Europe will experience, during the process. In the year 2012 there will be nationwide crop losses. The temperature, twenty years hence, in England will begin at 120F and constitute the start of the irreversible stage of temperature increase. Throughout England, at this time, there will be widespread flooding, together with a phenomenon of frequent large-scale fires that may be likened to the spontaneous forest fires which occur in Canada/North America after prolonged arid conditions.

Heat energy of the planet grows and evolution's delicate heat transfer mechanisms disintegrate!

Total planetary heat energy, weather system heat exchange and progressive weather system instability.

The weather systems of the northern hemisphere (and arctic), the southern hemisphere (and antarctic) and tropical zone have been evolved through geological time.

The transfer of heat energy, *within* and *between* these weather systems clearly interacts with the earth's careful conduction and movement of heat energy.

The delicate heat transfer and heat energy balances have evolved to form a balance between the earth's molten core, the 'apple skin thin' outer layer called the crust and the radiant heat from the sun.

The balances of heat energy involve heat energy transmission through the seas, sea floors, surface land masses, the moving molten fluid below the crust, and the heat energy of the earth's atmosphere. Through many millions of years the heat balance of the planet has been a *balance* of heat from the sun on the earth's 70% water/30% land surface and the heat *beneath* the earth's surface. The atmosphere has evolved a certain level of efficiency (through geological time) as a 'vehicle' for moving heat to and from different areas of the planet. The atmosphere's role in distributing heat *from* the warmer *to* colder areas of the planet *is* the stabilised pattern of weather that has evolved over many millions of years.

We, all of us, notice that heat moves from 'hot' locations to cold locations. We see this, for example, when the 'heat energy' in our cup of tea is transferred to the colder air that surrounds and is in contact with the tea. We also see heat transfer in our ovens when we notice the greater heat energy level at the top of the oven – warm air rises, of course. We also observe a similar circulation of heat when we 'heat' a pan of water. We see that when heat is added to the water (faster than it can lose it to its surroundings) the water will eventually boil. The ability of different liquids and gases to hold and 'move' heat clearly varies (this is known, simply, as specific heat capacity). As the water's circulation of heat gets faster, approaching boiling, we notice agitation of the liquid increases. We can clearly appreciate such simple phenomena without resorting to the laws of thermodynamics.

Hence air masses move warm air (and hence transfer heat energy) from the 'warmer' surfaces of the planet to the colder surfaces of the planet. (Also it is logical to realise that there is an obvious connection with the way molten liquid/fluid, beneath the earth's surface, moves.) The weather systems and the other Heat Transfer systems 'above', 'below' and 'at' the surface of the earth are very clearly *interlinked*. There developed a careful balance, over some 386 million years, that not only kept the surface of the earth stable but allowed the evolution of many forms of life.

The heat energy from the sun (to the earth) has remained constant. Yet activity on the earth's 'wafer-thin' surface is giving the planet ever increasing amounts of 'extra' heat energy that is unprecedented in the history of the earth's surface and atmosphere. (And if we go back to our very apt analogy of heating a pan of water – we know about the *'agitation'* of the liquid and we know nature cannot remove all this artificially produced heat.) There is nothing in space, around our planet, that can take away the extra heat.

If the maps showing radiated heat, from the earth's surface, are studied we can see the equatorial region of the planet ought to radiate the most heat. It can also be seen that the colder regions of the ice caps 'draw in' heat energy. So a circulation is clear,

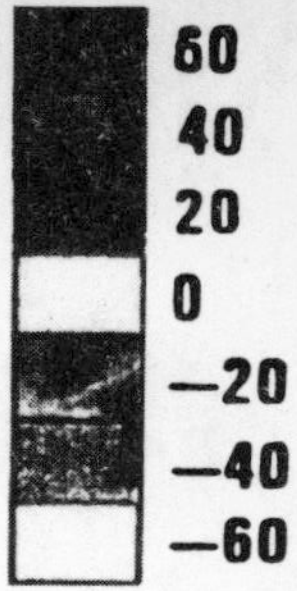

MAP TAKEN FROM A TEXT

WORDS AND FIGS. (EXCEPT 3RD COLUMN) ALIEN

Please note:

At 1993 Fluid of the upper mantle has begun
to change its pattern of movement and
circulation – as a result of 'holding' more heat.
By the process 'turning point' (2013) a 5 Degree
increase in the tilt will cause radical polarization of
weather systems – The planet's 'retained heat' will have begun
a geometric rate of increase, in line with the 'overall' stochastic
process parameters that are perceived.

K/Cal per cm per year

2013	1993
90	70
70	50
50	30
30	15
-30	-15
-70	-35
-90	-45

60
40
20
0
-20
-40
-60

in the way air masses move, that corresponds to this. So the air 'absorbs' and 'moves' heat energy as a key part of this process.

The oceans also move heat energy in this global heat transfer network. The *effect* of insulatory composites of various pollutants at key ocean bed locations is *yet* to be assessed. However it is easy to see that deficient or partially blocked heat 'outlets', on the ocean bed, will cause this geothermal energy to seek other 'outlets'. This process will 'stress' the earth's crust in new ways. As geothermal forces on the crust 'shift', fissures and plate boundaries will be stressed in new patterns.

Further study of the radiated heat energy shows that the earth's surface has become a great deal warmer in the interval 1973-1993. We can easily see that we have produced a great deal more heat – the carbon dioxide and ozone destruction shows us this. But is there any simple evidence to show that the efficiency of nature's methods of moving heat has diminished?

An obvious indicator of efficient and stable heat transfer is the weather over the last 20 years. The extremes of weather over the last 20 years show that 'something' is certainly causing progressive '*agitation*' of the planet's systems. Although somewhat simplified, the diagrams for polar and tropical weather systems *and* tropopause are useful. It is self-evident a 'stable' nature of air movements is consistent with a constant and *continuous* process of heat circulation.

However if one considers that the specific heat capacity or ability (of different gases) to hold heat energy varies, this can be a factor also. If one considers the map of radiated heat, the tropical regions of the earth have the greatest energy balance *need* to 'transport' heat energy. The radiated heat is clearly a phenomenon that takes place throughout the year, irrespective of season. With the vast destruction of the world's tropical rainforests the *oxygenation* of the tropical weather system is, therefore, severely diminished. This has caused the striation of the tropical tropopause into *five*, as it seems, vertical circulations of air mass. (There was previously *one* vertical circulation giving good heat transfer.) This will clearly have a drastic effect on the heat energy *absorption* and *distribution* that has existed previously.

One site of most obvious correlation can be seen at the 40K/cal per cm per year heat interface at the Sahara Desert in Africa. Remember the vast destruction of trees that existed previously. The trees had a vast oxygenation property that made the previously stable local atmosphere possible. It is observed that arid conditions and drought have intensified (causing many famines in Africa) in the last 20 years.

Concluding remarks

Many published papers, relating to 'Climate Change', conclude there will be very minor increases in global temperatures (typically of the order of 2.5 degrees). There are also other 'comforting' predictions regarding the change of key features in the earth's climate system. There seems to be a tendency to 'suspend' conclusions due to the 'need for gaining more data' and, of course, the need for 'a longer period of assessment' is often cited when conclusions are not stated.

Lengthy periods of data collection and analysis, to confirm statistical trends, do seem to be 'sound' practice. However there is a problem – the supposedly 'isolated elements' of the climate process *cannot* be treated as such. *The changes in these parameters are interactive in a way that makes drawing conclusions and acting on them urgent.*

Destruction of tropical rainforests, carbon dioxide acceleration, acceleration of population growth and the increasing planetary heat energy are just four parameters in climate change. The rates at which these parameters each escalate are *themselves* influenced by changes in *other* environment parameters and the inertia of their escalation. The inertia of many of these environmental elements is, either directly or indirectly, affected by man's activities. (One example being carbon dioxide – we produce it in countless millions of cars; presently seven billion humans produce it when 'breathing out'; and we *destroy* the trees which consume carbon dioxide and give us oxygen.)

The presently accepted computer models that deal with climate change are comforting to the extent that they do not alarm us with projected periods of crisis: 'happily we observe' that nothing really serious or 'irreversible' is likely to take place for *at least* twenty years. But the basis of models that deal with the *interaction of parameters* in the earth's climate system are clearly an immense simplification. The resources of many experienced mathematicians and vast computing capacity (such as the specially cooled CRAY mainframe computer in Cheyenne Mountain, USA) would be required to produce an appropriately adequate computer model. However even the 'writing' of comparatively simple computer models, based on 'straight-forward' mathematical functions, is a lengthy process. Once even a simple model is written, such as those often used for Computer Aided Engineering 'Simulations' (CAE), the process of 'proving out' or validating a model can lead to major changes before the model's simulated predictions conform to actuality.

If one were to consider a computer simulation model that could adequately represent nature's heat and energy transfer, there would have to be several mathematical equations (or functions). Each of these equations would represent how heat and energy moved through sea water, different parts of the atmosphere, land, ocean floors etc. Each single equation (or function) would need to be very complex.

Merely considering oxygenation (and therefore specific heat capacity) of the atmosphere – there will be a *seasonal change* (associated with the seasonal effect on planetary heat circulation) and there will be an on-going *permanent change* (associated with the loss of the prime oxgenators of the rainforests and proliferation of ozone-destroying catalysts which is gradually causing permanent changes in atmospheric 'specific heat capacity'). The equation for 'this' element's property has to represent its variability, as well as how its 'underlying trend' will *decline*. The equation for just this one element needs to be reasonably *accurate* – otherwise it will have a 'knock-on' effect causing ever increasing inaccuracies 'multiplied' throughout the other equations.

A simple analogy for the need for each equation to be reasonably accurate is easy to visualise. Several numbers when multiplied together continuously will give a *particular* answer. However in such a series of numbers if one, *and only one*, is changed, then the final result will be radically altered. In the analogy, the numbers are each an 'equation' which represents an element in the *chain* of the earth's Heat and Energy Transfers.

If one goes on to think how equations are 'arrived at', it becomes evident that 'raw data' and 'expert deduction' play a large part in the 'estimation' of an equation that is thought to describe a feature of the environment. Often the raw data is 'prepared' statistically using 'the Bell Shaped Curve' (or binomial distribution) of elementary statistics. The Bell Shaped Curve is often used and validated in manufacturing industries. (Such as what is known as Statistical Process Control.)

The bell shaped 'probability curve'

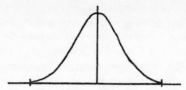

Yet even *simple* industrial processes can produce raw data which does not conform to the 'idealised' predictions of the probability curve. The probability curve is very useful as a starting tool in analysis and is often a primary resort. However, often the true nature of the raw data is biased away from the idealised distribution curve – such as the 'skewed' distribution. Also, the fluctuations in raw data can be a key property – such as Kurtosis.

A skewed distribution   Kurtosis

'Skewness' and 'Kurtosis' often occur in even *simple* processes – and can easily be 'missed' or misinterpreted.

If one considers data fluctuation, such as a 'spiky' trace instead of a nice smooth curve (which lends itself to easy analysis), 'Smoothing Functions' can be used to prepare data. For instance a 'spiky' and convoluted trace, if it is 'smoothed' enough times, will become a straight line! The *selection* of the *correct 'numerical methods'*, in the preparation of data, is a *very important first step*.

It is for these reasons that Scientists and Engineers, constructing computer simulation models, of quite simple systems, with only a few elements, often spend great time and effort redesigning and evolving these computer models to give realistic predictions that agree with known behaviour of the systems they model.

Clearly *practical* considerations of major 'human resource' and 'computing power' will necessitate massive simplification in Models that, say, predict global temperature increase. In these efforts, their spirit of environment consciousness should be commended. However, one must clearly see that if such a model predicts a one or two degree temperature rise in, say, ten years – this is really only *one* possible answer.

For instance, one approach to modelling a temperature-change process is to utilize the 'Physics' analysis of a 'forcing function' and *equate* a 'response' by holding all other climate parameters constant. Such an approach tends to discount many environmental parameters outright as well as ignoring the fact that these may change, escalate – and indeed trigger changes in yet other environmental parameters. Moreover the very real characteristic of the 'inertia' of these changes seems not to be dealt with at all.

Inertia in the behaviour of individual environmental features and 'inertia' of the whole system of climate change is *critical*. The inertia of the underlying processes which caused an 'apparently' sudden ozone depletion was clearly *inadequately* configured into the predictions for ozone depletion.

Can one consider a simple example showing 'inertia'? – The deoxygenation/*deforestation* process is an environmental parameter whose behaviour is influenced by 'inertia' and 'time' dependency.

For inertia, as a basic concept, we may think of a very heavy cylindrical 'roller' in a steel rolling mill. The roller fulfils exactly the same function as a cookery 'rolling pin' – except red/white hot steel ingots are being rolled thinner instead of dough or pastry. It will take a few hundred watts of energy (power) to *gradually* start and accelerate this massive roller to its top speed of rotation. It will take a similar amount of 'braking' energy to stop the roller *in a similar time* to that of start-up. However, in the steel rolling process, the roller can need to be *reversed* within half a second! This takes approximately half a million watts of power. (There is clearly a major inertia shift which causes a phenomenal increase in energy to counteract the inertia – from a few hundred watts to half a million watts.)

There is a valid energy analogy to the steel roller, in terms of the *accelerating* rate at which key rainforests are destroyed. It is not widely perceived that these trees are a critical part in nature's 'evolved' pattern of planetary heat transfer – their role is thought of primarily in agricultural terms and habitat for fauna. If the critical nature of these forests becomes widely perceived, *time* dependency of 'inertia' will require – '*Half a million watts of reversal activity*' NOT *a few hundred watts* (there is too little time).

We must understand a little more of *time* and *inertia* in an irreversible process. 'Irreversibility' in a process may be thought of as the 'point of no return' such that the process has achieved its own inertia and cannot effectively be 'switched-off'. To think about this a little more we must observe that many things in nature do not change at a constant rate – many processes start very slowly and finish incredibly fast. 'Inertia' and 'time dependency' will affect simple and complex systems similarly.

A kitchen sink may take two hours (some 7,200 seconds) to fill – if the faucet/tap leaks one drop per second. It is even a simple calculation to predict 'how full' the sink may be at a future time during its filling process. As the sink fills our '*deduced*' calculations, for our predictions, seem to fit *very well*. (As we observe the sink filling, we do *not* know the sink's 'overflow' is blocked. We have observed that there is only a *small* height difference between the overflow and the rim of the sink – however this was not thought to be significant, so it was *not* configured into equations of our computer simulation.)

The *entire* time history of the leaking faucet/tap filling the sink is, say two hours. From the beginning the deductions (for our computer simulation model) *seem* to be giving us good 'time' and 'water filling' predictions. However, as the water level increases, it will take us a few moments to realise the overflow is blocked! Yet a very few moments later the water *will* 'spill' over the sink's rim (and it will 'spill' *much* more water than one drop per second, as we all know). Here we see *time* and *inertia* – at the beginning (7,200 seconds ago) *one* second was *not* a significant time interval. *Yet now, at the end/collapse of the process (the point of overflow, that is) one second is a critical interval!*

We are lucky that our process is based on a sink, it has a large 'plugged' outlet – *we therefore do not need* to generate a *massive* reverse impetus to counteract the high system inertia in the last few moments. (Similar in effect to the massive energy needed to reverse the steel roller in *only* a moment.) *Again we are lucky it's a kitchen sink – we just 'pull the plug' and the water parameter just disappears from the system at phenomenal speed. However the earth does not have such a means of making all of the growing Heat energy disappear through a 'sink plug'.*

At the approach of disintegration of key environmental features, the inertia of all the process changes will not allow sufficient time for reversal. For instance, the critically located rainforests – these could *not* be 'instantly' regenerated and the detrimental effect, through their vast absence, on the climate system will not be instantly reversed. Many of the key environmental features will have reached the stage in their process where they cannot be 'switched off' or reversed.

The consequences of atmospheric and geothermal changes will begin to be perceived in weather and surface events, which will be located throughout the world. Given our escalating impact on environmental processes, particular catastrophic incidents that mark the disintegraion of these processes should *not* be called "acts of God" – humans are causing these changes. In fact consequences of atmospheric changes, causing famines etc should not any longer be called "acts of nature".

The Earth is man's home – he has nowhere else to go. The Earth was also the home of many species extinct and yet to be extinct. Many animals protect their environment in a territorial sense. Many animals will often sacrifice their own lives to protect their siblings, and in so doing, their descendents. We must ask ourselves:

Do we care less for our own descendants than they do theirs when we callously disrupt nature's delicate balances, evolved over millions of years?

These delicate balances have permitted the survival of oxygen-breathing life upon a stable earth's crust. If it is the most that you can do to plant just *one* tree, you must at least try to do this, in order to have some chance at averting what seems inevitable.

THE EARTH'S SURFACE IS MAN'S HOME,
WE HAVE NOWHERE ELSE TO GO. . . .

Appendix 1

Maps related to Section 5.0
Map 1 – process phenomena at 20 years.
Map 2 – safety zones at 20 years of process.
Map 3 – new land mass emergence.
Present land use and economy.
Land use by continent, presently and 20 years into process.
Figure 6 – loss of nutrient production at 20 years.
Figure 7 – loss of nutrient production at 20 years.

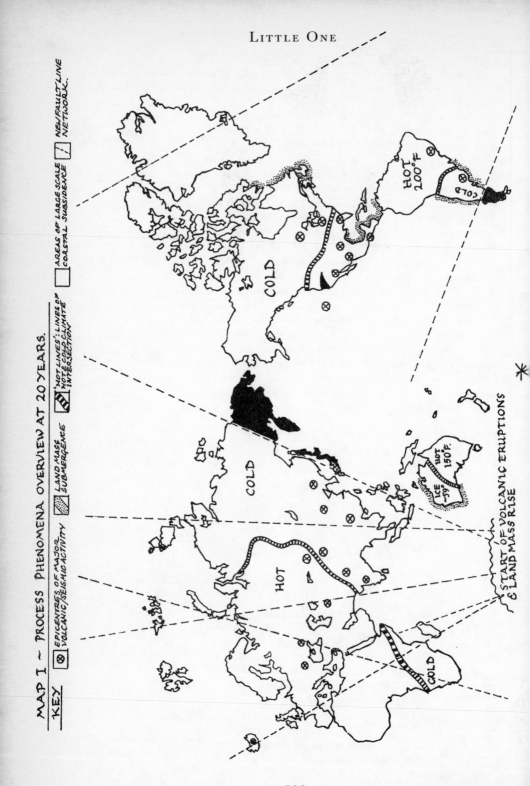

MAP I ~ PROCESS PHENOMENA OVERVIEW AT 20 YEARS.

KEY
⊗ EPICENTRES OF MAJOR VOLCANIC/SEISMIC ACTIVITY
▨ LAND MASS SUBMERGENCE
▨ 'HOT LINES': LINES OF HOT & COLD CLIMATE INTERSECTION
▢ AREAS OF LARGE SCALE COASTAL SUBSIDENCE
⟋ NEW FAULT LINE NETWORK.

COLD

COLD

HOT 200°F

COLD

HOT 150°F

ICE -5°F

COLD

HOT

COLD

START OF VOLCANIC ERUPTIONS & LAND MASS RISE

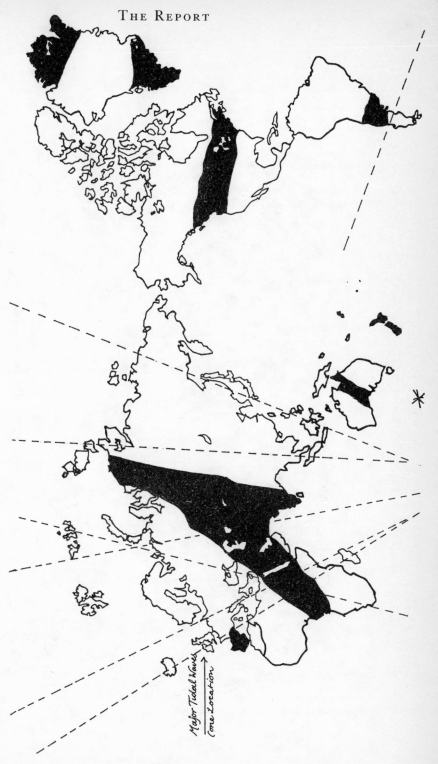

MAP 2

KEY ■ SAFETY ZONES ~ at 20 yrs.g Process. ☑ ~ DEVELOPING FAULT LINES

Major Tidal Wave.
Cone Location →

WORLD LAND USE & ECONOMY

KEY ▦ ~INDUSTRY. ▦ ~FARMING ☰ ~RANCHING ▨ ~Hunting, Fishing & ☐ Nomadic Herding Gathering

▨ ~ DESERTS

LAND USE BY CONTINENT & CAPACITY REDUCTION
AFTER 20 YRS. OF PROCESS

☐ NON-PRODUCTIVE ♠ FOREST Ⅲ PASTURE & GRAZING ⬇ CROPS & PLANTATIONS ≋ ARABLE

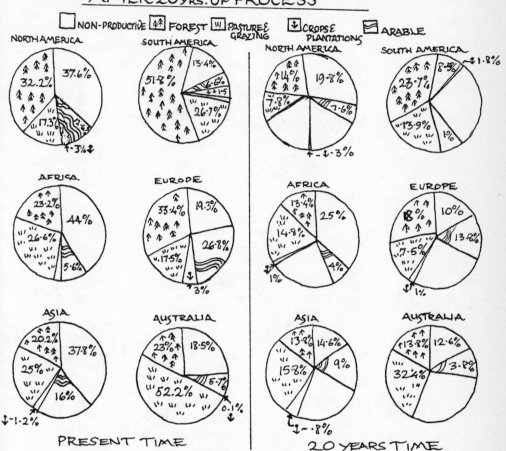

PRESENT TIME   20 YEARS TIME

I.E. NORTH AMERICAN FOREST ~ 32·2% DOWN TO 14%
OF CONTINENTAL LAND USE AT 20 YEARS.

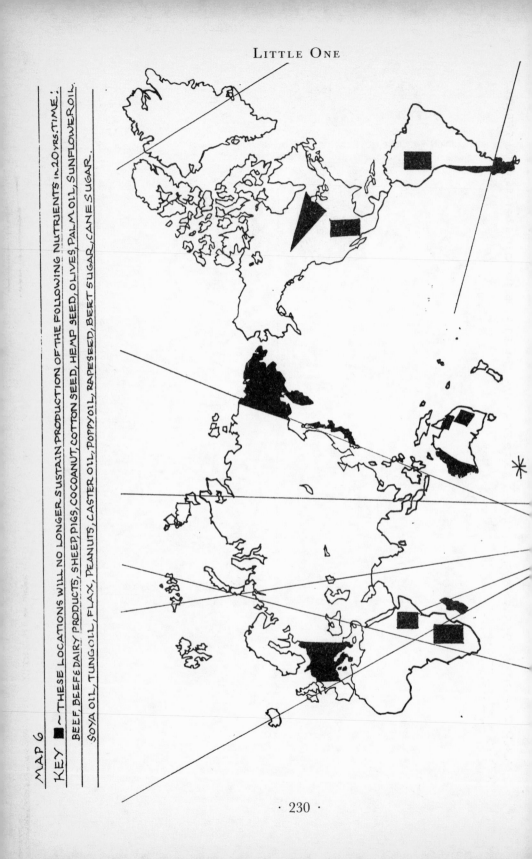

MAP 6

KEY ~ ■ ~THESE LOCATIONS WILL NO LONGER SUSTAIN PRODUCTION OF THE FOLLOWING NUTRIENTS IN 20 YRS. TIME :

BEEF, BEEF & DAIRY PRODUCTS, SHEEP, PIGS, COCOANUT, COTTON SEED, HEMP SEED, OLIVES, PALM OIL, SUNFLOWER OIL,

SOYA OIL, TUNG OIL, FLAX, PEANUTS, CASTER OIL, POPPY OIL, RAPESEED, BEET SUGAR, CANE SUGAR.

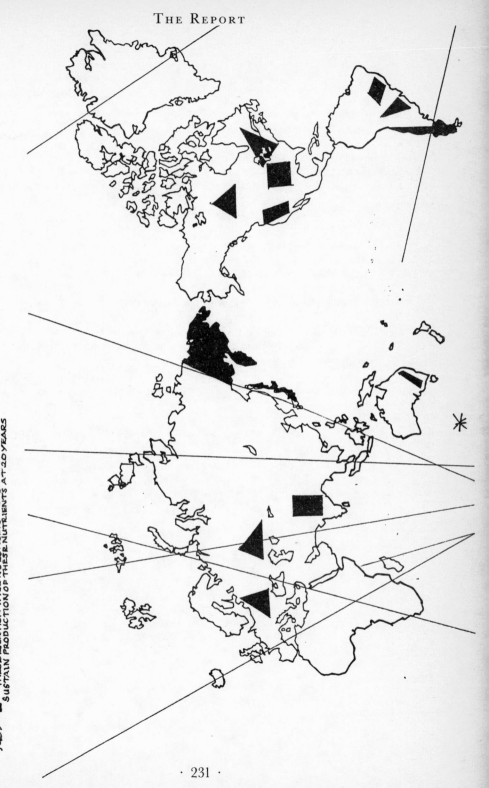

MAP 7.~WHEAT, BARLEY, RYE, CORN (MAIZE), SAGO, SORGHUM, MILLET, RICE, POTATOES, APPLES, CITRUS FRUIT, GRAPES.

KEY~ ■ ~ THESE LOCATION WILL NO LONGER. SUSTAIN PRODUCTION OF THESE NUTRIENTS AT 20 YEARS

Appendix 2

Notes on planetary phenomena and orbital mechanics interaction toward second stage of process.

Within the nineteen pages of notes included here (twenty pages in total), that were left in spirit by Albert Einstein are occasional annotations of my own. These are very brief, and may be identified from 'Marker Pen' lines having been drawn around them.

Own annotations – outlined/enclosed in Marker pen:

Page 2 – Comet, in star/planet section

Page 4 – Canonical could mean what is referred to as 'diskspace'

Page 5 – Striation of atmospheric gases, due to oxygen depletion during process

Page 7 – Correspondent to further changes in atmosphere *and* main diagram may be some sort of 'cracking tower' analogy for gaseous striation during oxygen depletion

Page 14 – Gravitational tearing effect of comet/star dwarf/planetary body.

Einstein's figures

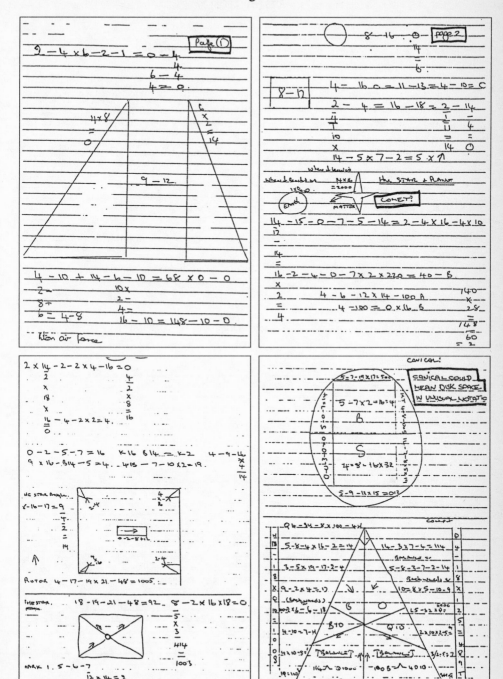

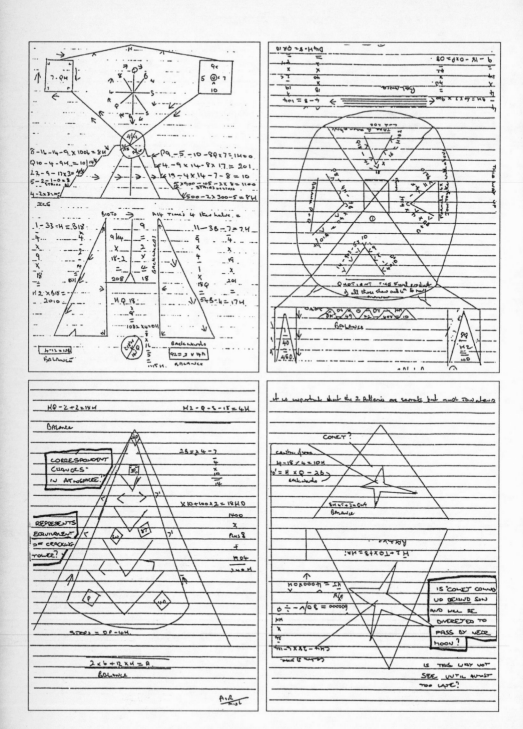

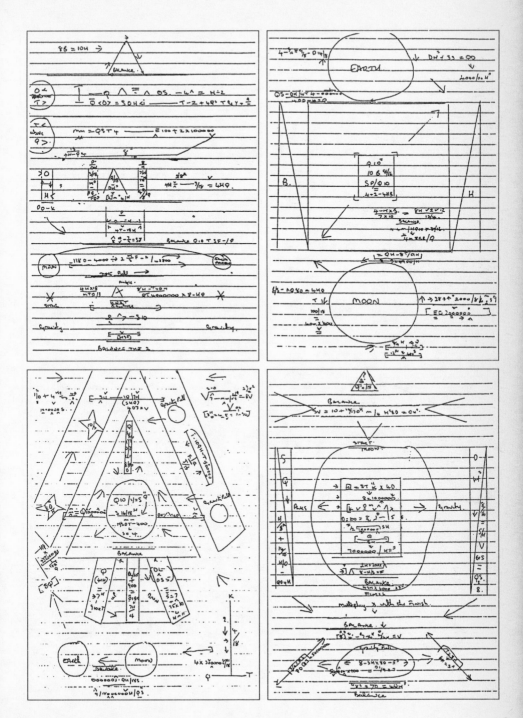

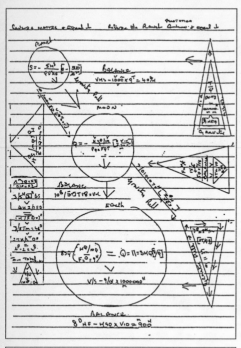

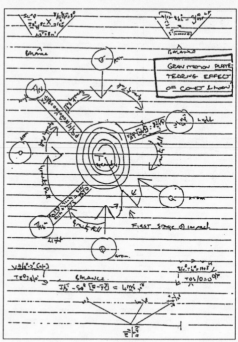

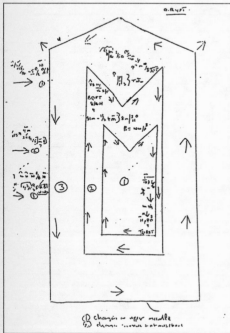

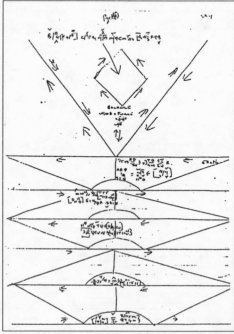

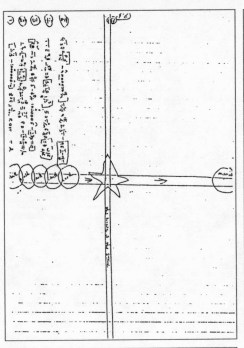

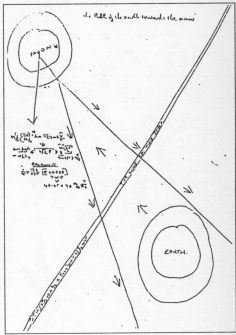

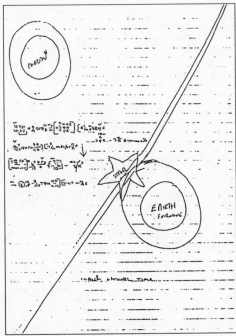

Appendix 3

Present day planetary climate and dependent phenomena

diagrams

1. Natural vegetation *and* Desertification, reduction and increase, respectively

2. Present climate temperature variances

3. Present climate distributions throughout world

4. Present population by Continent *and* present world-wide food consumption

5. Present self-sufficiency in food *and* present world-wide importance of agriculture

6. Present distribution, world-wide, of major volcanoes

7. Present distribution, world-wide, of major earthquakes

8. Present distribution, world-wide, of major rifts, major faults and mid-oceanic ridges

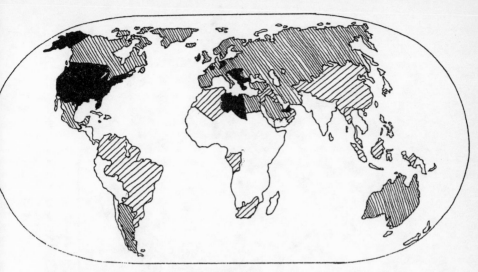

WORLD FOOD CONSUMPTION ~ AV. DAILY FOOD INTAKE PER PERSON IN KILOCALORIES

▓ OVER 3,500 K.Cals.p.p. ▨ 3,000 K.Cals.p.p. ▧ 2,500 K.Cals.p.p. □ 2000 or LESS K.Cals.p.p.

WORLD FOOD INTAKE RATIOS   U.S.A ~ 3,645   U.K ~ 3,256

Highest {
EAST GERMANY ~ 3,814
U.A.E   ~ 3,733
GREECE   ~ 3,688
U.S.A.   ~ 3,645
BULGARIA   ~ 3,642
}

Lowest {
GUINEA   ~ 1,776
GHANA   ~ 1,759
ETHIOPIA   ~ 1,749
CHAD   ~ 1,717
MOZAMBIQUE   ~ 1,595
}

WORLD POPULATION BY CONTINENT

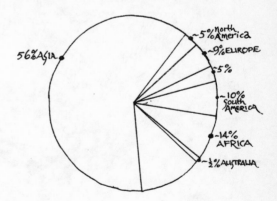

~ 5% North America
~ 9% EUROPE
~ 5%
~ 10% South America
~ 14% AFRICA
~ ½ % AUSTRALIA
56% ASIA

WORLD MAP: EARTHQUAKES

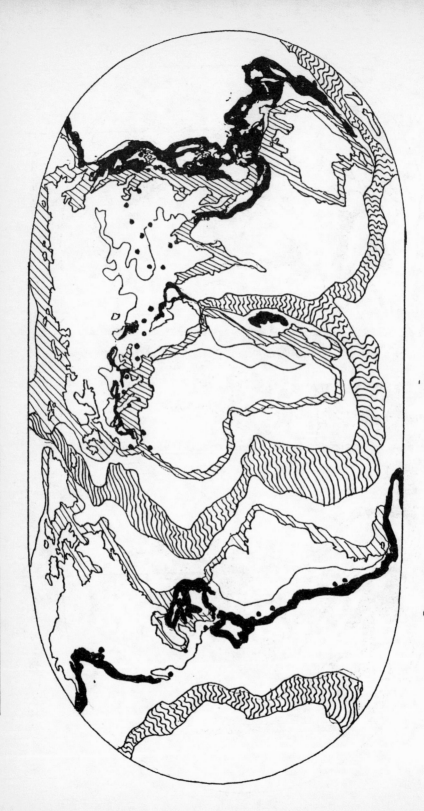

KEY: □ Submarine Zones ⊡ PRINCIPAL EARTHQUAKE ▨ MID-OCEANIC RIDGES (VOLCANIC)
of Mobile Land Areas   AREAS

▨ Submarine Extensions of Mobile Land Areas

DISTRIBUTION OF SHIELDS, RIDGES & FAULTS

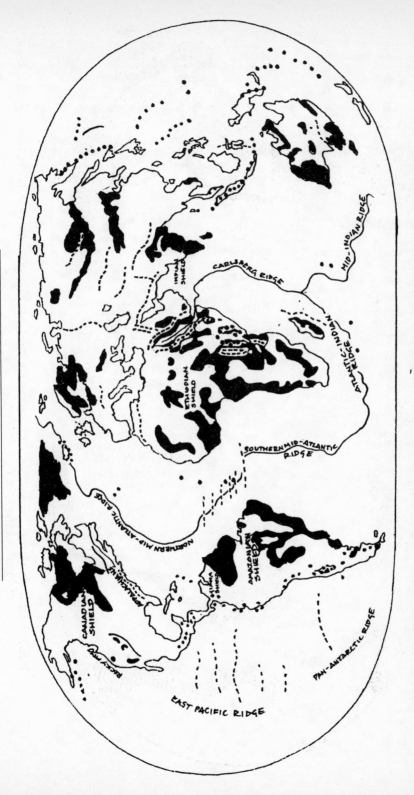

KEY: ■ ~ SHIELDS (PRE-CAMBRIAN)   ⊡ VOLCANOES & MAJOR CENTRES OF MAJOR EARTHQUAKE ACTIVITY   ▨ MAJOR FAULTS   ▨ MID-OCEANIC RIDGES

Appendix 4

Representative fauna depletion at end of first process stage. (Twenty years hence).

1. Based on the standard zoogeographical classification of environments, certain representative fauna will be quoted and a percentage of the population's *reduction* will be quoted

(a) PALAEARCTIC:

Roe Deer	− 10%
Fly Catcher	− 90%
Warbler	− 15%
Dunock	− 80%
Wild Ass	− 50%
Hedgehog	− 20%
Edible Dormouse	− 5%
Wild Sheep	− 60%

(b) NEARCTIC:

Beaver	− 15%
Tiger Salamander	− 10%
Pronghorn	− 50%
Skunk	− 25%
Mocking Bird	− 10%
Bison	− 45%
Turkey	− 30%
Rattlesnake	− 35%

(c) ORIENTAL:

Gibbon	− 55%
Orang Utan	−100%
Tree Shrew	− 40%
Tiger	− 90%
Fairy Bluebird	− 90%
Indian Elephant	− 60%
Peacock	− 45%

(d) ETHIOPIAN

Secretary Bird	− 90%
Sable	− 60%
African Elephant	− 85%
Potto	−100%
Zebra	− 60%

(e) NEOTROPICAL

Anteater	− 45%
Toucan	− 95%
Howler Monkey	− 90%
Guinea Pig	− 95%
Tapir	−100%
Sloth	− 90%
Rhea	−100%

(f) AUSTRALIAN

Duck-Billed Platypus	− 80%
Bird of Paradise	− 75%
Kangaroo	− 95 to 100%
Sugar Glider	−100%
Koala Bear	−100%
Cassowary	−100%
Kiwi	− 40%
Tuatara	− 70%

Representative 'endangered animals' extinction at twenty years of process (SEE LOCATION MAP).
  (1). Polar Bear (Thalarctos Maritimus) – EXTINCT
  (2). Audoulin's Gull (Larus Audouinii) – EXTINCT
  (3). Addax (Addax Nasomaculatuo) – EXTINCT
  (4). California Condor (Gymnogyps Californianus) – EXTINCT
  (5). Whooping Crane (Grus American) – EXTINCT
  (6). Galapago Penguin (Spheniscus Mendiculus) – EXTINCT
  (7). Vicuna (Vicugna Vicugna) – EXTINCT
  (8). Giant Otter (Pteronura Brasiliensis) – EXTINCT
  (9). Mountain Gorilla (Gorilla gorilla berengei) – EXTINCT
(10). Monkey Eating Eagle (Pilhecophage Jeffreyi) – EXTINCT
(11). Kakapo (Strigops habroptilus) – EXTINCT
(12). Long-tailed Ground Roller (Uratelornis Chimera) – EXTINCT
(13). Snow Leopard (Panthera unica) – EXTINCT
(14). Blue Whale (Balaenoptera Musculus) – LIMITED SURVIVAL*
(15). Thylacine (thylacinus cynocephalus) – EXTINCT

* note *certain* mammals and fish species will survive by finding *habitable zones* at distances near and far from the hot climate intersection lines.

REALMS of NATURE (ZOOGRAPHICAL) : FAUNA DEPLETION 20 yrs. INTO PROCESS

KEY : A~PALAEARCTIC. B~NEARCTIC. C~ORIENTAL. D~ETHIOPIAN. E~NEOTROPICAL
F~AUSTRALIAN

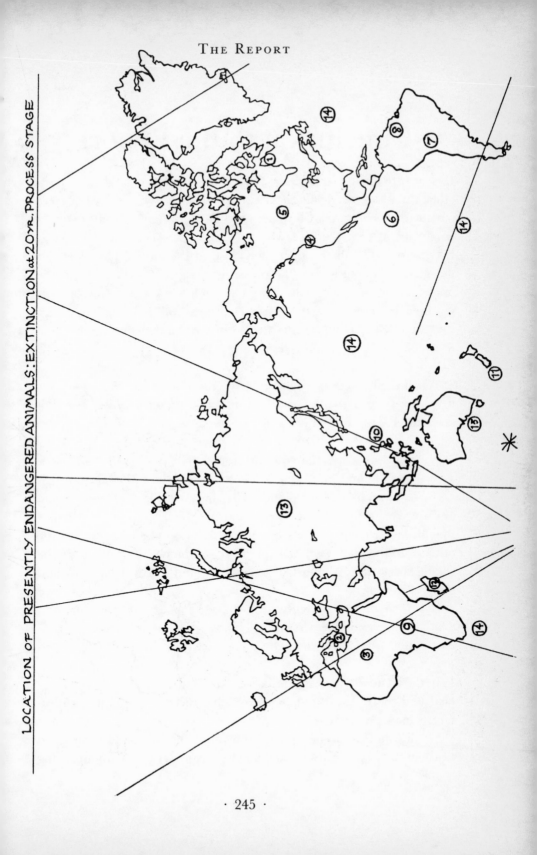

Conclusion to the Report

It is clear to me now, that if the Earth goes out of its orbital axis by an-other three degrees in the next twenty years we will be five degrees outside our orbital axis. Two main problems will arise from that:

1. Gravity will pull the Earth too close to the moon. This does not mean we will collide, but the pressure this gravity will exert on the inner part of the Earth will cause earthquakes and tidal waves. Our weather will change to the extremes of heat and ice. The fault lines that already exist will be enlarged so that when the comet comes, the destruction will be much worse.

2. When the comet does come in fifty years' time we will be too near its pathway and the devastation and destruction it will cause will leave the Earth uninhabitable.

The rainforests were created by Mother Earth and God for a reason. They keep life and nature in balance. Look at how they form a belt around the middle of our planet. The sheer weight of all those trees, and the geographical position of that weight, is important. Reduce that belt of weight and combine that as one influence with all the others and the planet will not spin in space the way it is meant to: the rainforests form a weight-belt balance around Earth. Change it and she will wobble.

In Africa the past twenty years have brought worse famine and death than ever before. Count how many trees have been cut down in that period. Just in the last ten years, more trees have been destroyed than ever before.

In the past twenty years India has experienced more flooding, more heat and more death and pestilence than ever before. India's rain-forests have been cut down.

South America has been plagued by more disease, famine, heat and death in the past twenty years than ever before. It goes without saying that the South American rainforests are the biggest in the world. One whole acre is felled every minute. People think they will not be affected. Think again.

You might believe that living in England, or other countries far from the tropical rainforests, you will be immune to the effects of such destruction. Wrong. The effects will reach us too: Mother Earth drew no national boundaries. Did the radioactive pollution from Chernobyl care where Russia ended and Scotland began? No. Do not doubt it – we too will experience floods, heat waves and inevitably, disease.

Please realise that none of this can be stopped unless the rainforests are put back.

It is the rainforests that keep us in balance. Once they are depleted beyond a certain point, our Earth will move another three degrees out of orbit: life will end.

Life will end.

We live because of the Earth. We stand on the Earth. We are fed by the Earth. We are watered by the Earth.

We must give her back her trees.

We must stop destroying the rainforests.

*　　*　　*

I will not be here in fifty years but my grandchildren will, as will yours. They must not be allowed to drown in tidal waves or be crushed to death in earthquakes. They must not live what lives they have scraping for food and starving. Our children are our responsibility. We have to choose now what world they will live in. It is those of us alive now who can prevent those who will live then from being the last people to walk on this Earth.

We can save ourselves and our planet. It is not too late.

Without the knowledge that is being brought to us from a distant place we would have been too late. It is important that when the time comes, we listen to White Arrow and his friends. White Arrow can not stand under the Earth and tilt her back again, but he *can* help us. Many millions of people have prayed to God and Mother Earth, knowing in their hearts that she cannot sustain us if we continue to make her sick. Those prayers are being answered now. We *decided* to pray. From our own free will we prayed. If help comes in answer to our prayers but in a form we never expected we must decide again. Will we decide to ignore the help because it steps out of a spaceship?

The governments who, so far, have done little to stop the continued rainforest destruction know they are putting profit before survival. They *know* there is serious danger in allowing it to continue, yet they stay silent. Why? The trees keep falling. Why?

How much is money really worth?

We must ask these people why they still allow the destruction to continue.

We must support any organisation which helps the rainforest as much as we can. An acre of forest costs £25.00. If millions of people gave just a penny each, the rainforests could begin to recover within ten years.

White Arrow's report already shows that we only have ten years left to stop the trees being killed and only eighteen years for the re-forestation to have any effect.

I have learnt many things from White Arrow. Some are terrible things that are coming. Some of the things he has shown me are already on this world but are not common knowledge because they are being kept secret from us by those who govern us. By keeping us in ignorance they are only serving to further our destruction.

The Earth is a living planet.

She gives us life.

Give her back her trees.

WE CAN AVOID OUR OWN DESTRUCTION

PART FIVE

With the drawing of this Love and the voice of this Calling
We shall not cease from exploration
And the end of all our exploring
Will be to arrive where we started
And know the place for the first time

T.S. Eliot: Little Gidding

Epilogue

<u>DECEMBER 1992</u>

It's Christmas now.

I am coming to the end of the first stage of a journey that's leading me to some land I have never seen. I only know that I must make this journey, and follow the path I find myself on. Some of what lies ahead has already been shown to me and I am aware of the bandits and sunsets that lie in wait. I know of strange encounters by magical waters, of pyramids, jungles, fearsome nights and awesome storms. I can see a revolution that will cross my path and leave it churned and muddy and I know of stations along the way where I will be fed and refreshed by people from other lands.

The son of a Red Indian Chief will accompany me every step of the way.

I turn to him now. He stands by the door, his arms crossed over his chest. What will he say, this being who through my feeble hand has written these words? This Spirit of wisdom who has come willingly to our world with so much help when help is what we most need and with so much to say at time when we most need to listen.

The people will want to know who you are, White Arrow. This book must now end, I know that, but what have you to say?

Softly, in many languages, I hear him speak.

Hardly above a whisper, he says, *'Our Father, who art in Heaven.'*

*   *   *

This is but the start of a story that must be told.
Ann's journey continues.

Appendix

Letters and ancillary documents reproduced from the originals.

May 5, 1993

Dear Mrs Walker,

I enclose a publication list and a copy of a recent book chapter concerning the fossil fuel CO_2 problem. The 280 ppm figure is the estimated preindustrial CO_2 level as determined from data on air bubbles trapped in ice cores. (See refs. 3-5 in my paper.)

I am not sure what your probability density function is or what it might imply about a crisis some 20 years from now. I myself think that there will be a crisis, but it will be brought on rather gradually over the next 100 years or so by the continued burning of fossil fuels. I hope the enclosed paper will help to explain my point of view.

Sincerely,

Associate Professor of Geosciences

Dear Mrs Walker

Your letter to Mr Franklin Perez, the former President of the Fort Belknap Community Council has been referred to me.

I would be happy to correspond with you or meet with you to discuss "the meaning (and verification) of certain tribal symbols . . . associated with . . ." (our) "grouping (Tribal)."

The United States Army gave my Grandfather, an Assiniboine named His Black Horse, the name Thomas H. Rain in 1890. I am a University Graduate, a Native Assiniboine speaker, a Language Teacher, a member of the Advisory Board of the Plains Indian, Buffalo Bill Historical Center, Cody, Wyoming, and I am a personal acquaintance of Lord John Jacob Astor VII. I have personal contacts in all Northern Plains Tribes. What I don't know, I can find out.

Extending my hand to you in friendship, I remain:
Sincerely yours,
Administrative Manager

11 August 1992

Dear Mrs Walker

Colonel Orellana, the Wing Commander here at Wright-Patterson, has referred your letter to me for reply. These types of inquiries are normally routed to the Public Affairs Office, which responds by enclosing the attached fact sheet on Project Blue Book. The information stated therein is, in fact, accurate. Project Blue Book was headquartered at Wright-Patterson until 1969, at which time the project was terminated and all records transferred to the National Archives in Washington D.C. The Air Force made its decision to discontinue the project after concluding that the UFOs reported and investigated to date gave no indication of posing a threat to national security.

We experienced a resurgence of interest in the Roswell incident in the wake of the recent publication of the book UFO Crash at Roswell. *Although the book claims that materials of some sort were flown to Wright Field sometime in 1947, those of us who work at Wright-Patterson today are unaware of the existence of any such material, nor do we know anything about the disposition of same, if in fact it was ever here in the first place. Your drawings are quite interesting, but I'm afraid we can do nothing to help clarify or confirm their significance.*

The address for the Modern Military Branch of the National Archives, should you wish to contact them, is: 8th Street and Pennsylvania Ave N.W., Washington DC 20408.

Sincerely

LOIS E. WALKER
Historian
I Atch
Project Blue Book Fact Sheet

7/29/1991

To Whom It May Concern:
The attached Eagle Feather War Bonnet in the possession of Mrs Ann Walker, Middlesex, England is a personal gift to Mrs Walker from the Assiniboine Medicine Lodge Society, Montana.

Signed
TA Shunga Saba – His Black Horse
Keeper of the Assiniboine Medicine Lodge

June 2 1993
Ms. Ann Walker

Dear Mrs Walker
Thank you for your letter of April 21, 1993, to Dr. Wes Huntress and for the documents regarding "Orbital Mechanics Projected Atmospheric/Surface Compliance and Distortions" mathematical theories.
These documents seem quite intriguing, even more so if they are in fact copied from Albert Einstein's original documents. I have made your orbital mechanics materials available to researchers in the Solar System Exploration and Space Physics Divisions for their review.
Once again, I appreciate your consideration in sharing these documents with NASA. My best wishes for a happy and successful year.
Sincerely,

Chief, Policy and Plans Branch
Office of Space Science and Applications.

6 January 1993
REF: MZC/CS/fel

Dear Mrs Walker,
The Office of the Secretary-General of the United Nations passed
on to this office your draft report on the irreversibility of stochastic
climate change process and your letter dated 24 September 1992. We
look forward to receiving the final version of the report when it will
be available. You may wish to send it also to the Intergovernmental
Panel on Climate Change at the following address:

> *c/o World Meteorological Organization*
> *41, Avenue G. Motta*
> *1211 Geneva 20*

Concerning your request for a "position" on new species of trees,
we suggest that the FAO is the organization within the UN system
best able to brief you on such a specific matter. The address of its
Forestry Division is:

> *Via delle Terme di Caracalla*
> *00100 Rome, Italy*

I wish you all success in your undertaking.

Yours sincerely,

Executive Secretary

cc:
Director, EOSG, UNHQ

4 February 1994

Dear Mrs Walker,

*Deputy Minister Dan Goodleaf has asked me to reply to your
letter of January 4, 1994. He thanks you for providing him with a
copy of your book "Heaven Can Come Later" and your recent study
on Global Warming. He has passed them on to this Department's
Environment Division for study.*

Yours sincerely,

*Philippe Cousineau
Executive Assistant
Deputy Minister's Office
Indian and Northern Affairs, Canada*

APPENDIX

References

The following list of references was compiled on completion of The Report in order to aid those readers who wish to further understand information summarised in The Report, and to help those already in the field of science to validate White Arrow's words. Further and more precise detail will be contained in the author's next book, in preparation.

Theoretical

1. Geothermal density, pressure changes in mantle and core:
"Theory of Energy and Mass Transfer"
by A. V. Lykov and Y. A. Mikhaylov
Prentice – Hall (LC 61:17006)

2. Process parameters and probability density factors behind 20 year irreversibility of process:
"The Theory of Stochastic Processes"
by D. R. Cox and H. D. Miller
Methuen (England) 1965 publication copyright

3. Hamiltonian systems, Hilbert space transformations, stability of periodic orbits, lusternik – Schnirelmann theorems, and topological connotations:
"Riemannian Geometry"
by Wilhelm Klingenberg
'De Gruyter Studies in Mathematics -1'
Walter De Gruyter (Berlin) 1982
ISBN 311-008673-5
LC 82-9772

4. Partition functions, thermodynamic systems, thermodynically isolated systems – macro canonical distributions, 'lagrange or undetermined multipliers, Einstein's models on solids, Vapour pressure of an Einstein solid:
"Introductory Statistical Mechanics"
by R. E. Turner and D. S. Betts 1974
University of Sussex Press
ISBN 085621-0196

General
* *"Handbook of Physical Calculations"*
by Jan J. Tuma
McGraw-Hill 1983
ISBN 007-065439-5
LC 82-9002

* *"Handbook of Numerical Calculations in Engineering"*
by Jan J. Tuma
McGraw-Hill 1989
ISBN 007-065446-8
LC 88-25944

* *"Engineering Mathematics Handbook" (3rd Edition)*
by Jan J. Tuma
McGraw-Hill 1987
ISBN 007-065443-3
LC 86-10349

* *"Modelling and Analysis of Dynamic Systems"*
by Charles M. Close and Dean K. Frederick
Houghton Mifflin Company (Boston) 1978
ISBN 0-395-25040-4
LC 77-74421

* *"An Introduction to the Numerical Solution of Differential Equations" (Revised Edition)*
by Douglas Quiney
Research Studies Press Ltd 1987
ISBN 0-086380-0556
LC 87-4922

* *"Fundamentals of Operations Research"*
by Russel L. Ackoff and Maurice W. Sasieni
John Wiley and Sons Inc 1968
LC 67-27271

* *"Measurements and Control Techniques in Rolling"*
Commission of European Communities Information Symposium, Luxembourg, 2
and 3 September 1981
Butterworths 1982
ISBN 408 221 577

* *"Earthquakes: A primer"*
by Bruce A. Bolt
W. H. Freeman 1978

* *"Volcanoes and Earthquakes/Geologic Violence"*
Gordon B. Oakeshott
McGraw-Hill 1976

* *"Earthquake Prediction"*
by Tsuneji Rititake
Elsevier Scientific publishing company (Amsterdam) 1976

References

* *"Continents in Motion"*
by Walter Sullivan
McGraw-Hill 1974

* *"Specialist Techniques in Engineering Mathematics"*
by A. C. Bajpai, L. R. Mustoe and D. Walker
John Wiley and Sons, 1980
LC 80-41274
ISBN 0-471-27907-2

* *"A Geology of Engineers" (Sixth Edition)*
by F. G. H. Blyth and M. H. de Freitas
Edward Arnold 1974
ISBN 0 7131 24407

* *"The World Ocean: An Introduction to Oceanography" (2nd Edition)*
by William A. Anikouchine and Richard W. Sternberg
Prentice Hall, 1981

* *"Geographical Variation in Coastal Development"*
by J. L. Davies
Longman, 1980

* *"The Water's Edge: Critical Problems of the Coastal Zone"*
Edited by Bostwick H. Ketchum
M.I.T. Press, 1972

* *"The Weather Machine"*
by Nigel Calder
Viking Press, 1974, (and B.B.C. 1974)

* *"Times of Feast, Times of Famine: A History of Climate Since the Year 1000"*
by Emmanuel Le Roy Ladurie
Doubleday, 1971

* *"Climates of Hunger: Mankind and the World's Changing Weather"*
by Reid A. Bryson and Thomas J. Murray
University of Wisconsin Press, 1977

* *"The Science and Wonders of the Atmosphere"*
by Stanley David Gedzelman
John Wiley and Sons, 1980

* *"Geocryology: A Survey of Periglacial processes and Environments"*
by A. L. Washburn
John Wiley and Sons, 1973

* *"Introduction to Chemical Engineering"*
by L. Bryce Anderson and Leonard A. Wenzel
McGraw-Hill, 1961
LC 60-53472

* *"Topics in Transport phenomena: Bioprocesses, Mathematical Treatment and Mechanisms"*
Edited By Chain Gutfinger
Hatstead Press, 1975
ISBN 0-470-33712-5
LC 75-15867

* *"Partial Differential Equations of Applied Mathematics"* (2nd Edition)
by Erich Zauderer
John Wiley and Sons, 1989
ISBN 0471-61298-7
LC 88-37525

* *"Numerical Methods for Partial Differential Equations"* (2nd Edition)
by William F. Ames
Academic Press Inc., 1977
ISBN 012-056760-1
LC 77-5786

* *"Probability, Random Variables and Stochastic Processes"* (2nd Edition)
by Athanasios Papoulis
McGraw-Hill, 1984
ISBN 007-048468-6
LC 82-14927

* *"An Introduction into Stochastic Control Theory"*
by Karl J. Astrom
Academic Press Inc., 1970
ISBN 012-065650-7
LC 70-105908

* *"Stochastic Optimal Control: Theory and Application"*
by Robert F. Stengal
Wiley – Interscience publication, 1986
ISBN 0-471-86462-5
LC 86-9096

* *"Nonlinear Dynamical Systems"*
by Peter A. Cook
Prentice-Hall, 1986
ISBN 013-623 216-7
LC 85-19283

REFERENCES

* *"Modelling and Simulation"*
by J. R. Leigh
Peter Peregrinus Ltd., 1983
ISBN 0-906048-95-8

* *"Statistical Methods for Comparative Studies"*
(Wiley series in Probability and Mathematical Statistics)
by Anderson, Auquier, Hauck, Oakes, Vandaele and Weisberg
Wiley Interscience Publications, 1981
ISBN 0-471-04838-0

* *"Comparative Statistical Interference"*
by Vic Barnett
John Wiley and Sons, 1972
ISBN 0-471-05401-1

* *"An Introduction to Probability Theory and its Applications – Volume II"*
(Wiley series in Probability and Mathematical Statistics)
by William Feller
John Wiley and Sons, 1965

* *"Elements of Queuing Theory With Applications"*
by Thomas L. Saaty
Dover, 1983 (unabridged reprint of McGraw-Hill 1961 Edition)
ISBN 0-486-64553-3

* *"Sequential Methods in Statistics"*
(Monographs on Applied Probability and Statistics)
by G. Barrie Wetherill
Chapman and Hall
ISBN 0 412 21810-0

* *"Introduction to the Theory of Distributions"*
by F. G. Friedlander
Cambridge University Press
ISBN 0-521-28591-7

* *"Applications of the Theory of Distributions in Mechanics"*
by W. Kecs and P. P. Teodorescu
Abacus Press, 1974
ISBN 0 85626-006-1

* *"Multivariable Calculus"*
by Lawrence H. Corwin
Marcel Dekker, 1982
ISBN 0-8247-6962-7
LC 81-5399

LITTLE ONE

* *"Handbook of Mathematics" (3rd Edition)*
by I. N. Bronshtein and K. A. Semendyayev
Van Nostrand Reinhold, 1985
ISBN 0-442-21171-6

* *"Numerical Analysis" (Second Edition)*
by Burden, Faires and Reynolds
Pringle, Weber and Schmidt, 1978
ISBN 0-87150-314 – X
LC 80-29558

* *"Heat Transfer"*
by Alan J. Chapman
Macmillan Publishing Company (New York), 1960

* *"Fundamentals of Heat Transfer"*
by Frank P. Incropera and David P. De Witt
John Wiley and Sons, 1981
ISBN 0-471-08961-3
LC 80-17209

* *"Heat Engines"*
by F. Metcalfe
Cassell Ltd. (London), 1960 Publication Copyright.